PERL

The Programmer's
⇒ Companion ⇒

PERL

The Programmer's
Companion

NIGEL CHAPMAN

JOHN WILEY & SONS

Chichester • New York • Weinheim • Brisbane • Singapore • Toronto

Copyright © 1997 by John Wiley & Sons Ltd,
Baffins Lane, Chichester,
West Sussex PO19 1UD, England

National   01243 779777
International (+44) 1243 779777

e-mail (for orders and customer service enquiries): cs-books@wiley.co.uk

Visit our Home Page on http://www.wiley.co.uk or http://www.wiley.com

Other Wiley Editorial Offices

John Wiley & Sons, Inc., 605 Third Avenue,
New York, NY 10158-0012, USA

Wiley-VCH Verlag GmbH, Pappelallee 3,
D-69469 Weinheim, Germany

Jacaranda Wiley Ltd, 33 Park Road, Milton,
Queensland 4064, Australia

John Wiley & Sons (Asia) Pte Ltd, 2 Clementi Loop #02-01,
Jin Xing Distripark, Singapore 129809

John Wiley & Sons (Canada) Ltd, 22 Worcester Road,
Rexdale, Ontario M9W 1L1, Canada

British Library Cataloguing in Publication Data

A catalogue record for this book is available from the British Library

ISBN   0 471 97563 X

Produced from PostScript files supplied by the author
Printed and bound in Great Britain by Bookcraft (Bath) Ltd, Midsomer Norton, Somerset.
This book is printed on acid-free paper responsibly manufactured from sustainable forestry,
for which at least two trees are planted for each one used for paper production.

Contents

Preface

The aim of this book is to introduce programmers to Perl, and Perl to programmers. It offers an invitation to look at a programming language that is different from the everyday ones, and can save you an awful lot of time and programming effort. You probably want to get on and find out about that programming language, but before you start chapter 1, spare a little time to read this preface, which tells you some useful things about the book.

Perl: The Programmer's Companion is not a tutorial on computer programming. It is a book aimed at people who already know something—possibly quite a lot—about programming, and at least a little about computer science. I assume that you have some experience using another programming language—probably C, C++ or Java—and that you are familiar with basic programming concepts, such as functions and abstract datatypes. I also assume that you enjoy programming computers, even if you find that these days you don't have much time for the enjoyable bits.

Perl: The Programmer's Companion is not an exhaustive reference to the Perl language. If you have Perl, then you have that already, in the form of the on-line manual. This can be transformed into several formats, possibly the most useful of which is a set of HTML pages, which can be navigated and searched with your usual Web browser. It is the most complete and up to date reference for Perl, and should include any information specific to your system.

Perl: The Programmer's Companion differs from most other offerings on the same subject by being written by someone who doesn't mind being described as a computer scientist. It is customary for computer scientists to treat Perl as an aberration and to ignore it as much as possible. Perl enthusiasts, for their part, tend to treat computer scientists with scorn, and accuse them of being detached from the real world, and generally no fun. I hope that this book may do something to reconcile the two factions, by showing that Perl is a worthy object of anyone's attention, and that a broader computer science viewpoint can provide some context for understanding and making judgements about Perl.

There appear to be two views of what Perl is. One school of thought, based on the fact that Perl was born in Unix, inherits many features from the Unix shells and tools like sed and Awk, and has a high level of support for interacting with that operating system built in to it, holds that it is primarily a Unix system administration tool. The other school of thought holds that Perl is a general-purpose programming language, whose slightly unusual nature should not prevent it being taken as seriously as C++, Modula-3 or Java. This book is based on the second view. Accordingly, where, for reasons of space or to avoid overwhelming you with detail, I have omitted some features of Perl, I have chosen to leave out features which are dependent on Unix. This may seem like heresy to some experts, but I hope you will agree after reading this book that, if you strip out all the Unix dependencies from Perl, you are left with a powerful and useful language, and one that can be used to advantage under any operating system.

Presentation

In the first half of the book, I make extensive use of syntax diagrams to describe Perl constructs and idioms. You may already be familiar with these diagrams in some form. The following tutorial describes the specific notation employed in this book.

A syntax diagram is a mechanism for describing how syntactical structures, such as expressions or statements, are built up out of smaller structures. If we suppose for the moment that a pizza is a syntactical structure, the following diagram provides a description of one, reading from the bottom up.

To find out what constitutes a legal pizza, you start at the double arrow head on the left and follow any route through the diagram to the two facing arrowheads at the right. Thus, one sort of pizza consists of a ⟨base⟩, followed by a ⟨topping⟩ and some mozzarella; another consists of a ⟨base⟩, followed by a ⟨topping⟩ then another ⟨topping⟩, yet another ⟨topping⟩, and the mozzarella, with some parmesan on top; and so on. The loop in the diagram means that you can repeat as many ⟨topping⟩s as you like; the line straight across that short-circuits the parmesan means that it is optional.

You will see that there are two sorts of symbol in the diagram: mozzarella and parmesan are written undecorated, to indicate that they cannot be broken down any further, but ⟨base⟩ and ⟨topping⟩ are written in italics and enclosed in angle brackets, to indicate that they are themselves made up out of smaller constituents. They could be described by further diagrams; for example, ⟨topping⟩ might have the following syntax diagram:

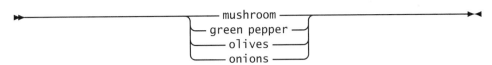

Branching diagrams like this indicate choices. Branches and loops may be combined in the same diagram, and occasionally, a symbol may appear on the backwards part of a loop, where it serves as a separator between repeated elements. Some diagrams cannot be fitted across a page in one piece and have to be broken; a single arrowhead at the right hand end of a diagram shows that the next line, which begins with a single arrowhead, too, is a continuation of the same diagram.

Some constructs are too simple to need diagrams to describe them. In that case, they can be described just by writing down the symbols that make them up. For example, a basic pizza might be

⟨*base*⟩ `mozzarella`

where the ⟨*base*⟩ is

`dough tomatoes`

Where syntax diagrams describe Perl constructs rather than Italian food, they show the order in which symbols appear reading from left to right, down the page, rather than from bottom to top.

For my programming examples, I have preferred realistic complete programs, even where they may be quite lengthy, to isolated fragments of code that illustrate a particular point of syntax or usage. Because Perl can be so concise, you will sometimes find that the program is shorter than the explanation of what it does.

Because I believe that you can learn from mistakes, I sometimes give examples of errors or things I consider bad practice. These are identified by having large black crosses alongside, like this:

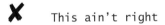 `This ain't right`

▷ You will also see indented passages like this set in smaller type than the surrounding text, with triangles at the beginning and end. Apart from this one, these passages are either somewhat tangential or highly detailed. They may be omitted at
◁ first without great loss.

▶ Other passages are delimited by filled-in triangles, like this. These present comparisons with other programming languages, usually C, C++ or Java. Such comparisons are intended to help orientate programmers who are familiar with these languages,
◀ but may not make much sense to those who are not.

Where it matters, Perl is the language and `perl` is the implementation. The language is Perl as it was redefined when version 5 of `perl` was released. The name Perl5 is used when it is necessary to distinguish it from its predecesor Perl4, but Perl on its own always means Perl5.

A final point about the presentation: while I never intentionally lie to you, sometimes I simplify matters to begin with, by describing a special case of some feature or construct, or omitting some of its optional elements. Usually, the general form is described later, although sometimes extra details are only introduced gradually, and you may be referred to the reference material for the last word.

Acknowledgements

Anybody writing a book about Perl—indeed, anybody using Perl—owes a debt to its creator, Larry Wall, without whom there would be nothing to write about, and to the many Perl programmers, some of whom are mentioned in the text, who have developed Perl modules to extend the power of this remarkable language. The scripts in this book have all been developed and tested on an Apple Macintosh computer, using the excellent MacPerl port of Perl, written by Matthias Neeracher, to whom, also, thanks are due. I owe a similar debt to Donald Knuth, Leslie Lamport and the many talented people who have contributed to the development of TeX and the LaTeX document preparation system, which I used to typeset this book. I am particularly indebted to Mark Wooding for his syntax package, which I have used extensively, and to Andrew Trevorrow, for his OzTeX implementation of TeX for the Mac.

I am grateful to Chris Benson, whose suggestions and comments on the manuscript led to many improvements, and to Malcolm Beattie for his careful review of the final draft. (Needless to say, the responsibility for any remaining errors and infelicities is mine.) Finally, I have to thank Gaynor Redvers-Mutton for making me write a book people might like to read, instead of the one I wanted to write.

Introduction

Perl is an extraordinary programming language: you can use it to do extraordinary things, like analysing, taking apart, and transforming text in a host of ways; or performing complex transactions over computer networks; or bringing World-Wide Web pages alive with interaction; or producing prototypes of complex systems in a fraction of the time it would take you to write them in C. And, with all this, Perl is free, and it's available for almost all types of computer and operating system.

This book contains many examples of extraordinary things being done with Perl. For instance, in chapter 10, you will find a fifteen-line Perl script which retrieves a week's radio programme schedules from a World-Wide Web site over the Internet. This retrieval involves a series of network interactions using a protocol which, while relatively simple, is not trivial. Not only can the task be achieved with such a short piece of Perl code, it was achieved by someone with no experience of network programming, and little knowledge of the protocols involved.

A more mundane example is provided by a Perl script I recently wrote to systematically change the names of a large collection of files, because the conventions used for naming the output files from one program were different from those used for the input files of another one. (You can find a simplified version of this script in chapter 6.) The problem could hardly be more ordinary; what is extraordinary is the ease with which Perl enabled me to solve it. If I had had to write a C program to do this, I would probably have found an excuse not to. The fiddlesome task of building and taking apart strings as arrays of characters and passing them to the right system call would just have been too much to face. If I had had to write it in C++, I would still be trying to identify the best set of abstractions to implement as classes. There is no shell or command interpreter on the Macintosh system I was using, and even on a Unix system, a combination of tools would have been required to accomplish this conceptually simple task. Twelve lines of Perl, written in as many minutes, has to date saved somebody from having to rename several thousand files, one at a time, by hand.

In the wider world, software consultants who specialize in Perl routinely report saving their clients large amounts of money (I have seen 'hundreds of thousands of dollars' mentioned more than once) by writing simple Perl scripts to automate tasks that would otherwise have required a team of specialist programmers to develop a system especially for the purpose. The Human Genome Project, which aims to produce a map of the complete DNA sequence of humans, uses Perl extensively to manipulate the massive quantities of data it generates. By facilitating the translation of data between different formats, so that it can be exchanged between researchers at different institutions around the world, Perl helped make possible the international collaboration that is essential to a project of such magnitude.

Or consider the World-Wide Web. If the Web was just a global hypertext network, consisting of linked pages of information that you could browse over the Internet, it would be useful, but the ability to run programs on a Web server—the machine where information resides—in response to a request from a browser provides a whole extra level of utility and flexibility. It makes possible something as simple as providing a visitors' book on your Web page, or as complex as a 'shopping cart', allowing visitors to select a number of products while browsing an online catalogue and then order and pay for them all by credit card. The mechanism which makes it possible for such programs to be run from a Web page is called the Common Gateway Interface (CGI), which is a standard way of arranging for programs to be executed on the server machine and for data to be passed from the Web page to the program and back again. This data is passed in several ways, but anything passed to a CGI program must be encoded using special conventions for embedded spaces and other special characters; anything passed back has to be in the form of a Web page with HTML commands. Thus, CGI programs must do a lot of processing and formatting of text—just the sort of thing, as we shall see, that Perl is extremely good at, and as you may have found out, C, Pascal and similar languages are extremely poor at. Without Perl, it is doubtful whether there would be such a rich variety of interaction based on CGI available on the World-Wide Web.

Perl is also extraordinary in the literal sense: it is out of the ordinary, in its syntax, its data types and its underlying design philosophy. There have always been maverick programming languages that offer an alternative to the commonly used, established languages, and Perl is one of these. It does incorporate ideas from the main streams of programming language development, but it combines them with features of natural languages, as well as other mavericks, and utilities such as `sed` and `grep`, which are not usually thought of as programming languages, in its own… extraordinary way, to produce something special.

You may ask, Why step outside the mainstream? Change and adventure provide one answer; the ease with which Perl gets your jobs done provides a more compelling one. A deeper reason is that mainstream programming languages are letting us down. For a start, much of the time they are addressing the wrong problem. They are designed with big, complicated and ambitious programs in mind, that have tight performance constraints, and require a disciplined team of skilled programmers to produce. Such programs can be important, but not all programs are like that. A lot of programs are much more modest things, which do vital but unexciting jobs, like reformatting data files, generating statistical summaries from a collection of fixed-format records, or searching a file system for files of a certain size. Jobs like this don't really need the same sophisticated techniques of software construction as large scale reliable programming, and yet they can consume a quantity of time and effort wholly disproportionate to their innate difficulty if you have to tackle them with a language designed with these sophisticated techniques in mind. Perl is far better for such jobs, because it provides the tools you need, with no extraneous machinery to get in your way.

How is this achieved?

The most attractive and powerful feature of Perl is its support for high-level datatypes. These include fully dynamic list structures, associative arrays ('hashes' as they are called in Perl), and strings of characters. Powerful operations are supplied for working with these types of data; strings are especially well catered for, with extremely sophisticated pattern-matching and replacement operations available.

These built-in data structures are adequate as they stand for many of the tasks Perl is usually put to. Providing similar facilities in a mainstream language requires either writing some dull code that implements textbook data structures and algorithms, or mastering a complex class library like C++'s STL. If you need to implement more elaborate data structures, Perl provides references, which are rather like pointers, but safer. Their presence obviates the need for raw pointers and the attendant potential for mischief. This in turn makes automatic storage management feasible, thereby taking another burden off the programmer, and removing a potential source of obscure runtime errors.

But that is not the end of it. Perl is extensible. The object-oriented features introduced into the language with version 5 make it possible to produce libraries of re-usable code, referred to as modules in the Perl world. Many such modules exist, covering an enormous range of areas, including database access, networking and inter-process communication, security and encryption, image manipulation, and, of course, CGI programming. The extension mechanism also makes it possible to write modules in languages other than Perl itself, providing access to low-level system facilities or interfaces to other programming languages, while still presenting a uniform interface to Perl programs. A large collection of modules is available via the Internet. When you start using these modules in your Perl programs, the limits of what you might consider a problem that does not demand the complexity of a mainstream programming language suddenly expand to encompass all these areas.

Almost everyone would agree that all this is excellent, but some aspects of Perl are more controversial. Probably the first thing about Perl that will strike anyone used to conventional programming languages is the way in which just about every character available on the keyboard has been pressed into service: Perl source code is peppered with $, @, %, and \, with a sprinkling of ^, ? and #. The result looks positively bewildering to the neophyte. You will soon find that all the strange characters are meaningful and that, in many cases, they actually help make your scripts easier to understand.

One of Perl's strongest challenges to contemporary orthodoxy is its loose attitude to typing and declarations. By default, variables do not need to be declared before they are used (although you can ask `perl` to impose this restriction for you, if you find it helpful); the same variable may be used at different times to store values that, in most programming languages, would be considered to have different types; the same value may be interpreted differently depending on the context it is used in (for example, the string of characters 3.142 may be used as a floating point approximation to π if you apply any arithmetical operation to it). The virtue of such permissiveness is that you don't have to bother with any declarative rubric, you can just get on with your computation. Whereas a considerable body of opinion holds, rather vociferously, that strong typing helps prevent programming errors, there is little solid evidence to support the claim, and the popularity of type-casts in C programs suggests that a strongly enforced type system may be seen as more of a hindrance than a help by many practising programmers.

Even Perl's defects are out of the ordinary. If you read the Perl on-line documentation, you will find the phrase 'There's more than one way to do it' enshrined there as the Perl motto. The profusion of ways of doing the same thing springs from a desire to provide a means of programming expression that is as natural as possible for as many programmers as possible. This sounds like a laudable aim, but it could be argued that, whereas novice programmers might find difficulty discovering any way of carrying out a particular task in a programming language, experienced programmers are more likely to be able to think of too many ways, and to be in danger of suffering a design paralysis in the face of trying to choose among them. A language which provides a dozen sensible ways of adding one to a variable if a certain condition holds does not help matters. You might well argue, though, that an inability to choose between options is, perhaps, more the programmer's problem than the programming language's.

▷   The possibility of making choices about how you express your computation means that questions of *style* can arise in Perl programming, and style, in turn, implies questions of *taste*. You can look at just about any piece of Perl code and say to yourself 'I'd rather that was more succinct' or 'less cryptic' or 'more like C++' or 'less like C++' or whatever. You will find that there are some things that most Perl programmers consider 'good' style, but just as with writing, there are—and can be—no universally agreed rules.

The Perl in this book is written in a style best described as neo-classical post-retropunk. It makes no claims to be the best style, and you will probably develop
◁   your own (ultra-post pre-techno-modern, perhaps).

In common with other languages providing built-in support for high level datatypes and operations, Perl does not offer performance comparable to that of hand-crafted programs written in a more conventional language. For the tasks it is best suited to, this is unlikely to be a problem. For example, the performance of CGI scripts is more or less irrelevant, since the perceived response is dominated by network and server delays. Perl is usually compiled into a parse tree, which is then interpreted, although a compiler which translates it into C is also available. The interpreted approach has advantages (for any programming language) since no machine dependent and bulky binary versions of the program are ever produced, and more information about the source can be available at runtime.

▷ There is some terminological confusion between a Perl *program* and a Perl *script*. Some authorities will try to tell you that the term 'script' should be used for source programs in languages that are interpreted, and 'program' should be reserved for those that are compiled. This is nonsense, since there is nothing inherent in any language that determines whether it is interpreted or compiled. In practice, the terms are used more or less interchangeably in the context of Perl; if there is a rational distinction, it is that 'script' should be used when the emphasis is on the ◁ text of the code, whereas 'program' embraces its execution and behaviour.

As I mentioned at the outset, Perl is free. Free of charge, free of restrictions on redistribution, and free of restrictions on what you do with it, subject only to a few eminently reasonable ones, which amount to saying that if you change it, you cannot claim that your version is Perl any more. This open-handedness encourages Perl programmers to adopt a suitably liberal attitude to distributing their Perl scripts and modules. Perl is also free of the control of any standards organizations, and is thus free to grow and change.

Perl has been described—possibly humourously—as a post-modern programming language. 'Post-modern' may seem like an odd term to apply to a programming language, but, in its popular connotations it does capture some of the extraordinariness of Perl. Since it escaped from the philosophers and critical theorists, the term has come to mean any and all of: eclectic, playful, iconoclastic, logically illogical, illogically logical, unexpected, challenging, paradoxical and probably something to do with new media and the Internet. All of which could describe Perl. Post-modern ideas, especially in architecture, are also seen as being at odds with the Modern ideas that gave rise to tower blocks and austere functional design. In much the same way, Perl's funky, relaxed approach to programming offers a challenge to the stern, mathematically and managerially inspired orthodoxy of software engineering, and opens up a space for playfulness and paradox. People like Perl for just that reason and…it works and gets the jobs done anyway.

Making It Happen

Getting the job done is central to Perl: whatever else it may be, Perl is not an academic language, fit only to be contemplated and analysed, with footnotes. If you are to get anything out of it at all, you need to be able to run Perl scripts.

The first thing you need, then, is a `perl` system. If you do your computing on somebody else's machines—your firm's, college's or any other institution's—you will need to ask your system administrator whether `perl` is available. A conscientious system administrator will have installed the most recent version.[1] If yours has not, try to persuade them to do so, but do not accept anything less than version 5.001, or you will miss most of the fun. If you do your computing on your own machine, or have a less than conscientious system administrator, it will be necessary to obtain a version of `perl`. If you have Internet access, this is easy—see page 251. If not, you may be able to find it on a CD-ROM, or perhaps get it from a friend.

Installation on most platforms is simple, although the procedure will vary. On Unix, and systems that resemble it, it is necessary to build the system from sources, but a makefile is provided. For other systems, `perl` is distributed as a binary, and installation usually just means putting it and its associated libraries and documentation in a suitable place. An installation script is provided for systems like Windows, where more complex procedures are needed.

Having installed `perl`, you will need to consult the documentation for your platform to discover the details of invoking it to run your scripts. The system was originally developed on Unix, where the command line rules, so the standard way of running a Perl script is to put the text of the script into a file, using an editor, and then to type a command line, consisting of the name of your `perl` system, followed by some switches (which control different aspects of the execution process), the name of the file containing your script, and any arguments (usually the names of data files) you wish to pass to it. Thus, on a Unix system, I might type

```
perl -w myscript.pl data1 data2
```

in response to the command line prompt, to get the script in the file `myscript.pl` executed, with extra warnings enabled by the -w switch, and the filenames `data1` and `data2` passed as arguments to the script. Different systems have different conventions for naming commands and files, and different ways of identifying switches, but the general approach is the same.

▷   A Unix convention is that, if the very first thing in a file is the magic combination of characters #!, the rest of the first line is treated as the pathname of a program, possibly followed by some arguments. When you type the name of a file beginning with #! at the command line prompt, the program named on the first line is executed and passed the rest of the line, the name of the file and any additional arguments

---

[1] 5.004 is in its β-testing phase at the time of writing, and should be available when you read this.

typed on the command line. This convention is used to enable you to execute Perl scripts as if they were system commands. A file called /wombles/orinoco/snooze beginning with a line such as

```
#!/usr/bin/perl -w
```

and containing a Perl script can be made executable by setting the appropriate permissions. If the directory /wombles/orinoco is on your search path, typing

```
snooze forty winks
```

at the command line prompt is equivalent to invoking perl using the command line:

```
/usr/bin/perl -w /wombles/orinoco/snooze forty winks
```

(The exact pathname of the perl system may be different from /usr/bin/perl on your system. Your system administrator will be able to tell you what it is.) On some systems that do not support it directly, this mechanism is partially simulated to provide a way of embedding options and arguments in the source of a Perl script.

On a system such as MacOS, where there is no command line, invocation will be different. MacPerl, the MacOS port of perl, is invoked like all Macintosh applications by double-clicking its icon. Commands can then be selected from menus to open a script, set options, and run it. Anyone familiar with the standard MacOS interface elements should have no trouble using MacPerl. A Perl script can be saved in a form called a 'droplet', which can then be invoked by dragging and dropping files on to its icon; the names of the files are then passed to the script as if they had been typed at the command line on Unix.

You may also find that, if you use one of the more powerful editors, it is possible to invoke perl directly from within your editor, and have it take part of your edit buffer as either a Perl script or as the input to a script. Details will again vary, and you will have to consult the editor's documentation.

Although I try not to prejudice my account in this book in favour of any particular system, when I have to refer to command line options or other aspects of perl invocation, I will use the terminology of the Unix version, since this is consistent with most of the Perl documentation. However, if, for example, I refer to using the -w switch, you should understand that what follows also applies if you select Compiler Warnings from the Script menu in MacPerl, or do whatever the equivalent is on your machine.

It is no accident that I have used -w as an example switch; the warnings it enables are a useful aid to diagnosing errors in Perl scripts. You should routinely use this switch. Another switch that aids debugging is -d, which causes your script to run under the Perl interactive debugger. Opinions differ on the usefulness of interactive debuggers: I know people who cannot manage without them, and others who never use them at all. If you fall into the former class, you will find that the Perl debugger offers all the facilities for setting breakpoints, single-stepping execution, and examining the state of memory that you would expect. Even if you never use a debugger for debugging, it can sometimes offer useful insights into what is going on inside your script when it executes.

The Perl documentation comes as part of the distribution. It is organized in sections; the `perldebug` section describes the debugger. Another useful section is `pertraps`, which describes common errors you might make. The documentation is distributed in a form that can be converted into HTML, Unix man pages, or LaTeX source, or viewed by special reading software. Once again, the details will vary with platforms and individual installations. However, one thing is sure: if the documentation is absent, you should complain. It is the definitive source of information on the Perl language and the `perl` system.

Simple Text Processing

2

I could begin my description of Perl in a time-honoured way, by describing the syntax of each of its constructs, starting with the simplest and most basic, and showing how each can be used to achieve some desired computational effect. This is not very appropriate for Perl: one of the things that makes Perl so easy to use is the wealth of shortcuts and defaults it provides to make the code for common tasks concise and natural. Giving a full description of every construct with its defaults would probably give the impression that Perl was nothing but a bag of special cases and exceptions, without necessarily showing you either the underlying structure of the language, or the usefulness of those special cases.

Alternatively, I could begin by showing you a program that writes a simple message to the terminal, and use it to explain all the red tape necessary to put together a simple program. However, in Perl, there is no such red tape, and such a program would be as simple as

```
print "Follow that Camel!\n";
```

so it doesn't teach us anything much.

Instead of using either of these approaches, I shall begin by looking at some patterns of usage, or *programming idioms*, where special cases of some constructs are combined to produce a specific class of computations. In this case, the class of computations will be text processing jobs, similar to those you might perform with an editor. (Perl makes a very good editor, although it is a great deal more, too.)

Introducing Perl via idioms is not just a matter of expository convenience. Combining idioms is a good way of writing Perl programs.

Each idiom possesses its own syntactical structure, which can be described with the aid of a syntax diagram, just as well as individual language constructs can.[1] For example, the first idiom I will describe has the following structure:

---

[1] If you skipped the preface, and are not familiar with syntax diagrams, you will have to go back to page x to find out about them.

►►──────── while ─ (< >) ─ { ─ print ┬─────────────┬ ; ─ } ──────►◄
                                        └─ if ─ ⟨*pattern*⟩ ─┘

A couple of examples are:

```
while (<>)
{
   print;
}
```

and

```
while (<>)
{
   print if /blue/;
}
```

It doesn't take much insight to see that these programs take the form of a loop that will be executed repeatedly while some condition holds, and that each time round the loop something may be printed, but what and when?

As I explained at the end of chapter 1, when `perl` is called upon to execute your script, a collection of command line arguments may be passed to it. A script may interpret its command line arguments in any way it likes, but often they are treated as filenames, so that the computations specified in the script may be applied to the contents of a collection of files.

A loop introduced by `while (<>)` exemplifies this behaviour; it works its way through all the files identified by the command line arguments, reading one line every time round the loop. The loop finally terminates when all the lines in all the files have been read. Within such a loop, the statement

```
print;
```

prints the line that has just been read to the standard output, usually your screen. Thus, the complete Perl script

```
while (<>)
{
   print;
}
```

has the effect of printing the contents of all the files named as command line arguments to the standard output.

▷ If the string consisting of a single minus sign (–) is used instead of a filename, it is interpreted as the 'standard input'. Standard input is also used if there are no command line arguments. The interpretation of this concept is system-dependent: it often means the user's keyboard, but if your system supports i/o redirection and pipes, it may be a file or the output of another process. Again, you will need to consult your system documentation to find out exactly what standard input means ◁ to you.

What happens if you add the optional clause, introduced by `if`? As you would suppose, this makes the printing occur only if a certain condition holds. Many different sorts of condition may be specified in Perl, and conditions may be used in several different contexts. In this idiom, we are using a condition to control the execution of a single print statement; our conditions will specify a pattern, and be satisfied when the current input line contains a string described by that pattern.

You will almost certainly have come across the idea of describing sets of strings by a pattern before, probably in the context of searching in a text editor or file scanning program, or possibly in the lexical analysis phase of a compiler. The patterns you use in these areas are usually specified in some notation derived from the mathematical concept of *regular expressions*. Regular expressions are used as the basis of patterns in Perl, too. The language provides many convenient extensions to the mathematicians' basic regular expression notation, but these simple patterns are already very useful by themselves, so we will start by looking at how they are provided and used in Perl.

Regular Expressions

Regular expressions provide a way of writing down a compact description of a potentially infinite set of strings with a certain structure, such as 'all words beginning with a capital letter and ending in s' or 'all numbers beginning 01 or 02, followed by any number of digits'. We can use regular expressions in our first Perl programs to specify that only lines containing certain strings should be printed.

The Regular Operators

The regular expression notation is an algebraic one, which means that complicated descriptions can be constructed as expressions built up out of simpler sub-expressions combined by operators, just as complicated arithmetic expressions can be built up out of simpler ones using the familiar arithmetic operators $+$, $-$, $\times$, and $/$.

In order to build expressions out of sub-expressions and operators, we need to have some simple elements to start off with. In arithmetic, we start with numbers; in regular expressions, we start with individual characters, which just describe themselves. Thus `B` is a regular expression, describing the letter B.

▷ There is a potential problem here, in distinguishing between the expression and the letter it describes. I will use the fixed width 'teletype' font used for program fragments for expressions, and the ordinary text font for what it describes.
◁

There are only four operators for combining sub-expressions in the basic notation. The first of these, called *alternation* and written |, specifies a choice between the strings described by two regular sub-expressions. You can read | as 'or': the expression 0|1 describes either 0 or 1. Just as we can string together operators of the same precedence in arithmetic, as in $2 \times 3 \times 4 \times 5$, so we can string together a set of alternatives: I|B|M is a regular expression describing any of the initials of International Business Machines.[2]

The second operator is *concatenation*, signified by writing regular expressions one after another. The combined expression describes strings whose first part is described by the first sub-expression, second part by the second expression, and so on. If the sub-expressions are just single characters, concatenation allows us to write expressions to describe single strings; for example IBM describes the string IBM.

In general, though, we can describe more interesting sets of strings by combining sub-expressions which themselves use concatenation and alternation. Once we can write expressions using more than one operator, it becomes necessary to specify the relative binding powers of operators. Does IB|M describe the strings IB and M, or IB and IM? By convention (and in Perl), concatenation binds more tightly than alternation, so the first interpretation is correct. You can use brackets to alter the binding, just as you would in an arithmetic expression such as $5 \times (8 - 3)$. Thus, I(B|M) would be the expression you needed to describe IB and IM. Because of this convention

    IBM|Apple|Motorola

is a regular expression describing the names of the three partners in the AIM PowerPC consortium, and

    IB(M|Apple|M)otorola

describes IBMotorola (two different ways—no harm in that) and IBAppleotorola. Notice that I have not put any spaces in these expressions: a space is a character just like any other and will normally be interpreted as part of the expression: I B M does not describe IBM, with no spaces between the letters, only I B M, with spaces. (However, we will see later that when you use a regular expression in Perl you can, if you wish, specify that spaces should be ignored and used for layout purposes instead.)

The most powerful regular operator is *repetition*, written as a postfix *. That is, the operator is written after the sub-expression to be repeated,[3] so if *R* is some regular expression, *R** describes zero or more occurrences of the string described by *R*. Going back to sub-expressions consisting of one character, X* describes any number (including none) of kisses. The repetition operator is more binding than either of the other two, so, for repetition of more complex

---

[2]The use of any company name or trademark in this section, or elsewhere in this book, does not imply anything other than a lack of imagination on the part of the author.

[3]Postfix operators are not that common, but this isn't one of Perl's innovations; the notation dates right back to the first work on regular expressions.

strings, brackets have to be used: IBM!* describes IBM with an arbitrary number of exclamation marks; (IBM!)* denotes an arbitrary number of repetitions of IBM!—perhaps the refrain to one of their famous company songs (*repeat ad libitem, to fade*). The babble on a trading floor might be described in part by

```
((Buy|Sell) (ten|twenty|fifty|a hundred)!)*
```

The last of the simple regular operators is again postfix, and represents *option*: if a sub-expression is followed by a ?, then the string it describes may be missing. Thus IB?M describes IBM and IM. The binding power of ? is the same as that of *.

▷ Regular expressions can be given a precise mathematical definition, in terms of set theory. If you have a taste for such things, consult a textbook on formal language theory or compiler construction. If not, you can just rest assured that there is some solid theory that tells us how powerful regular expressions are, and that the algorithms used by perl for matching regular expressions are correct. ◁

Regular expressions are used for many things in Perl, especially carrying out searching and replacement operations on text. If[4] you write a regular expression between two slash characters, you have a *pattern*. The strings described by the regular expression are said to *match* the pattern. Generally, we also say that a string matches a pattern if it contains a substring that matches the pattern. For example /blue/ is a pattern; it is matched by (among an infinite number of other strings):

```
blue
blues
only blue will do
the bluebells of Scotland
```

but not by any of

```
red
bluto
b l u e
Blue
```

We are now in a position to understand the full Perl idiom introduced at the beginning of this chapter, where the print statement is qualified by if and a pattern. The effect will be to print only those lines which match the pattern. For example, the program

```
while (<>)
{
  print if /blue/;
}
```

will print only those lines of the files named in its command line arguments which contain the string blue. Thus if the input comprised the nine lines:

---

[4]But not only if: see page 17.

```
blue
red
bluto

blues
only blue will do
b l u e
the bluebells of Scotland
Blue
```

the program would print the first, fifth, sixth and eighth. Notice that the blank line is still a line, but, of course, it does not match the pattern, and that pattern-matching is case-sensitive.

There won't be too many explicit examples of Perl scripts in this section, but you should remember that any regular expression becomes a pattern if you enclose it in slash characters, and then you can fit it into the idiomatic framework to get a program which prints lines that match the expression, so any example of a regular expression implies an example script.

▷ The simple notation I have described is a surprisingly powerful one, which allows me to write down expressions for many complex and interesting sets of strings. It is not possible, though, to describe strings with an arbitrarily deeply nested structure such as correctly bracketed expressions. The expression <*>* denotes an arbitrary number of <s followed by an arbitrary number of >s, but does not stipulate that the number of <s should be equal to the number of >s. It is impossible to express such constraints in the regular expression notation. (So you can't write down a regular expression describing all correctly formed regular expressions.) Compiler writers often use regular expressions to describe the lexical structure of a programming language—what constitutes a legal identifier or a numeric constant and so on—but not its syntactical structure—how expressions are built from sub-expressions, ◁ structured statements from simple statements, and so on.

Character Classes, Repetition Counts and Escapes

The simple notation is adequate, but it can be cumbersome. Try, for example, writing a regular expression to describe identifiers consisting of an upper- or lower-case letter, followed by any number of letters, digits, or underlines; or a string constant consisting of up to 255 characters enclosed in double quotes. You can do it all right but you will need a wide sheet of paper if you want to get it all on one line. Consequently, you will rarely see patterns in Perl scripts that use only the four basic regular operators. Although these are necessary and sufficient, Perl provides various extensions to the basic notation. Most of these extensions are also supported by other programming languages and utilities that make extensive use of regular expressions, but Perl has more extensions than anyone else.

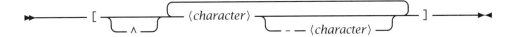

Figure 2.1 Character classes

The first is a compressed notation for a set of alternatives, each consisting of a single character, such as A|E|I|O|U, which describes any upper-case vowel. Instead of this, you can write [AEIOU]. That is, a string written inside square brackets describes a *character class*, which is matched by any single character in that string.

Sometimes, it is easier to say what a string is not than what it is. In general, doing so lets in all sorts of complications and difficulties, but for the simple case of a set of characters, it is not problematic. The expression [^AEIOU] describes any character *except* an upper-case vowel. In general, if the first character of a string inside square brackets is ^ (this character may look like either a circumflex accent or an up-arrow on your keyboard), then the expression describes any single character other than those in the remaining string. You should realize that this 'other than' pre-supposes that we know what the set of all possible characters is. In practice, it will be the character set used by your computer system.

Even with these notational extensions, large sets such as that consisting of any upper- or lower-case letter can only be described by long cumbersome regular expressions. To cope with such cases, in a character class you may abbreviate a range of characters by specifying the first and last separated by a hyphen. For example [0-9] matches any digit, being a shorthand for [0123456789], which in turn is a shorthand for 0|1|2|3|4|5|6|7|8|9. Here again, there is a pre-supposition: that the ordering of characters is defined. Again, in practice, it will be the ordering of characters in your system's character set, considered as small integers. Thus, character ranges are machine-dependent. You can be pretty sure that [0-9] is any digit, but while [a-z] almost certainly includes any lower-case letter, it may include other things as well.

You can combine ranges and single characters into one expression just by concatenating them within the square brackets. Thus, [a-zA-Z_] describes any letter or underline character, so a complete expression for the structure of Perl names is [A-Za-z_][A-Za-z0-9_]*. Square brackets bind like ordinary brackets, so the repetition applies to all of the second character class, as required. You can negate ranges specified this way, too, so [^A-Za-z0-9_] is any character that could not appear in a name.

The syntax diagram in figure 2.1 summarizes the possible forms of character classes, as described so far.

Certain character classes are so commonly used that Perl provides special shorthands for them: \d stands for any digit (it is equivalent to [0-9]); \s stands for any white space character (space, newline or return, tab or form-feed);\w stands for any 'word character'. What this actually means is any letter (upper or lower case), digit or underline. Each of these shorthands has an inverse, which uses the same letter in upper case: \D stands for any single character except a digit, \S, any single character except a space character, and \W, any single character except a word character. These so-called *escape sequences* may be used inside square brackets. For example [\d,] stands for a digit or a comma.

An extreme shorthand is employed for the class of (nearly) all characters: a dot (.) stands for any single character except[5] a newline, so .* stands for any string without embedded newlines. You cannot use this shorthand inside square brackets—what would it mean? Instead, a dot just stands for itself within a character class, so [\w.] stands for any word character or dot.

A second set of extensions allows you to write regular expressions involving repetition. We already have the * operator to express an arbitrary number of zero or more repetitions. Quite often, you want to describe something repeated one or more times. You can do this: \w\w* is one or more word characters, for example. Expressions of this form are rather awkward, though, so Perl provides a postfix + operator, which is used just like *, but signifies one or more occurrences of the expression preceding it. Thus, \w+ is the usual regular expression employed to describe a word.

Writing a regular expression to describe a fixed number of occurrences of something is tedious and long-winded: six digits would be \d\d\d\d\d\d, and 256 characters...Well, you do it. In Perl, you may follow a sub-expression with a repetition count enclosed in curly brackets. For example, the previous examples could be written simply as \d{6} and .{256}. You can have counts within counts, so ((Hip!){2}Hooray!){3} matches three cheers for Perl. The notation is generalized to deal with between *m* and *n* occurrences of a sub-expression, where *m* and *n* are arbitrary positive integers. Thus [1-9]\d{2,4} describes any decimal number between 100 and 99999. If the second number is omitted, then it is taken to be infinity: \d{3,} is any string of three or more digits. You should be able to see that * is equivalent to {0,}, + to {1,} and ? to {0,1}.

By now, you may be wondering how to write down a regular expression which includes one of the characters like [,], *, ?, and so on—so-called *metacharacters*—which form part of the regular expression notation itself. In general, if you want a metacharacter to stand for itself within an expression, you put a backslash (\) in front of it. Thus, whereas camel? stands for came and camel, camel\? stands for the interrogative camel?. If you put a \ before any character that is not a metacharacter, the \ is ignored. (Therefore, \\ means \, whether you consider \ a metacharacter or not.) Inside square brackets, only ∧, - and] need escaping in this way, and then only in places where they could be performing their metacharacteristical function: you don't

---

[5]Usually—see page 124.

need to put a \ in front of ∧ unless it immediately follows the opening [, nor in front of – unless it appears between two characters. As a special concession, you don't even need to escape] if it immediately follows the opening [. Or you could always put \ in front of these characters within square brackets, anyway.

A similar problem arises with / characters within a pattern delimited by slashes. If your regular expression contains slashes, then when you try to turn it into a pattern, `perl` has no way of distinguishing between those inside the expression and the one that ends the pattern. This is a problem with URLs. A regular expression describing the URL of John Wiley and his sons' computer books Web page just consists of the URL itself (with the dots protected by \s):

```
http://www\.wiley\.co\.uk/compbooks/
```

If you simply put slashes round this and plug it into the script framework, you get a bunch of syntax errors:

✗
```
while (<>)
{
    print if /http://www\.wiley\.co\.uk/compbooks//;
```
✗
```
}
```

Because the pattern ends after the colon, everything else on the line appears to be rubbish divided by rubbish. Again, a solution is to put \s in front of the /s, but the result is not very nice:

```
print if /http:\/\/www\.wiley\.co\.uk\/compbooks\//;
```

A better solution is to use a different character to delimit the pattern. In fact, the form of pattern I have described is just one of those helpful shortcuts that Perl provides. In general, a pattern begins with the letter m (the 'match' operator). The next character is taken as the delimiter, and the pattern extends from the first character beyond it to its next occurrence, presumably at the end. Only if the delimiter is a / can you omit the m, as I have done up to now. To make the previous example more readable, it could be written like this:

```
print if m!http://www\.wiley\.co\.uk/compbooks/!;
```

Actually, I just lied again. If the character following the m is one of (, {, [and <, the pattern extends to the matching closing bracket), },] or >, respectively. This may sound extravagant, but it is quite neat and makes patterns easy to read:

```
print if m{http://www\.wiley\.co\.uk/compbooks/};
```

As well as protecting metacharacters and providing shorthands for some character classes, backslash escapes are used to allow you to include characters that are hard to write in a regular expression. For example \t denotes a tab, \n a newline and \r a carriage return. For any character *x*, \c*x* represents

\t	tab
\n	newline (see text)
\r	carriage return
\f	form feed
\b	backspace (see text)
\a	bell (the a stands for alarm)
\e	escape
\c$x$	control-x, for any x
\0$d_1 d_2 d_3$	character with code $d_1 d_2 d_3$ in octal
\x$d_1 d_2$	character with code $d_1 d_2$ in hexadecimal

Table 2.1   Character Escapes

the character you get by holding down the control and x keys at the same time, so \cU represents control-U. More generally, \x$d_1 d_2$, where d_1 and d_2 are hexadecimal digits ([0-9a-f]), represents the character whose internal code is the hexadecimal number $d_1 d_2$; if you prefer octal, \0$d_1 d_2 d_3$ (the character after the backslash is a zero, not a letter O) is the character with octal representation $d_1 d_2 d_3$. If d_1 is zero, you can leave it out.

Table 2.1 lists all the available escape sequences of this nature. You will probably be aware that the meaning of newline is system-dependent: on Unix it is the same as linefeed, whereas on MacOS it is the same as return, and under MS-DOS and Windows it is the two-character combination of both of these.

The sequence \b only stands for a backspace within square brackets; outside them it means something completely different, which can be illustrated with a simple example.

Suppose somebody has given you a huge file containing a list of song titles, one per line, and you want to extract the titles of blues songs. This cannot be done mechanically, of course, because titles often give nothing away about the songs, but you could make a rough start by searching for the words 'blue' and 'blues'. You might try the following:

```
while (<>)
{
  print if /[Bb]lues?/;
}
```

This would certainly select *Hambone Willie's Dreamy-Eyed Woman's Blues*, and a thousand similar titles, but it would also select *The Bluebells of Scotland*, a fine song in its place, but not, as far as I know, a staple of the blues repertoire. What you want is a pattern that is matched by 'blue' or 'blues', but only when they occur as entire words. You can use \b to achieve this, because, outside square brackets, \b is a regular expression that matches the empty string, only when it occurs between a character that could belong to a word and one that could not. That is, \b matches at the point between a \w and a \W (in either order). Thus, a better pattern would be /\b[Bb]lues?\b/.

If you examined the output from a program using this new pattern, you would find that most of the real blues songs have titles that end in the word 'blues', and that most titles with the word 'blue' in are not real blues songs at all. Therefore, a better option might be to look for lines with 'blues' at the end. You can do this using another special character. $ is a regular expression that matches the empty string just before the newline on the end of a line. (Later, we'll see how to do pattern matching on any string; if there is no newline, $ matches the end of the string.) Pragmatically, a good pattern for the blues aficionado would be /[Bb]lues$/.

▷ This example illustrates a general point about specifying patterns. The first two patterns select more titles than you want: in the jargon, they produce 'false positives'; the third pattern will miss some titles, such as *I'll sing the blues for you*; it produces 'false negatives'. (Actually, all of the patterns produce false negatives, since none of them would select *If I had possession over Judgment Day*, a blues song if ever there was one.) Whereas in tidy examples in books you can produce patterns that select just what you want, in real examples involving text, you often have to choose between false positives and false negatives. Which is worse depends on the ◁ consequences of the incorrect results.

You would expect there to be some way of matching the empty string at the start of a line, and so there is. The character ^ fulfils this function outside of square brackets. Thus, for example, the following script prints only lines containing nothing visible:

```
while (<>)
{
  print if /^\s*$/;
}
```

That is rather pointless, but you might well want to print only the other lines—the ones that do contain something visible. We need a new idiom for this, one which prints lines that *don't* match a pattern. It isn't much different from the one we have used so far.

```
▶▶──── while ─ ( < > ) ─ { ─ print ┬─────────────────┬ ; ─ } ───▶◀
                                    └─ unless ─ ⟨pattern⟩ ─┘
```

Unsurprisingly, replacing 'if' by 'unless' reverses the sense of the condition. (It's more surprising that so few programming languages let you do that.) So, this script strips out blank lines:

```
while (<>)
{
  print unless /^\s*$/;
}
```

▷ You could be forgiven for wondering why ∧ and $ are used instead of some other \ escapes. Well, Perl just isn't consistent; in this case, there is an established tradition within the Unix world of using these two characters for these purposes. Familiarity was preferred over regularity. This will not be very comforting to those of you who ◁ have never seen a Unix system.

Making Changes

No program we have seen so far does anything more than print selected lines from some data files. The selection criteria are sophisticated, and the operation can be useful, but it is hardly the stuff of great programming. We need, at the very least, to be able to change things.

To illustrate the most basic changes Perl can make to text, we need a new idiom.

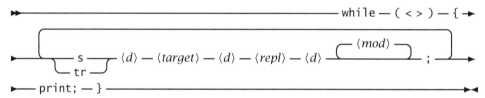

Once again, the `while (<>)` introduces a loop that operates on each line of a set of files named on the command line (or its equivalent). In this case, before printing each line, Perl makes some alterations to it.

Substitution

Each `s` introduces a *substitution* operation. (We'll get on to `tr` later.) The ⟨*target*⟩ is a regular expression, delimited by the first two ⟨*d*⟩s, which can be any character, but most people usually use slashes, as with patterns. The replacement, which extends to the final ⟨*d*⟩, specifies text to be put in place of the string in any line which matches the target pattern. If there is no match, nothing happens.

▷ As with search patterns, if you find it more agreeable, you can use matched pairs of brackets to delimit your target and replacement. In that case, despite the syntax ◁ diagram, each has its own pair of brackets, as in `s{this}[that]`.

For example, reverting to my file of song titles, instead of printing only the lines ending in 'blues', I might prefer to print the whole file, and flag the selected lines, preparatory to doing a proper scan by hand. This Perl script adds a distinctive string to each selected title (and canonicalizes to a capital B).

```
while (<>)
{
  s/[Bb]lues$/Blues <<<<<<<<<<<<<<<<<<<<<<<</;
  print;
}
```

It produces output like this:

```
Hambone Willie's Dreamy-Eyed Woman's Blues <<<<<<<<<<<<<<<<<<<<<<<<
The Bluebells of Scotland
```

If more than one substitution is given, they are done in the order they appear in the script.

A very simple application of this idiom is the correction of habitual typing mistakes. Like most self-taught touch-typists, I have a collection of words I often mis-type: 'language' comes out 'langauge' as often as not, 'regular' is 'regualr', and 'mathematical' 'amthematical' in most of my first drafts. I would like to correct these all in one go by applying a Perl script to the files I have typed, but the following one does not quite achieve the desired effect.

✘
```
while (<>)
{
  s/langauge/language/;
  s/regualr/regular/;
  s/amthematical/mathematical/;
  s/Langauge/Language/;
  s/Regualr/Regular/;
  s/Amthematical/Mathematical/;
  print;
```
✘
```
}
```

No, it's not the missing \bs in the target—they don't matter here, I'd want to make the correction to 'langauges' anyway. The trouble is that each substitution will only be performed on the first occurrence of its target on each input line. There's no problem with 'regualr langauges', because the two mistakes match different patterns, but if, as is only too likely, I had typed

```
regualr expressions describe regualr langauges
```

only the first 'regualr' would get corrected. To ensure that every occurrence of a target is replaced, you can append the ⟨*mod*⟩ g (for 'global') after the replacement, as in

```
s/regualr/regular/g;
```

and similarly for the others. Now the only problem is that I can't apply the program to this chapter, or it will destroy all the examples.

At this point, you probably want to protest that any self-respecting text editor can do substitutions like this—and searching for regular expression patterns, if it comes to that—and you would be right. However, Perl has two advantages. First, for large files with a lot of substitutions, it can be a lot faster, and you can use a Perl script in batch mode while you get on with something else. Second, and more importantly, Perl can carry out its substitution operations as part of a program doing many other sorts of operation to achieve effects impossible in even the most powerful editors, as we will see. Perl is a programming language, after all.

Back References

Still at the editor level, you probably know from experience that, when the target of a substitution describes more than one string, it is often necessary to be able to refer back in the replacement to the matching sub-string that was actually found. Going back to an earlier example:

```
s/[Bb]lues$/Blues <<<<<<<<<<<<<<<<<<<<<<</;
```

What if I didn't want to change every lower-case b to B? I would like to be able to have the replacement consist of whatever I found originally, with the chevrons appended. In a replacement text in Perl, you can refer to 'whatever I found originally' in two different ways. If you like succinct notations and don't mind them being cryptic, you can use the sequence $&, like this:

```
s/[Bb]lues$/$& <<<<<<<<<<<<<<<<<<<<<<</;
```

If you prefer something more readable and don't mind the extra typing, you can call it $MATCH like this:

```
s/[Bb]lues$/$MATCH <<<<<<<<<<<<<<<<<<<<<<</;
```

Before you can use the long name, though, you do need some red tape at the head of your program. (I know I said Perl doesn't have any, but this enables an optional facility.) Just put the incantation

```
use English;
```

near the beginning of your script. In chapter 9 you will find out exactly what it does, but for now, suffice to say it lets you call $& $MATCH. There are other names with both cryptic and long-winded versions. Generally, I shall tell you about both, but use the long ones.

Since there are only two possible targets, Blues and blues, it would have been quite painless to flag my titles without changing them simply by using two substitutions. Here is an example where this would not be feasible:

```
s/^[\d.]+/($MATCH)/
```

Any collection of numbers and dots at the beginning of a line (maybe a sub-sub-section number, like 4.53.11) will be put in brackets (perhaps to bring it into conformance with somebody's house style).

More complex substitutions can be achieved by referring to individual pieces of $MATCH within the replacement. To do this, you first need to have a way of breaking up a regular expression into pieces. This is done by isolating each part you want to extract as a sub-expression, enclosed in brackets. For example, suppose you had written a regular expression for Web page or FTP URLs (Uniform Resource Locators):[6]

```
(http|ftp)://(\w+\.)*\w+(/\w+)*/?
```

These brackets are there because they have to be to make the operators bind correctly. If I want to use this pattern to break out the domain name and pathname from a URL, I must add extra brackets round the corresponding sub-expressions, like this:

```
(http|ftp)://((\w+\.)*\w+)((/\w+)*/?)
```

In a replacement text, you can use the special sequences \$1, \$2,... to refer to the actual string which matched the first, second,... bracketed sub-expression. Sub-expressions are numbered by counting opening brackets from left to right. This expression breaks down like this:

$$(_1http|ftp)_1://(_2(_3\w+\.)_3*\w+)_2(_4(_5/\w+)_5*/?)_4$$

When it is used to match `http://www.wiley.co.uk/compbooks/cpp`, \$1 acquires the value `http`, \$2 `www.wiley.co.uk` and \$4 `/compbooks/cpp`. What about \$3 and \$5? These sub-expressions are the operands of a * operator, so the sub-expressions themselves are matched several times. What actually happens to \$3 and \$5 is that they are set to the last string matched, so they get `co.` and `cpp`. Using this behaviour is likely to get you into trouble, so it's better to stick to sub-expressions with a clearly defined matching string.

If the following script is run on a file of URLs, it will print just the domain name of each:[7]

```
while (<>)
{
  s!(http|ftp)://((\w+\.)*\w+)((/\w+)*/?)!$2!;
  print;
}
```

▷ You *can* distinguish between brackets that are being used for precedence reasons and those that are being used to delimit the sub-expressions whose matching strings will be assigned to \$1, \$2, and so on. The sequence (?: acts just like an opeing bracket; it is matched by an ordinary closing bracket, but it is not counted when the matching strings are extracted. I could have written my regular expression as

---

[6] If you don't know what a URL is or looks like, you may have missed something important that has been going on in the world lately. Consult a good book on the World-Wide Web or HTML; a couple are mentioned in chapter 11.

[7] Actually, it won't necessarily, because the regular expression isn't adequate to deal with the full range of possible domain names and pathnames, but I abhor gratuitous realism.

```
(http|ftp)://((?:\w+\.)*\w+)((?:/\w+)*/?)
```

and then, when it was successfully matched, $1 would hold the protocol, $2 the domain name, and $3 the path name. I find this so hard to read that I prefer to live with the extra sub-expressions.

A closely related but subtly different feature is the ability to refer back *within a pattern* to strings matched by bracketed sub-expressions earlier in the pattern. This allows you to write regular expressions to describe structures featuring exactly the same (arbitrary) string repeated. For example,

```
\w+ and \w+
```

describes any two words joined by the conjunction 'and'. If you want to stipulate that both words are the same, you can use a back-reference to the first to describe the second. However, you don't use $1 for back-reference within a pattern, you use \1 (and \2,... if you need them). You can rationalize this by saying that the back-reference is being used differently in the different contexts, once as a string and once as a regular expression; or you could just assume that $1 and its friends cannot be set until the pattern-matching operation is complete. Either way, just remember to use \1 within a pattern and $1 everywhere else. (Yes, we have by no means exhausted the possibilities of $1.) As with $ back-references, you must bracket sub-expressions to make \ back-references work.

The regular expression needed for pairs of identical words connected by 'and' is

```
(\w+) and \1
```

The difference between the two sorts of back-reference is illustrated in the following script:

```
while (<>)
{
  s/(\w+) and \1/$1 twice/;
  s/(\w+) and (\w+)/$2 and $1/;
  print;
}
```

This code reverses pairs of different words, turning 'Marks and Spencer' into 'Spencer and Marks', and collapses identical pairs, taking 'Saatchi and Saatchi' into 'Saatchi twice'.

Translation

A specialized form of substitution consists of the systematic replacement of one character by another, wherever it occurs. A common requirement for this *translation* operation occurs when you want to turn every upper-case letter in some string into its lower-case equivalent. This is tedious and repetitive to express using the substitution operator. For this example, I would need 26 substitutions:

```
s/A/a/g;
s/B/b/g;
```

and so on.

The `tr` operator is provided for just such translations. Syntactically, it resembles the substitution operator, but both its arguments are interpreted as strings, although a hyphen can be used as a shorthand for strings consisting of a range of characters. The effect of `tr/ABC/XYZ/` is to scan the current line for occurrences of any of A, B or C, and replace them with X, Y or Z, respectively. In general, the line is scanned for any character in the first string, which is replaced by the corresponding character in the second string. Transforming upper-case letters to lower-case letters would normally be done with `tr/A-Z/a-z/` (where I take it that EBCDIC is not normal).

Translation can be used to write an instant `rot13` translator:

```
while (<>)
{
  tr/A-Za-z/N-ZA-Mn-za-m/;
  print;
}
```

What13? I have it on good authority that `rot13` is an encoding scheme used by contributors to some Usenet newsgroups to encipher material they think might be found offensive by some readers. It works by replacing each letter with the one 13 further on in the alphabet, so A becomes N, and so on, until M becomes Z; after that, the translation wraps round, so that N is mapped to A, O to B, and so on. The script just given achieves exactly this rotation, preserving the case of letters and leaving all other characters alone (again, assuming ASCII is the character code). Because 13 is half of 26, the same program can be used to encrypt and decrypt messages; it will change

```
Amuse yourself for hours!
```

into

```
Nzhfr lbhefrys sbe ubhef!
```

and back again. (Imagine that.)

Translations are implemented with a table, so this script is not only easier to write and understand than any messing about with modular arithmetic on character codes would be, it's faster, too.

The `tr` operation has some useful qualifiers and (naturally) short cuts. If you append a `c`, then the string of characters to be replaced is complemented— that is, the translation is applied to any character *not* in the string. This is most useful in conjunction with the fact that if the second string is shorter than the first, the second is padded out with copies of its last character. Hence

```
while (<>)
{
  tr/.;?!,: \t\n/X/c;
  print;
}
```

is a better way of dealing with potentially offensive Usenet postings—it Xs out everything except white space and punctuation. This example also shows that the escapes for single characters work in the argument to tr; those such as \d and \w, which represent whole character classes in regular expressions, do not.

The qualifier s replaces runs of the same replaced character by a single one.

```
tr/ \t/ /s;
```

This translation squashes (hence the s) runs of spaces and tabs into a single space; it can be used to undo the right justification of crude word processors that don't do it properly.

Finally, if you append the qualifier d, then short replacement strings are not extended; instead, any character belonging to the search string that does not have any corresponding replacement is deleted.

```
tr/0-9/0-7/d;
```

deletes the digits 8 and 9, a crude but effective way of ensuring that numbers are octally legal.

Introducing Filehandles

All the scripts that you have seen so far have selected and transformed lines from the files whose names are specified as the command line arguments when they are run. It isn't long before you begin to wish for a more flexible way of specifying which file your input should come from. In Perl, objects called *filehandles* play a central rôle in allowing you to control input, and also output.

A filehandle takes the form of a name, usually written entirely in upper-case, such as STDOUT, STDERR or MYFILE. This convention prevents name clashes between filehandles and other program entities. You associate a filehandle with a file using an open statement, which, for simple uses, has the form:

►——————— open — ⟨*filehandle*⟩ — , — ' ⎽⎽⎽⎽⎽⎽ ⟨*filename*⟩ — ' —————————◄
                                      ⎣ > ⎦

For example,

```
open INFILE, 'myfile.data';
open OUTFILE, '>results';
```

The > in front of the file name in the second example causes the filehandle OUTFILE to be opened for output. (If the file already exists, it is truncated to zero length.) In its absence, as in the first example, the filehandle is opened for input. If you have a filehandle that has successfully been opened for input, one thing you can do with it is place it between angle brackets in the condition of a while loop:

```
open INFILE, 'songs.data';
while (<INFILE>)
{
  print if (/[Bb]lues$/);
}
```

performs the search for blues titles on the file called songs.data, instead of the files named on the command line. Here, the result is a less flexible program, but later we will see that explicit use of filehandles can greatly increase the flexibility of Perl.

In the example just given, I have started to move beyond my basic file processing idiom. As you can see, some initialization can be performed before entry to a loop, and the angle brackets can contain the name of a filehandle, instead of being empty.

You can also use a filehandle in a more general version of the print statement: the word print can optionally be followed by a filehandle that has been opened for output and a list of strings to be printed instead of the current line:

We will see in the next chapter how to write down the strings in question.

The filehandles STDOUT and STDERR are opened for output for you by the system. STDOUT is normally the default, as we have seen. STDERR is the 'standard error' stream, a Unix concept in origin. It is usually associated with your terminal, even when STDOUT has been assigned to some other file or device, so you can send messages independently of your program's regular output. Note the absence of any comma after the filehandle.

▷ Another filehandle that may be automatically opened for you is called DATA. This filehandle may be used to read data that is contained in the same file as your Perl script. If you wish to do this, you must separate the script from its data by placing the special token __END__ (that's END with two underlines in front and two behind) between them. For example:

```
while (<DATA>)
{
  print if (/[Bb]lues$/);
}
__END__
Blues fell this morning
I'll sing the blues for you
Hambone Willie's Dreamy-Eyed Woman's Blues
Dry Spell Blues, Parts I & II
```

```
The Bluebells of Scotland
Crossroads blues
If I had possession over Judgement Day
```

This may look like something from the days of stacks of punched cards and OS/360 JCL, but it can be very convenient for testing your scripts, and saves you having to ◁ keep track of special files of test data.

Comments and Layout

Even though the language features described in this chapter only allow you to write very simple Perl scripts, it is as well to get into the habit of documenting your code. Perl scripts can include comments, which are introduced by a # sign and extend to the end of the line. This allows you to include blocks of commentary by prefacing each line of a paragraph with a #—a task which any self-respecting editor will do for you—or to annotate individual statements. I offer no recommendations about what should go into your comments, beyond that it should be intelligent and helpful. Most individuals and organizations develop their own conventions, guidelines and habits. I'm not even going to say that you *must* include comments in your scripts. You know best.

▷   Indeed, you will notice that no script in this book is annotated with Perl comments. This is because I prefer to put most of the commentary in the text, and to make use of the typographical possibilities of a book for making annotations within a script more readable.

In chapter 8, you will meet an alternative mechanism for documenting Perl code, known as a pod, which is similar in spirit to 'literate programming' systems. These allow you to intermingle text and code in a natural way, and to generate a program's ◁ formatted documentation from its source.

Like comment conventions, program layout is a matter of taste and house style. Some guidelines are included in the Perl on-line documentation, but they will not suit every occasion and temperament. Not all are followed in *Perl: The Programmer's Companion*, for example.

If you do believe in comments, then you can include them within a regular expression. Since complicated regular expressions can be quite obscure, doing so can help make your scripts more readable. A comment with the form:

```
(?# ⟨comment text⟩ )
```

can appear anywhere within a regular expression, and will be ignored. Embedded comments of this form are not very attractive, though, and a better alternative is to append the qualifier x to your expression. If you do so, white space inside an expression is ignored, instead of being treated as part of the expression; this allows you to lay out your expression more attractively. In addition, you can add comments in the usual form, extending from a # to the end of the line. If you do need something to match a space in a regular expression modified by x, you just need to put a \ before it. An example of a commented regular expression being used within a substitution is the following:

```
#  Extract the path name from a URL
 s[#  An http or ftp URL
    (http|ftp):// # The protocol
    ((\w+\.)*\w+) # Domain name
    ((/\w+)*/?)    # Path name
 ]
 [$4]x;
```

Scalar Values and Variables

3

Perl makes a fine off-line text editor, but if that were all there was to it, nobody would get very excited. What makes Perl so powerful is that its editing operations are combined with other, equally sophisticated, text, file and process manipulation facilities, within the framework of a flexible and extensible programming language.

More Statements

To do more than the simple text processing of the previous chapter, we need some extra forms of statement. First, we can generalize the loop that scanned the files:

▶▶─────────── while ─ (─ ⟨expression⟩ ─) ─ { ─ ⟨loop body⟩ ─ } ───────────◀◀

where the ⟨loop body⟩ has the form:

▶▶─────────────────── ⟨statement⟩ ───────────────────◀◀

as, indeed, will all the Perl scripts we see for a while.

The statements in the loop body are executed repeatedly in order, as long as the expression is true, in a sense to be described later. So far, the only form of expression I have used to control a while loop consists of a pair of angle brackets, <>, optionally containing a filehandle. In either case, the expression is true until the associated files are exhausted. These expressions are also used for their side-effect, the reading of a line of input. We will soon see other forms of expression that can be used to control a loop.

Statements can take several forms; a while loop is itself one possible form. Another is a qualified simple statement:

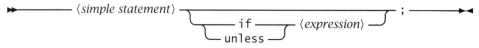

▶ As in C and C++, each simple statement is terminated by a semicolon; semicolons are statement terminators, not separators as they are in Pascal and its descendants, but you may, if you like, omit a semicolon immediately before a closing curly bracket, so it looks as if they are separators. Awk and BCPL fans will be disappointed to ◀ learn that you cannot omit a semicolon at the end of a line.

In the last chapter, the only forms of simple statement were substitutions, translations, and print statements. All of these can optionally be made to depend on a condition specified after if or unless. As well as these statements, we will soon be using *assignment* statements, with the form:

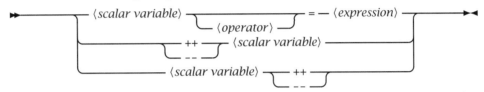

(More complex forms of assignment statement and while loops are possible, as are other loops and control structures; all will be described in due course.) An assignment is considered simple, so it can be followed by an if or unless qualifier.

The use of several statement forms in the context of an extended file processing idiom is illustrated in the following script:

```
$blues = $total = 0;
open INFILE, 'songs.data';
while (<INFILE>)
{
  $total = $total + 1;
  $blues = $blues + 1 if /[Bb]lues$/;
}
print STDOUT "There were $blues blues titles out of $total\n";
```

Scalars

No prizes for guessing what the script above does; it illustrates several distinctive features of Perl.

Scalar Variables

Although I am using variables to count the total and matching lines, there are no declarations. Perl variables need not be declared explicitly; when you need a variable, you can just use it. Two things follow from this: first, there is no way for the perl system to check whether you have mis-spelled a variable's name, although if you enable the compiler's warnings you will be told if you only ever use a name once or use the value of a variable that has not previously been assigned to, which is enough to catch many such errors. Second, no type information is statically associated with a variable name at compile time, at least, not in any conventional sense. Variables do carry a broad indication of their type in the form of the symbol preceding their name. You cannot have failed to notice that the line-counter variable is referred to as `$total`. The `$` indicates that this is what Perl calls a *scalar variable*. For the sake of your sanity, it is probably best to consider the name of the variable to be `total`, and to read the `$` as 'the scalar'. There can be other things called `total`, and other ways of obtaining a scalar value from a different type of variable.

Most valid names consist of a mixture of letters, digits and underline characters, but if a name begins with a digit, it can only contain digits. `$1` and `$2`, which we met earlier, are in fact scalar variables. Upper and lower case letters are distinct: `$svar`, `$Svar` and `$SVAR` are all different scalar variables. A name may consist of just a single punctuation character or mathematical symbol, which you still put a `$` in front of when you use it, as in `$!` but most such names have pre-defined meanings, and you should not try to define them for your own purposes. Most of them also have more readable equivalents if you `use English`.

▷ Sometimes, even the exceptions have exceptions. Although the Perl documentation states that 'Names which do not start with a letter, underscore, or digit are limited to one character', there is a collection of built-in variables with names like `$^I` and `$^W`. It turns out that the ^ and following character are translated by `perl`'s lexical analyser into the corresponding control character, such as tab for `^I`, so in some ◁ sense these sequences do conform to the stated rule.

Perl does use keywords, such as `while` and `if`, but these are not reserved words in the conventional sense. You can have a scalar variable called `while` if you insist, because it will be used as `$while`, without conflict. However, a filehandle carries no such identifying prefix, so it is possible for filehandle names to clash with reserved words. This is one reason why filehandles are usually written entirely in upper-case.

'Scalar' is a term borrowed from mathematics, where it means an individual value, as opposed to a vector consisting of several values. In Perl, scalars are numbers or strings. Inclusion of strings among scalars might be considered an abuse of terminology, since a string is an ordered sequence of several characters, but in Perl you cannot manipulate single characters (as distinct from strings of length one), but you usually treat a string as a single value.

Any scalar variable can hold any scalar value. There is no distinction between numerical and string variables, and conversion between the two types of scalar is carried out automatically whenever it needs to be. There is therefore virtually no such thing as a compile-time type error in Perl.

▷ A scalar variable can also hold something called a reference, which is used to con-◁ struct complex data structures. We will not need references until chapter 7.

Numbers and Arithmetic

In a programming language that does not distinguish between string and numerical types, it is not surprising that there is no distinction between different types of numerical value, such as floating point numbers and integers (never mind the ghastly multitude of numerical types in C and C++). By default, all arithmetical operations are carried out on double precision floating point numbers, however that is interpreted on your machine.

▷ You can put

```
use integer;
```

at the head of your program to make perl use integer arithmetic, if you are only working with whole numbers. This gains you a little speed, and means you can stop
◁ worrying about precision.

Perl has taken most of its arithmetical apparatus from C, with syntax and semantics mostly intact. Numerical constants can be written as conventional decimal numbers, like 1996 and 3.142, or you can use scientific notation, with e introducing an exponent, as in 2.998e8, for (an approximation to) 2.998×10^8. If you are that way inclined, you can use hexadecimal constants, by prefixing 0x to a string of hexadecimal digits ([\da-fA-F]+), as in 0xff1b2, or octal constants, just prefixed with a leading 0, as in 0377. You can break up long numbers to make them more readable by using underlines to separate groups of digits: 1_967_452, for example.

Table 3.1 summarizes Perl's arithmetical operators, their precedence—highest at the top, with precedence levels divided by horizontal lines—and meaning. It also includes some logical operators, which will be discussed shortly. Only a few of the arithmetical operators need any extra comment at this stage.

Unexpectedly in a primarily non-numerical language, exponentiation is built in as the ** operator .

The left and right shift operators, << and >> can be used to perform multiplication and division by powers of two as well as manipulation of bit masks. Using anything but an integer as the right operand is not very sensible. You can do it, but the result will not mean anything.

The 'bit-wise' operators ~, & and | evaluate their operands and then combine them by complementing, AND-ing or OR-ing each bit. They are only really suitable for masking and combining bit vectors.

There are a few built-in arithmetic functions, which are listed in Table 3.2. For now, call a function by following its name with an argument in brackets, as in log($x). There is more to be said on the subject of function calling syntax, though. In the table, where an argument is shown as $x, any arithmetic expression can be used; in the second column, x means the value of $x.

Operator Symbol	Meaning	Comments
++	Increment	Prefix and postfix forms
--	Decrement	Prefix and postfix forms
**	Exponentiation	
~	Complement	See text
!	Logical negation	
+	Numerical affirmation	Occasionally necessary to disambiguate expressions
-	Arithmetic negation	Unary operator
*	Multiplication	
/	Division	
%	Remainder	
+	Addition	
-	Subtraction	
«	Shift left	See text
»	Shift right	See text
<	Less than	
>	Greater than	
<=	Less than or equal to	
>=	Greater than or equal to	
==	Equal to	
!=	Not equal to	
<=>	Comparison	See text
&	Bit-wise AND	
|	Bit-wise OR	
^	Bit-wise XORExclusive OR	
&&	Logical AND	Lazy—see text
||	Logical OR	Lazy—see text
=	Assignment	
⟨op⟩=	Assigning operators	See text
not	Logical negation	Low precedence version of !
and	Logical AND	Low precedence version of &&
or	Logical OR	Low precedence version of ||

Table 3.1   Arithmetical and logical operators

Typical call	Result	Comments
atan2($x, $y)	$\tan^{-1}(x/y)$	Result is in radians and between $-\pi$ and π
abs($x)	$|x|$	Absolute value
cos($x)	$\cos x$	x in radians
exp($x)	e^x	
int($x)	$\lfloor x \rfloor$	Truncates towards 0
log($x)	$\log_e x$	
rand($x)	random number r	$0 \le r \le x, x > 0$
rand	random number r	$0 \le r \le 1$
sin($x)	$\sin x$	x in radians
sqrt($x)	$\sqrt{x}$	$x \ge 0$

Table 3.2   Built-in arithmetic functions

Truth Values and Operators

Perl does not have a Boolean type, as found in Pascal or C++; there are no Boolean constants `true` and `false`; any expression can be used as a condition. If it has a numerical value it is considered false if it evaluates to zero; if it has a string value, it is false if it is the empty string, with no characters, or if it consists of the single character 0. Any other value is true. By 'false' and 'true', we mean that the value will cause a condition to fail or succeed, respectively. When you use a pattern in a test, as we did in the previous chapter, it returns true or false depending on whether it matches or not.

The numerical comparison operators <, >, <=, >=, == and != return a true value if they succeed, false if they fail, so they can be used as conditions, for example, to control a while loop. Notice, if you have never used C, C++ or Awk, that equality is ==. A single = is used for assignment, as in Fortran. You cannot string together comparisons the way a mathematician or BCPL programmer would: constructs like $a < $b < $c are illegal, so at least they are not interpreted in the wrong way. The expression $a <=> $b returns −1, 0 or 1, depending on whether the value of $a is less than, equal to, or greater than that of $b. Respectively. This operation can be useful to avoid repeated comparisons.

The 'logical' operators !, && and || are used to combine conditions in the style of Boolean algebra. Using the bit-wise operators for this purpose would not necessarily produce the required results: ~1 is not equal to 0, in particular, so the negation of a true value is not necessarily false. !, && and || produce the right answers. Furthermore, && and || perform *lazy evaluation*: they evaluate their second operand only if necessary. Since $exp_1 \&\& exp_2$ is false if exp_1 is false, exp_2 will only be evaluated if exp_1 is true; similarly ||'s second operand will only be evaluated if its first is false. Finally, these two operators return as their value the last operand they evaluated, which you will see, if you think about it a moment, is consistent with the interpretation that anything not false is true. The behaviour forms the basis of some highly characteristic Perl idioms. A simple example is

```
$x > $epsilon && 1/$x
```

which returns the quotient 1/$x, unless $x is less than or equal to some value $epsilon, presumably chosen to be the smallest value which will prevent the division misbehaving. If $x is less than this value, the result is set to a false value to indicate the fact, and because of laziness, the division is not carried out.

The operators not, and and or have exactly the same meaning as !, && and ||, but with a much lower precedence. The Perl idiom *par excellence* makes use of or and its lazy behaviour:

```
open INFILE, 'songs.data' or die "Could not open 'songs.data'\n" ;
```

The call to open returns true or false, depending on whether it succeeds or fails. So, if the call succeeds, that is that; if it fails, the other operand of or must be evaluated. It is a call to a system function die, which terminates execution, pausing only to print an error message. The overall effect is that the program opens the file or dies (as it were). You have to use or instead of ||, unless you add brackets, because the precedence of operators means that

```
open INFILE, 'songs.data' || die "Could not open 'songs.data'\n" ;
```

would be parsed as

```
open INFILE, ('songs.data'||die "Could not open 'songs.data'\n") ;
```

—an unlikely file name.

Assignment

Often, as in the line counting program, once you have evaluated an expression, you assign the result to a variable. Simple assignment is performed by the = operator, as in the line

```
$blues = $blues + 1 if /[Bb]lues$/;
```

As you can see, an assignment can be performed conditionally, by appending if and a condition, just as printing was performed conditionally in the scripts in the previous chapter.

Following the tradition of Algol68 and C, an assignment in Perl is an expression, returning the value of its left hand side after it has been updated, so it can be used as a sub-expression within a more complex expression, if you like to do things like:

```
$n = ($y = $z +5) + $x;
```

or, less controversially, as in the line counter,

```
$blues = $total = 0;
```

which initializes both variables to zero.

Also in the Algol68 and C tradition, Perl supports composite assigning operators, such as += and *=. If ⟨*op*⟩ is an operator, the effect of

⟨*variable*⟩ ⟨*op*⟩= ⟨*expression*⟩;

is the same as

⟨*variable*⟩ = ⟨*variable*⟩ ⟨*op*⟩ ⟨*expression*⟩;

so I could have written

```
$blues +=  1 if /[Bb]lues$/;
```

An assigning operator is a single lexical item; you must not leave any space between the ⟨*op*⟩ and the =.

Later, we will see that the left hand side of an assignment can be something more complicated than just a variable. In such cases, the left hand side is only evaluated once when a composite assigning operator is used, with a slight gain in efficiency. Be careful if you habitually depend on the side-effects of expression evaluation. (Better still, stop depending on them.)

The term *l-value* is widely used to mean something you can assign to. A scalar variable is—or, more correctly, *has*—an l-value. So does an assignment expression: it is the l-value of the target of the assignment, which means you can copy something and update the copy in one fell swoop. Doing such a thing with numbers is probably inviting accusations of obscurity:

```
($x = $y) *= 3;
```

is a byzantine way of assigning $y*3 to $x. When we come to look at operations on strings in the next section, such combined operations may seem more defensible.

Perl provides an additional shorthand form of assignment for the addition and subtraction of one from a variable (or other l-value). ++$x is the same as $x += 1: it adds one to $x and returns its new value; $x++, on the other hand, also adds one to $x, but the value of the expression is the old value of $x, not the new one. I could (and usually would) have written the update to my blues counting variable as

```
++$blues if /[Bb]lues$/;
```

Think of prefix and postfix ++ as pre- and post-increment operations; the -- operator is available similarly for pre- and post-decrement.

▶ The increment and decrement operators are also found in C and C++. C++ programmers are usually in the habit of preferring pre-increment over post-increment wherever possible, especially when the operation is used on its own as a statement. This
is because of the overhead of the copying operation implied by post-incrementation.
In Perl, not only is there no question of an expensive copy constructor being called
behind the scenes, but a post-increment is optimized into a pre-increment when
that can be done without altering the semantics. I continue to prefer pre-increment,
◀ but there is no virtue in doing so.

Although an assignment is an expression, as these examples show, it can
be used on its own as a statement, and usually is. In fact, any expression
can be used as a statement. Indeed, the only form of simple statement is an
expression, which you presumably evaluate for some side effect. (Well, there
is goto, but nice programmers don't, so I'll ignore that.) Even print is an
expression, inasmuch as it returns a non-zero value when it succeeds. We
saw other examples of expressions being used as statements in the previous
chapter, because a substitution operation is also an expression; its value is
the number of substitutions performed. Here is an extended version of my
typing corrector, which counts the number of mistakes (only a couple of the
substitutions have been shown this time):

```
while (<>)
{
  $subs += s/([Ll])angauge/$1anguage/g;
  $subs += s/([Rr])egualr/$1egular/g;
  print;
}

print STDERR "$subs substitutions\n";
```

This really does do what I claim, even though it looks as if I have made
the most elementary of programming mistakes by not initializing the counter
variable. In Perl, scalar variables are automatically initialized to zero the first
time you use them for arithmetical purposes. This behaviour is guaranteed,
not a quirk of implementation, but explicitly initializing them yourself does no
harm, and may make your scripts more perspicuous. If you activate compiler
warnings, you will be told about uninitialized variables—after all, the default
is not always what you want.

Before it is used, a variable has an undefined value; certain operations also
return an undefined value as their result under exceptional circumstances.
You can test whether a variable is defined or not by passing it to the function defined, which returns true or false appropriately. (If you reason that
passing a variable to defined is using it, and ought to cause it to be initialized
to zero and become defined, you are not yet used to Perl.) Clearly, for simple
variables this test is of limited usefulness, but we will meet it again later.

You can explicitly undefine a variable, or create an undefined value using
the function undef, which may be passed an argument, which it will cause to

become undefined, or be used without arguments to generate an undefined value. Thus `defined(undef)` is always false, and you can use `undef` when you need an undefined value to indicate the failure of some operation.

Strings

Consider the statement

```
print STDOUT "There were $blues blues titles out of $total\n";
```

It does what it appears to: if `$blues` is 50 and `$total` is 190, it produces

```
There were 50 blues titles out of 190
```

on the standard output, even though `$blues` and `$total` occur within the " symbols, which as you would expect, delimit the string. To see exactly what is going on, we need to step back and look at the several ways Perl lets you write down strings.

You can write strings in several ways, which are broadly divided into two categories,[1] called *literal strings* and *interpolated strings.* The simpler are the literal strings, most often written as a sequence of characters between single opening quote symbols ('), such as

```
'Totally weird'
```

Within a literal string in single quotes, almost every character stands for itself (literally), the only exceptions being that \' is used to include a single quote within the string, and consequently it may be necessary to use \\ for \ if it occurs just before the closing quote symbol. Otherwise, nothing is treated specially, not even \n, so

```
print 'All on one line\nSecond line\n'
```

will produce the output

```
All on one line\nSecond line\n
```

(with no newline on the end). You can, however, include newlines within a string, like this:

```
print 'All on one line
Second line
'
```

to get

---

[1] There is actually a third category—deeply beloved of Unix Perl programmers—that of strings with 'command interpolation', which are constructed from the output of a system command. Some other systems are also capable of supporting command interpolation, but not all. Consult your local documentation to see whether yours does. Naturally, the commands that you can interpolate are specific to each system.

```
All on one line
Second line
```

As in any programming language that allows multi-line strings, if you miss out the closing quote of a string, perl will cheerfully swallow up everything it finds as if it was part of your string, until it reaches the next quote symbol. In Perl, the error message you eventually get is, at least, quite clear.

If you don't like ' as a delimiter, you can write literal strings in the form

q ⟨*delimiter*⟩ ⟨*characters*⟩ ⟨*delimiter*⟩

As with patterns specified with m, both delimiters must be the same, unless the opening one is some kind of opening bracket, in which case the closing delimiter will be the matching closing bracket. Examples are:

```
q!He's totally weird!
q[He's totally wired!]
```

Typically, you choose a delimiter other than ' so that you can include a ' inside your string without a backslash. If you are so unlucky that your new delimiter appears within the string, you can, of course, escape *it* with a backslash.

There is one other, vaguely disreputable, way of writing some literal strings. Any word (a string described by [A-Za-z_]\w*) is treated as a literal string if it could not be anything else, like a keyword, filehandle or, as we will see, a subroutine call. Obviously, this is an error-prone feature, but occasionally it is convenient, and many Perl programmers use it, at least sometimes. If you turn on compiler warnings, you will be told about any of these so-called *bare words*, in case they are mistakes.

Interpolated strings are different: whereas in a literal string the characters you type are exactly the characters that make up the string, in an interpolated string, two sorts of substitution are carried out on the written characters before the string's value is arrived at. The first is backslash substitution: all of the escape sequences listed in Table 2.1 are expanded, just as they are in a pattern replacement text. Secondly, any variables are replaced by their values. The simplest way to write down an interpolated string is to enclose it between double quote symbols ("). Thus, when I write

```
print STDOUT "There were $blues blues titles out of $total\n";
```

both sorts of substitution are carried out on the string before it is printed. The \n is replaced by a newline, and the values of the scalar variables $blues and $total are inserted into the string, replacing the names. This process of replacing variables by their values is referred to as *interpolation* (correctly, if pedantically) to distinguish it from the substitution performed by the s operation.

Wait a moment—the value of $blues is a number, like 50, not the string '50'. This is Perl; you don't need any explicit conversion to turn a number into its string representation. If you need a string and you have a number, the conversion will be done for you automatically.

As with literal strings, interpolated strings can be written with delimiters other than the standard ones, provided you use an explicit operator to introduce them. In this case, it is qq, as in

```
qq["She inherited a $million bucks"]
```

Here the double quotes are part of the string. As you should have supposed, and as this example illustrates, you can use brackets of the several kinds available to delimit the string, or you can use any single character at both ends if you prefer, just as you can with literal strings.

And just as you can with patterns and replacements. The similarity is no coincidence: patterns and replacements are a specialized sort of string. As we have seen, they are subject to backslash substitution; they may also be subject to variable interpolation. A replacement always is, unless single quotes are used to delimit it. If we have

```
$dollars = 1_000_000;
```

and the current line is 'You owe the tax man $amount', then

```
s'amount'$dollars';
print;
```

will produce the output

```
You owe the tax man $$dollars
```

whereas

```
s/amount/$dollars/;
print;
```

produces

```
You owe the tax man $1000000
```

The interpolation of variables in a replacement should come as no surprise. $1, $2, $MATCH, and so on, are scalar variables, and we have seen them being interpolated before.

Within a pattern, variable interpolation is done whenever a $ appears in a position where it could not be a metacharacter.

```
s/$dollars/2000000/g;
```

will change all occurrences of 1000000 into 2000000.

It may happen that you need to interpolate a variable into a string so that its value is immediately followed by some alphabetical or numerical character, for example,

      `"The distance is $distkm"`

where $dist holds the distance, and there should be no space between it and the km. (We write 70km, not 70 km.) How is perl to know you are not interpolating a variable $distkm? It cannot, so you must help by enclosing the variable name in curly brackets:

    "The distance is ${dist}km"

The $ indicating a scalar stays outside the curly brackets (otherwise they will be taken literally).

Only variables are interpolated into strings; if you write an expression within an interpolated string, such as

     "The distance is $dist*5/8 miles"

it will not be evaluated, so you would just get the string

    The distance is 64*5/8 miles

if the value of $dist was 64.

There are a few extra backslash escapes you can use in interpolated strings. They are most useful in conjunction with variables whose values you may need to modify before interpolation. The sequences \l and \u change the following character to lower or upper case if it is a letter. If you want to change the case of a whole sequence of characters you indicate its beginning with \L or \U as appropriate, and its end with \E. As you can see, these sequences are redundant if the enclosed characters are literal, but if they have been interpolated they may be useful. For example, if $ascii holds the string 'ascii', $character holds 'character' and $set holds 'Set', then

    print "The \U$ascii\E \u$character \l$set\n";

prints

    The ASCII Character set

More useful still is \Q. Within an interpolated string (including a search pattern) any metacharacters occurring in a substring between it and \E are stripped of their metacharacteristical meaning. Suppose I want to scan some Perl scripts looking for occurrences of the regular expression \b[Bb]lues?\b. Not something that matched the regular expression, but the regular expression itself. I could put in a lot of backslashes:

    print if /\\b\[Bb\]lues\?\\b/;

but that is not very pretty. Nor would it help me at all if (somehow, for some good reason) I had constructed the expression in a variable $blue_pattern and wanted to interpolate it:

     print if /$blue_pattern/;

This goes back to looking for strings matching the pattern. To get the desired effect, use \Q:

```
print if /\Q$blue_pattern\E/;
```

Apart from writing string literals and interpolated strings, another way of generating a string value is by reading a line from a file. An expression such as <INPUT> consisting of a filehandle in angle brackets has as its value the next line of the file associated with that filehandle. The empty filehandle <> has as its value the next line from the concatenation of the files named by the command line arguments. When you use this expression as the condition of a while loop, as we have done until now, all sorts of side-effects occur to produce the behaviour of the file processing idiom we have come to love. Anywhere else—at least in any context we know about yet—you just get the line, as long as there is one, and an undefined value if you have reached the end of the input.

Operations on Strings

Strings can be assigned to scalar variables.

```
$greeting = q#G'day#;
$greet_everyone = "$greeting all!";
$next_line = <INPUT>;
```

At the risk of over-stressing a point, there is no such thing as a string variable or a numeric variable. After the above code I could later write

```
$greeting = 58.7;
```

without a murmur of complaint from the Perl compiler, even if compiler warnings are enabled. I probably should not do anything of the sort, but the responsibility to ensure that my variables are only assigned semantically consistent values is mine.

A few operators are available for constructing expressions out of strings; such expressions can, of course, be used wherever a string is required, for example as an argument to print.

Concatenation of strings is written as an infix dot: $s1 . $s2 consists of all the characters of $s1 followed by all those of $s2. The precedence of . is the same as that of infix + and -. The assigning operator .= is available, and is often used to build up a string incrementally. The following script sticks together the first letters of each line of its input, in the manner of an acrostic.

```
while (<>)
{
  /(^.)/;
  $initials .= $1;
}
```

```
print "$initials\n";
```

The pattern is matched just for the side effect of setting $1 to the first character on the current line. Presented with the following eulogy (inspired by Lewis Carroll in his worst Victorian manner):

```
Post-modern language,
Eclectic in inspiration,
Reveal your potential---
Let loose information!
```

it would print

```
PERL
```

An operation for generating repetitive strings is written x (just a lower case letter x) which produces a string consisting of as many copies of its left operand as are specified by its right. Thus

```
('Hip! ' x 2 . 'Hooray! ') x 3
```

gives the three cheers for Perl I wrote a pattern to match in the last chapter. The precedence of x is the same as that of infix *. In some contexts, an x can look like part of a name, and a . can look like part of a number. Rather than try to work out which contexts these are, it is easiest to make a point of putting spaces before and after these operators.

Notice that there are operators for concatenating and repeating strings (. and x) and *different* operators for concatenating and repeating regular expressions (juxtaposition and postfix {n}).

Conversion between strings and numbers in Perl is free and easy—positively libertarian. If you use a number as an operand of an operator expecting a string, it will be converted to its conventional decimal representation. We have seen this with print, but it applies equally to . and x. 3 x 33 has the value 333333333333333333333333333333333333. Note that whereas 3.33 is an approximation to $3\frac{1}{3}$, 3 . 33 is the string 333. Hence the following script

```
$n = 3.33;
$n *= 3;
$s = 3 . 33;
$s *= 3;
print "n = $n; s = $s\n";
```

produces the output

```
n = 9.99; s = 999
```

Conversion from string to number is, as the multiplying assignment to $s shows, also performed silently when a numerical operand is needed and a string with the form of a number is supplied. Any string which does not have the form of a number can also be used in a numerical context, and some conversion will

Typical Call	Result
chr($x)	The character with code x in your machine's character set.
hex($x)	The number x interpreted as a hexadecimal constant.
oct($x)	The number x interpreted as an octal constant *unless* x begins 0x, when it is interpreted as a hexadecimal literal
ord($x)	The numerical character code of the first character of x

Table 3.3 Explicit conversion functions

be attempted, yielding zero unless the beginning of the string looks like a number. You can probably infer what the conversion code in the Perl interpreter looks like from this behaviour. If you activate the compiler warnings, you will be told if you attempt to use a string of the wrong form in a numerical context.

There is an exception. The operator ++ treats string operands in a unique, unprecedented and nicely useful way. Sometimes. If its operand has ever been used as a number, then the increment you would expect takes place. If its operand does not match the regular expression ∧[A-Za-z]*[0-9]*$, it is treated as zero, and you probably didn't mean to increment it. *But* if its operand does match that pattern, and has never been used as a number, a strange and wonderful thing takes place: digits at the end of the string are incremented, letters are incremented by converting them to the next letter of the alphabet; in both cases, if the incremented value would exceed the maximum character in a particular range ('9' for digits, 'z' for lower case letters, 'Z' for upper case letters), a carry takes place, with the last character wrapping round (to '0', 'a' or 'A') and the next character to the left being incremented in the same way. Thus, if $s holds '009' and has never been used numerically, ++$s is '010'; if $s holds 'Z', ++$s is 'AA'; and if $s holds 'Ac9', ++$s is 'Ad0'. You might use this behaviour to generate unique identifiers. The -- operator does not behave in the inverse way you might have hoped for.

There are a few functions which perform explicit conversions between strings and numbers. These are shown in Table 3.3.

You can use a string as a condition, when '' and '0' are false and anything else is true, and you can use comparison operators between strings. Here, the free convertibility between strings and numbers adds a complication, since there are two ways of comparing strings of a numerical form. Is '10' less than '2'? Obviously not, if you convert both to numbers, but equally obviously so if you compare them lexicographically. Perl avoids choosing between these two interpretations by providing two sets of comparison operators.

The numerical operators <, <=, >, >=, ==, != and <=> do arithmetical comparisons, and convert string operands to numbers if necessary. Corresponding to them, the string operators lt, le, gt, ge, eq, ne and cmp do lexicographical comparisons. They each have the same precedence as and compute the equivalent relations to their respective numerical counterparts. The following all return true: 'aa' lt 'ab', 'ab' lt 'abc', '10' lt '2' and '2.00' ne '2', although '10' < '2' and '2.00' != '2' are false. The operators force conversions on their operands, the operands do not force any reinterpretation of the operators. With no static type information, and with free convertibility between strings and numbers, it is, in general, quite impossible for the Perl compiler to tell you that you are using a numerical comparison operator when you should be using a string one. Comparing strings with < is a very easy mistake for a newcomer to Perl to make; it is up to you to know what you are doing, though.

Substitution and pattern matching provide the most flexible operations on strings in Perl, but there are some built-in functions that can also be useful. The number of characters in a string is returned by the function length: if $greeting holds 'What ho!', then length($greeting) is 8, and length("$greeting one and all!") is 21.

If you need to take strings apart and rebuild them, one option is to use the function substr, short for 'substring', since this is what it extracts. It can take either two or three arguments; the first is an expression that evaluates to a string, and the second is an offset indicating where in that string the substring is to begin; an offset of zero means the first character, one the second, and so on. If a third argument is present, it is the length of the substring.

For an example that is particularly easy to follow, suppose $numbers has the value '0123456789'. Then substr($numbers, 1, 3) is '123', the substring starting at offset 1 and extending for three characters. You can use a negative offset, in which case the starting character is counted from the end of the string: substr($numbers, -3, 3) is '789'. As you see, somewhat inconsistently, the last character is at offset -1, but then, it could hardly be at offset -0. You can use a negative length, in which case it is subtracted from the total length of the string to produce the length of the required substring: substr($numbers, 3, -3) is '3456789'. If the length you provide is too long, you get the substring from the offset to the end of the string— substr($numbers, 3, 35) is '3456789'—and if the offset is out of range— as in substr($numbers, 30, 5)—you get the empty string. If you activate perl's warnings, an out of range offset will cause a runtime error.

If you omit the third argument to substr, the extracted substring extends from the offset to the end of the string: substr($numbers, 5) is '56789'. In general, providing $n is in range, substr($s, $n) is equal to substr($s, $n, length($s)-$n).

The string returned by substr has an l-value, which means you can assign to it. If the first argument to substr has an l-value, this will update it. (If it hasn't, you will get a runtime error instead, which is no less than you will deserve.) Perl strings are real strings, not silly inflexible arrays of characters, so the new string you assign to a substring does not have to be the same length as the old one. For example, you can chop a chunk out of a string by assigning the null string to a substring, like this:

```
substr($numbers, 1, 3) = '';
```

leaves $numbers holding '0456789'. Or you can replicate a segment:

```
substr($numbers, 1, 3) x= 4;
```

turns the original $numbers into '0123123123123456789'.

The last two string functions we will consider are rather specialized: chop removes the last character of a string, chomp removes the last character if and only if it is a newline.[2]

Why would you want to do such things? Usually, it is because you are using a filehandle to read lines from a file and you want to treat the file as consisting of data records separated by newlines. Perl doesn't; it treats them as lines, each of which has a newline on the end as an integral part of it (with the possible exception of the last line in the file). By chomping off the newline, you bring the data into the format you conceived it as being in. The chop function is less discriminating, and will mess things up when the last line of your file does not have a terminating newline. This may happen quite often, depending on how your data files are prepared, and by whom. Chomping is thus safer than chopping, but chopping is more traditional—and also exactly what is required under some other circumstances.

You can leave out the argument to chomp or chop, and the function will operate on the current line... No, actually, it won't and it's about time you learned the truth about what happens with all those operations like print and s that don't take an argument and, so far, have conveniently worked on the current line of input.

These functions actually operate, in default of an explicit argument, on a built-in variable called, if you have put use English at the top of your program, $ARG, and $_ otherwise. If you use a filehandle in angle brackets as the condition in a while loop, then each time the test is evaluated, the next line is assigned to $ARG. Several other operations cause a value to be silently assigned to $ARG by default; pattern-matching, substitution and translation are applied to $ARG unless you stipulate otherwise, and several other functions operate on $ARG when no explicit argument is given. For example, all of the arithmetic functions of one argument listed in Table 3.2, may be called just by giving their name; log is equivalent to log($ARG), and so on.

This is all rather shocking to software engineers and conventional programming language experts, isn't it? Such serious side-effects and hidden arguments defy the tenets of most programming methods. But if you think of $ARG as being something like a pronoun—something like 'it', in fact—which refers back, in a well-defined manner, to the result of a recent operation—you will see that there is a precedent for such behaviour in natural languages, even if it is rare in programming languages. You can think of $MATCH, $1, and the others as being like pronouns, too. It's not so awful, really.

---

[2]Not quite only if: it removes the 'input record separator', which usually *is* a newline.

More About Substitution and Pattern Matching

So now you know that the pattern matching, substitution and translation operations from the previous chapter were all secretly operating on $ARG. What if you want them to operate on some other string? The string binding 'operator' =~ is provided for this purpose. I have put 'operator' in inverted commas here because, although =~ is syntactically an operator (with a high precedence, between that of ! and infix *), it is not something which takes some operand values and combines them into a result. Rather, it redirects the application of some other operator—perhaps the operation is its operand?

Coming up with a coherent explanation of the semantics of =~ considered as an operator is much more difficult than understanding what it does from a couple of examples. So, whereas

```
s/([Rr])egualr/$1egular/g;
```

fixes some typing errors in $ARG,

```
$the_line =~ s/([Rr])egualr/$1egular/g;
```

fixes the same errors in the string currently stored in $the_line. Similarly,

```
print if /[Bb]lues$/;
```

prints $ARG if it ends in Blues or blues, and so does

```
print $ARG if $ARG =~ /[Bb]lues$/;
```

$ARG does not have to be implicit, if you prefer to spell everything out.

The =~ operator does return a result; it is the result that would be returned by the operation on its right hand side. If you wanted to count the number of spelling corrections being made, the following would work just as well as the version given earlier:

```
$subs += $ARG =~ s/([Rr])egualr/$1egular/g;
```

The left hand operand of =~ can be any expression with an l-value. This begins to lead us towards the 'Guess what this does' style of programming:

```
$subs += ($the_line = $ARG) =~ s/([Rr])egualr/$1egular/g;
```

copies $ARG into $the_line and then changes all mis-spellings of regular in $the_line; $ARG retains its original value, so don't do this:

✗   `$subs += ($the_line = $ARG) =~ s/([Ll])angauge/$1anguage/g;`
✗   `$subs += ($the_line = $ARG) =~ s/([Rr])egualr/$1egular/g;`

The second assignment re-copies $ARG, so the first set of changes is lost. If you like these *portmanteau* constructions that do several things at once, you might approve of this:

```
$subs += ($the_line = <>) =~ s/([Ll])angauge/$1anguage/g;
```

that reads the line, assigns it and corrects it all in one. However, you may well
find that organizing the flow of control in your program once you have done
so is not easy. Sometimes it is better to plod along with the clichés.

▷ A strictly redundant operator !~ binds a string to a pattern match or substitution
and then logically negates the result, so

```
print $ARG unless $ARG !~ /[Bb]lues$/;
```

is the same as

```
print $ARG if $ARG =~ /[Bb]lues$/;
```

You already have ! and unless, which can produce any effect you could with !~,
but !~ allows you to stress the exceptional nature of your substitution's failure,
◁ where that is appropriate to making yourself clearer.

We saw earlier that interpolation only causes the substitution of variables'
values and not the evaluation of expressions. Some sophisticated substitutions
become possible if you treat the replacement in a substitution operator as an
expression, and evaluate it. To do this, you must add the qualifier e after the
replacement. Doing so would enable me to convert distances in kilometres into
miles:

```
s!(\d+)km!($1*5/8).' miles'!ge;
```

The pattern matches any number followed by km, setting $1 to the number of
kilometres. This is converted to miles by multiplying by 5/8 (causing an implicit
conversion to a numerical value) and then the string ' miles' is appended
(causing conversion back to a string). Notice that I have to use an explicit
concatenation operator, and enclose the string in quotes. When you use the e
qualifier, the entire replacement is treated as an expression, not just any bit,
like ($1*5/8), that looks like one.

▷ If the evaluated expression produces a string in the form of an expression, you can
evaluate that, in its turn, by appending another e after the first one. And so on. Such
tricks are beloved of fans of macro processors, but do not contribute to readable
◁ programs, and should probably be avoided, except for your own amusement.

Two Examples

To conclude this chapter, I will develop a couple of complete Perl scripts to
perform some real computation, albeit of a simple kind.
First, let us use the text manipulation facilities of Perl that we have learned
to perform a literary experiment. The writer William Burroughs is known for

his lurid visions of the universe, and for pioneering the use of certain semi-mechanical techniques of composition, such as the 'cut-up', a sort of literary collage, whereby new texts are assembled by cutting up and mixing together old ones, and the similar 'fold in', which he has described as follows:

> A page of text—my own or someone else's—is folded down the middle and placed on another page—The resulting composite text is then read across half one text and half the other. [...]In using the fold-in method, I edit, delete and rearrange as in any other method of composition.[3]

Perl can't help with the last part, but if you have text in machine-readable form, the purely mechanical business of combining halves of two pages is easily accomplished by a short script.

We will try to do a little better than you could by just putting the folded pages under a scanner. Instead of just breaking each line in the middle, we will break it between words, as near the middle as possible, so the combined halves will not contain any actual gibberish.

I begin by opening two files. Here I have wired their names into the code, which is obviously inflexible. In chapter 5 we will see how to explicitly open files named on the command line. First of all, I need to invoke the long names of built-in variables.

```
use English;
```

Now here is the cliché for opening a file or giving up if the open fails. I will try to be a little more helpful by including the error code in my dying message. The variable $OS_ERROR (also known as $!) is set to this value if the operation fails.

```
open TEXT1, "conrad" or die "could not open conrad ($OS_ERROR)\n" ;
open TEXT2, "cppx" or die "could not open cppx ($OS_ERROR)\n" ;
```

For this program, I will assume that both pages have the same number of lines, so I can just keep looping as long as one of them is not empty. My strategy inside the loop will be to break each line read from the filehandle TEXT1 into two approximate halves in the variables $left1 and right1, and each line from TEXT2 into $left2 and right2. I read from TEXT1 in the loop condition, which tests for the end of file by seeing whether the value read is defined, then read from TEXT2 and chomp both lines.

```
while (defined($right1 = <TEXT1>))
{
  $right2 = <TEXT2>;
  chomp $right1;
  chomp $right2;
```

---

[3]From *The Third Mind* by William S. Burroughs and Brion Gysin (John Calder, London, 1979).

Now I work out where the middle of the first line is and break it into two using
`substr`. I don't bother with the niceties of rounding, because we are going to
find an exact break point later by looking for a word break.

```
$half1 = int(length($right1)/2);
$left1 = substr($right1, 0, $half1);
$right1 = substr($right1, $half1);
```

Next, I pull any characters that could form part of a word off the front of the
right half and stick them on the end of the left half.

```
$right1 =~ s/^(\w*)//;
$left1 .= $1;
```

Now I do the same thing to the other line, except that I make sure that the right
half does not begin with a punctuation mark that might appear incongruous
when the two halves are concatenated.

```
$half2 = int(length($right2)/2);
$left2 = substr($right2, 0, $half2);
$right2 = substr($right2, $half2);
$right2 =~ s/^(\w*)[\.,\?!;]?//;
$left2 .= $1;
```

All that is left to do is write out the combined line and terminate the loop.

```
    print "$left1$right2\n";
}
```

Figure 3.1 shows the result of running this script over a page from that
bottomless well of textuality, Joseph Conrad's *Heart of Darkness*, and a page
from my own *Late Night Guide to C++* . The text has been formatted to fit the
page, but no other changes have been made. The result clearly needs some of
that editing, deleting and rearranging, but is quite promising in parts. Mostly
the parts Conrad wrote.

▷ If you take this sort of thing seriously, there is considerable scope for text mangling
and manipulation in Perl. Obvious extensions to the fold-in technique, such as
recombining the folded in text with itself, or recursing, converge to a stable state or
break up quite rapidly. However, there would seem to be potential in, for example,
randomizing the break points, or using more texts. A program called `travesty`
that attempts to produce new texts based on the frequency of word combinations
in an original is distributed with Perl. I found the results disappointing, although
the approach sounds promising on paper.

   If you get anywhere with this, mention *Perl: The Programmer's Companion*
◁ when you accept the *Prix Goncourt.*

For the less literary minded, here is a program more at one with the computing world, a world permeated with initials, from the utilitarian CCITT and

I started the lame engine ahead put in perspective. There is trader—this intruder," exclaimed the. Function libraries have been at the place we had left. "He must be, though, because functions save him from getting into trouble if, but not of data, only small manager darkly. I observed with assumed put in a library. The majority from trouble in is concerned with manipulating the particular data structures The current was more rapid now, the steamer to say, though, that re-use of stern-wheel flopped languidly, and I caught-orientation—it just isn't done the next beat of the boat, for in sober mechanisms. thing to give up every moment. It was life. But still we crawled. Sometimes that OOP is a revolution way ahead to measure our progress, before objects, every new project invariably before we got abreast. To simply is not true. The first was too much for human patience. The a new system to build is to resignation. I fretted and fumed and can be adapted. Adaptation may or no I would talk openly with Kurtz and extending, but it does conclusion it occurred to me that my of existing code. Furthermore, action of mine, would be a mere futility repertoire of data structures at knew or ignored? 'what did it matter list insertion function or a such a flash of insight. The essentials one they've done before, surface, beyond my reach and in to the new context. You can type. The ideas, algorithms and Towards the evening of the second day not the physical code itself. miles from Kurtz's station. I wanted introducing (or re-introducing) grave, and told me the navigation up there the new version, but it is be advisable, the sun being very low a component in a library, reading next morning will be suitable, and perhaps

Figure 3.1 A folded in text

ASCII, through the merely cute WYSIWYG, to the awful IMHO and OTOH that infest the Usenet newsgroups. Here is a first version of a script that reads a file containing a phrase on each line and extracts the initials of each word of the phrase.

Once again, I will use long names for built-in variables, but this is the last time I will explicitly show the red tape. From now on, you can assume it is always there.

```
use English;
```

The script uses the file scanning idiom, with each line being chomped.

```
while (<>)
{
  chomp;
```

I am going to remove words from $ARG one at a time until there is nothing left. I prepare for this by making sure there is nothing at the beginning of the line before any words—I want to make as few assumptions about the input as necessary.

```
s/^\W*//;
```

I remember the phrase and set a variable to hold the initials to the null string.

```
$phrase = $ARG;
$initials = '';
```

Now loop through this phrase, removing a word and any following non-word characters, by substituting the empty string, until there is nothing left. By bracketing the regular expression used in the substitution, I make sure that the word is remembered in $1. I include apostrophes in words, otherwise unexpected results are produced.

```
while ($ARG)
{
  s/^([\w']+)\W*//;
```

I use `substr` to extract the first letter of the word, and append it to $initials.

```
  $initials .= substr($1, 0, 1);
}
```

Finally, I print the phrase and its initials (in upper case), and loop for the next one.

```
  print "$phrase -> \U$initials\E\n";
}
```

The script produces output like this:

```
what you see is what you get -> WYSIWYG
what you see is all you've got -> WYSIAYG
what you get is not what you want -> WYGINWYW
```

I realize that anybody capable of reading this book could carry out this algorithm without the help of a computer, but later we will see how the script can be extended to build a more useful program that decodes the initials for you. We will also see some other, arguably better, ways of doing the job. (There is, after all, more than one way of doing it.)

Flow of Control

4

With the features described in the previous chapter, Perl is a recognizable programming language, although as yet we have seen only a little of its full extent. In particular, although its primitive data types and the operations on them have been described in some detail, the scripts you have seen rely on only a crude form of loop and the conditional execution of an individual simple statement for organizing the flow of control.

Before we can go on to look at Perl's structured data types, we must redress the balance by considering its repertoire of structures for controlling the flow of statement execution.

Conditionals

You will not get very far with a program in any language if it does not make choices. Because simple statements in Perl can do quite elaborate things, we have managed so far by qualifying simple statements with if and unless to make their execution contingent on the value of some expression. Sooner or later you will need to make the execution of a *sequence* of statements depend on a condition, or choose between two or more sequences to execute. For this, you will need the full conditional statement, which resembles those of most imperative languages. Indeed, for that reason, many programmers will prefer it to a qualified statement, even for a single statement.

The full syntax is:

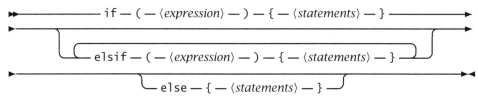

▶ The syntax is closest to that of C; if you are more used to Pascal you should note the absence of any explicit then keyword and the presence of brackets round the condition. As previously explained, this condition may be any expression—its result will be interpreted as false if it is 0, '0' or '' and true otherwise. Another syntactical detail you should note—C programmers included—is that the curly brackets ◀ are necessary even if only a single statement is controlled by the condition.

The semantics holds no surprises. The statements following the if are executed if the expression evaluates to true. Thus, the following adds one second to a time stored as a number of minutes and seconds in the two variables $mins and $secs.

```
if (++$secs == 60)
{
  ++$mins;
  $secs = 0;
}
```

If there is an else, the statements following it will be executed when the test following if fails, so the next code fragment sets $longer to whichever of two strings $a and $b is the longer, or to $a if they are the same length.

```
if (length($a) >= length($b))
{
  $longer = $a;
}
else
{
  $longer = $b;
}
```

The keyword elsif (note the spelling) is used when you have a series of mutually exclusive tests, to permit the elision of some curly brackets. This script prints a message determined by the form of each input line, as well as counting the lines that contain something it recognizes.

```
while (<>)
{
  ++$lines;
  if (/\d{4}\s\d{4}\s\d{4}/)
  { print "credit card number\n"; ++$matches; }
  elsif (m!http://((\w+\.)*\w+)((/\w+)*/?)!)
  { print "web page URL\n"; ++$matches; }
  elsif (m!ftp://((\w+\.)*\w+)((/\w+)*/?)!)
  { print "FTP URL\n"; ++$matches; }
  elsif (/^X+$/)
  { print "kisses!\n"; ++$matches; }
  else
  { print "unrecognized\n"; }
}
print "$matches matches in $lines lines\n";
```

Perl does not have a conventional switch or case statement, although `elsif` provides a reasonable alternative, and the optimizations usually performed on cases are performed on a sequence of `elsif` tests consisting of comparisons with constants.

You may use the keyword `unless` anywhere you can use `if`; the effect is to logically negate the condition. Sometimes this will result in a more natural formulation of your algorithm. Disappointingly, there is no `elsunless`.

The `if` construct is a genuine statement, not an expression, so it does not have a value. This seems a little unsporting. However, there is a conditional expression, which steals its repulsive syntax from C.

⟨*test*⟩ ? ⟨*expression₁*⟩ : ⟨*expression₂*⟩

A snappier way to set `$longer` is:

```
$longer = length($a) >= length($b)? $a: $b;
```

 You can achieve the effect of some conditionals using Boolean operators; the paradigm of this is the idiomatic code for opening a file or calling `die` if the attempt is unsuccessful (see page 36). You have to be careful, though. Thinking about Boolean algebra and implication may lead you to suppose that you can replace

⟨*test*⟩ ? ⟨*this*⟩ : ⟨*that*⟩

by

    (⟨*test*⟩ && ⟨*this*⟩) || ⟨*that*⟩

Sometimes you can, but not if ⟨*this*⟩ might legitimately evaluate to zero or the empty string. Consider:

```
$non_negative = $a < 0 ? 0 : $a;
```

and

✗   `$non_negative = ($a < 0 && 0) || $a;`

Because you want to return 0 for negative numbers, the `&&` clause always evaluates to 0 one way or another, so `$non_negative` is always set to `$a`. So the conditional expression is not redundant after all.

Loops

More About While Loops

We know that to achieve any non-trivial computation we must be able to execute statements repeatedly while some condition holds. For the ascetic programmers among us, the simple while loop, as we have seen it already, is enough.

However, forcing every repetitive computation into a while loop with a single exit can be awkward, leading to duplication of code or the artificial use of flags and state indicator variables. Although the programming theorists tell us that loops with a single entrance and exit are easiest to reason about (i.e. to get right), most programmers find the ability to break out of a loop, abandon an iteration, or repeat an iteration without testing the condition can be convenient for dealing with exceptional occurrences. Perl provides these facilities and more. Here is its while loop in its full glory:

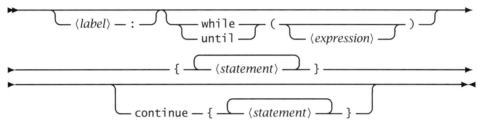

Although I will refer exclusively to a 'while loop', you will see that the keyword `until` can be used instead of `while`, with the effect that the loop is executed repeatedly as long as the controlling expression is false.

▶ Do not confuse an until loop with Pascal's repeat...until loop. In Perl, the condition is always checked before the loop, so an until loop may never be executed, if the condition is true when it is first entered. To achieve the effect of a loop that is always executed at least once, you must use a different device, which will be described later.

◀

As with the if statement, the curly brackets around the loop body are compulsory, even if the loop body is just a single statement. You can, though, use `while` and `until` as qualifiers after a single simple statement, the same way I used `if` and `unless` in chapter 2. This provides an opportunity for you to emphasize the action over the repetition where that is appropriate. For example

```
print while (<>);
```

is another version of the file copying program from chapter 2.

The additional syntactical features of the while loop introduced here only make sense in conjunction with some new statements, which you can only use inside a loop.

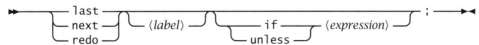

The simplest of these is `last`, which causes an immediate exit from the loop; `next` and `redo` are a little more subtle. Both cause the current iteration to be abandoned, but whereas `next` causes the controlling expression to be tested to see whether to start another iteration, `redo` just goes back to the start of the loop body, without doing the test.

You can exercise fine control over the effect of `next` with the continue block, which may follow the loop body proper. It is always executed just before the condition is tested, so under normal circumstances it is just an annexe to the loop body. If you execute a `next` command, though, the continue block is executed, although the rest of the body is skipped. A `redo` or `last` command skips the continue block.

If the expression controlling the loop is omitted, it is taken to be `true`, so a loop beginning

```
while ()
```

is an infinite loop. Unless your program is intended to execute forever, there must be a `last` statement in the loop, or some other form of abrupt exit.

It may seem unlikely that all these loop features could be required at once, and the following example *is* a wee bit contrived, but you should be able to see the usefulness of the various constructs, even if you can think of another way of writing the loop.

I am going to construct a simple interactive command interpreter. All it is actually going to let you do is control the value of a variable, using the commands `up`, `down` and `zero` to add one, subtract one, and set its value to zero, respectively. Use your imagination to magnify this into something like an interactive debugger. I will provide a `quit` command to terminate the interaction, and a shorthand command !, which will cause the most recent command to be repeated. More precisely, it will cause the most recent *legitimate* command to be repeated, because I will diagnose and reject illegal input. After each command, the variable's current value is to be printed.

I will begin by explicitly initializing the variable whose value is being changed by the commands, and another one which I will use to remember the previous command, in case it has to be repeated. As you are aware, this initialization is superfluous, but it makes it clearer what is going on.

```
$n = 0;
$last_cmd = '';
```

I will use $ARG to hold the current command; I need to prime it before entering the loop, so I prompt for the first command. Some systems buffer terminal output and only actually transmit a line to the terminal when a newline is sent. I want the prompt to appear on the same line as the user's response, though. I can guarantee that terminal output will appear immediately by assigning a true value to the built-in variable $OUTPUT_AUTOFLUSH, also known as $|.

```
$OUTPUT_AUTOFLUSH = 1;
print "$n\ncommand?  "  ;
chomp($ARG = <STDIN>);
```

I set up an infinite loop to read commands from the user.

```
while ()
{
```

The command just read is tested against each legitimate possibility in turn.
The first few don't deserve any commentary.

```
if ($ARG eq 'up')
{ ++$n; }
elsif ($ARG eq 'down')
{  --$n;  }
elsif ($ARG eq 'zero')
{  $n = 0; }
```

The repeat is more interesting. First, I have to see whether there is anything to
repeat, by checking whether $last_cmd still holds the empty string. If it is no
longer empty, then I assign its value to $ARG; I now want to proceed exactly as
if the last command had just been entered again, so I jump back to the start of
the loop with redo.

```
elsif ($ARG eq '!')
{
  if ($last_cmd)
  {
    $ARG = $last_cmd;
    redo;
  }
```

If there is nothing to repeat—! is the first command, so $last_cmd is empty—I
inform the user, and go straight on to the next iteration.

```
  else
  {
    print "No previous command to redo\n";
    next;
  }
}
```

If the command was quit I do so by leaving the loop without staying on the
order of my going.

```
elsif ($ARG eq 'quit')
{  last;  }
```

I don't know how to deal with any other command, so I print a message and go
on to the next iteration.

```
else
{
  print "Unknown command <<$ARG>>\n";
  next;
}
```

I only reach the statement following these tests if I have dealt with a legal command; in that case, I want to remember what it was. If I had an error of any sort I do not want to remember it—presumably the user does not expect to be able to repeat an error. Therefore, the assignment to $last_cmd should be inside the loop body. However, the current value of $n should be printed and a new command read even if there was some error, so these actions belong in the continue block.

```
    $last_cmd = $ARG;
}
continue
{  print "$n\ncommand?   "  ;  chomp($ARG = <STDIN>); }
```

The syntax diagram tells you that a loop may be labelled. These labels are not the labels recidivistical programmers go to; they are special, and may only be used with the loop transfer statements. As the second syntax diagram shows, each of last, next and redo may be followed by a label; the diagram cannot tell you that this label must be the label on a loop the transfer appears inside. Syntactically, a loop label is just a name, with no identifying prefix corresponding to the $ on scalar variables. It is customary to use all upper-case letters for them, both to make them stick out, and to avoid clashes with reserved words. Using loop labels has two purposes. First, it provides documentation, clearly linking a transfer of control with the larger structure it occurs in. Second, it permits you to exit from several layers of nested loop. The most common use of this facility is for abandoning a computation when some abnormal condition is detected.

An easily understood example of the usefulness of a multiple loop exit is provided by a simple script that compares two files whose lines are sorted in lexicographic order and prints lines that occur in both files. Because the files are sorted, the task is easy: you read each line of the first file in turn. For each line, you read and discard lines from the second file as long as they are less than the current line from the first, since they cannot possibly match. You then compare the current lines from the two files; if they match, you print them, otherwise you go back and get the next line from the first file. Provided there are no duplicate lines in either file, and you prime the current line from the second before you start, all goes well, until one or other of your files runs out. You do not know which file is shorter, so you may encounter an end of file condition reading from either. If you have ever tried this, you will probably have discovered that trying to test for the end of both files in one or other of the loop headers will leave you tied in knots, probably repeating the test in several places. It is far easier to detect the end of file when it occurs, and abandon processing there and then. If it is in the inner loop, this means abandoning both loops. A labelled last statement will do this just fine.

Assuming you have successfully opened filehandles FILE1 and FILE2, the following code will print matching the lines.

```
    $line2 = <FILE2>;
```

```
LINE:
while (defined($line1 = <FILE1>))
{
  while ($line1 gt $line2)
  {
    last LINE unless defined($line2 = <FILE2>);
  }
  print $line2 if $line1 eq $line2;
}
```

▷ If you studied the syntax diagram for the while loop at all carefully, you may have been mildly astonished to discover that you can have a while loop with no `while`. It is not a mistake, it is Perl. A sequence of statements enclosed in curly brackets and possibly labelled is a loop that executes once—unless the curly brackets are doing something syntactical like delimiting one of the clauses of a conditional. You may object that any sequence of statements is a loop that only executes once, but you would be wrong, because in a loop, you can use the control transfer statements `last`, `next` and `redo`. In the absence of a loop condition, this may look suspiciously like something nasty and unstructured, and it is. You wouldn't catch me doing that
◁ sort of thing.

Before leaving the while loop, there is one additional pattern-matching idiom that should be mentioned. Just as you can add a g qualifier to a substitution to make 'global' changes, you can add one to a pattern. At first sight this makes no sense at all: a pattern matches or it doesn't; how can it match globally? In general, it cannot do so meaningfully, but in a loop, a pattern may be matched by a different substring in its target each time round the loop. Each time it will set $MATCH and its friends, and 'remember' where the match occurred; next time round, it will start looking for a match where it left off, only failing when it has run out of matches. This iterative matching behaviour is what the g qualifier does to a pattern matching operation.

Here is an improved version of the script to extract the first letters of phrases, which shows this behaviour in action.

```
while (<>)
{
  chomp;
  $initials = '';
  while (/([\w']+)\W*/g)
  {
    $initials .= substr($1, 0, 1);
  }
  print "$ARG -> \U$initials\E\n";
}
```

Unlike the previous version, this script does not have to take apart $ARG, nor worry about ensuring that leading punctuation or spaces are removed to make sure that the string will eventually diminish to the empty string. Each time the pattern is matched, $1 is set to a word, as required. The loop is exited when there are no words left to match.

For Loops

You might think that the richness of Perl's while loop would be enough for anybody, but there is another form of loop, the for loop. This construct only really comes into its own in conjunction with arrays, which will be introduced in the next chapter. It is derived from C's for loop, which provides a more general iterative construct than the simple counting loops in other languages, so it can sometimes provide a more compact formulation of your algorithm than a while loop. Whether or not the result is more readable is a matter of opinion, and will depend on how much time you have spent writing C, C++ or Java programs.

The syntax is as follows:

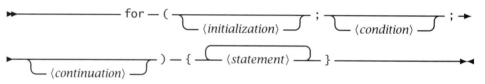

where ⟨*initialization*⟩, ⟨*condition*⟩ and ⟨*continuation*⟩ are all expressions. The loop is exactly equivalent to one of the form:

Because of this equivalence, last, next and redo can be used inside a for loop; because the ⟨*continuation*⟩ is performed just as a continue block, it will always be executed after a next.

A for loop *can* be used in Perl for simple counting loops. Then, the ⟨*initialization*⟩ sets up a counter variable, the ⟨*condition*⟩ tests it against a final value, and the ⟨*continuation*⟩ adds or subtracts a constant increment:

If the ⟨*increment*⟩ is one you will probably prefer to use ++ instead of += 1. For example:

```
for ($i = 1; $i <= 10; ++$i)
{
    print "$i times table\n\n";
```

```
    for ($j = 1; $j <= 10; ++$j)
    {
      $m = $j * $i;
      print "$j x $i = $m\n";
    }
    print "\n\n"
}
```

To demonstrate that a for loop can do more than count through some numbers, I rewrote the command line interpreter using a for loop instead of the while loop. To prove a point—I'm not saying which—I also removed all the control transfer statements and used state variables instead.

```
use English;

$last_cmd = '';
$n = 0;
$OUTPUT_AUTOFLUSH = 1;
for ($redoing = $quitting = 0;
     !$quitting and ($redoing or
     (print "$n\ncommand?  " and chomp($ARG = <STDIN>)));
     $last_cmd = $ARG if $redoable)
{
  $redoing = 0; $redoable = 1;
  if ($ARG eq 'up')
  { ++$n; }
  elsif ($ARG eq 'down')
  {  --$n;   }
  elsif ($ARG eq 'zero')
  {  $n = 0; }
  elsif ($ARG eq '!')
  {
    if ($last_cmd)
    {
      $ARG = $last_cmd;
      $redoing = 1; $redoable = 0;
    }
    else
    {
      print "No previous command to redo\n";
      $redoable = 0;
    }
  }
  elsif ($ARG eq 'quit')
  { $quitting = 1;  $redoable = 0; }
  else
  {
    print "Unknown command <<$ARG>>\n"; $redoable = 0;
  }
}
```

Block Expressions

Some programmers favour a style of programming in which a sequence of statements culminating in an expression is used in place of a simple expression. We all use functions for this purpose, but some languages allow you to put such a block in any syntactic context where an expression could be used. Algol68 springs to mind as an example, and BCPL programmers will remember `valof...resultis`. Perl, too, has this facility.

A construct of the form

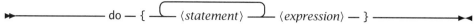

causes the statements to be executed, and then returns the expression as its value. Presumably, the value of the expression depends on side effects of the execution of the statements.

▷ Do you want to be absolutely accurate? Remember that any expression is actually a statement in Perl, so what you have inside the curly brackets of a do block is a sequence of statements. The returned value of the block is the value computed by the last statement executed. There may be conditionals among the statements, so the last value computed may not be an expression at the end of the block. Readability and style considerations suggest that, if you use do blocks, they should have the form shown in the syntax diagram. There is no semicolon after the final expression because of the rule that semicolons may be omitted before a closing curly bracket.

◁

A common use of a block of this sort is to make the test of a while loop occur after some statements have been executed, instead of at the very beginning of the loop. This may help you avoid `last` statements and continue blocks, if you do not like them. I could, for example, have written my command interpreter with a loop header consisting of a do block:

```
while (do {
        print "$n\ncommand?   ";
        chomp($ARG = <STDIN>);
        $ARG ne 'quit'
     })
```

The test for the quit command, and the associated `last`, can be removed from the loop body, and the continue block can be dispensed with. A do block would also have made the for loop version of this program more readable.

A second use of a do block depends on an anomaly in its behaviour, which might just have been put there on purpose. If you put a `while` or `until` qualifier after a do block, then it is repeated, just as any simple statement consisting of an expression would be, except that the do block is evaluated before the test. This property of do blocks gives you a way of writing those loops that must always be executed at least once, in the style of Pascal's repeat...until and (as it happens) C's do...while. Since I have never yet written such a loop in any programming language that didn't turn out to be wrong, I will omit any examples.

▷ A similar facility for generating a single value from a sequence of expressions is provided by Perl's comma operator. If an expression has the form

⟨*expression*₁⟩ , ⟨*expression*₂⟩

then the first expression will be evaluated, presumably for its side effects, since the result will be thrown away and the second expression will be evaluated to get the result of the whole expression. Except that the comma is so heavily used in the syntax of Perl that this will only be the case if it occurs in the right context. Even where there is no such confusion, the comma is a very insignificant operator and the sequencing is easily overlooked. Although the essence of Perl programming is to do whatever you like that works, this is one construct I would advise against.
◁ There are other ways of achieving the same effect.

Subroutines

Subroutines, routines, functions, procedures…whatever you call them, and whether you consider them to be an indispensable mechanism for abstracting over statements and expressions, a handy way of breaking your program into manageable pieces, or a way of optimizing the size of your program…Perl has got them.

When you declare a subroutine (let's call them that, for consistency with the keyword used to declare them) you give a name to a sequence of statements. The syntax could hardly be simpler.

sub — ⟨*name*⟩ — { ⟨*statement*⟩ } —

The keyword sub tells you and perl that this is a subroutine declaration, the ⟨*name*⟩ is the name you wish to give to your subroutine, and the statements in curly brackets are the body of the subroutine. Using the name (calling the subroutine) will cause the body to be executed. You have abstracted away the details of the computation performed by the statements, allowing you to refer to the entire computation by the single name; or, if you prefer, you have written the code for the function body once, and can invoke it many times using a subroutine call.

Although Perl provides a confusing variety of notations for calling subroutines, for those without arguments, using its name followed by an empty pair of brackets () as a statement or an element of an expression is adequate for now. For example, I might declare a subroutine, based on an example from chapter 3, to translate distances and speeds from metric to imperial units.

```
sub km_to_miles {
  s!(\d+)km!($1*5/8).' miles'!ge;
```

```
    s!(\d+)kph!($1*5/8).'mph'!ge;
    print;
}
```

Implicitly, it works on $ARG and prints the line produced by the translation. I might call it like this:

```
km_to_miles() while (<>);
```

You might object that in such a trivial context, there is no point in using a subroutine, but I hope that it is not necessary to labour the point that for real programs, abstraction is a necessity if we are to cope with complexity. Although the examples exhibited so far are trivial, Perl is not a toy, and realistic Perl scripts can attain a level of complexity that demands the use of the program structuring capabilities of subroutines.

If you accept that point, you will probably object more strongly that abstracting a statement sequence by giving it a name is hardly adequate. Subroutines must be able to return results, so that they can be used as functions to abstract over expressions; they must have local variables, so that their internal computations can be confined without affecting the program's global state; and they must be able to take arguments, so that they can provide parameterized abstractions, which capture the effect of an infinite family of computations, differing only in the values of some variables provided by the caller.

Strange as it may seem, you cannot understand Perl's method of passing arguments to subroutines before you know about its array data structure, but results and local variables are simple.

Locals are introduced by the keyword my:

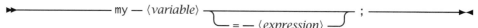

For scalars, the ⟨*variable*⟩ includes the $ prefix; other kinds of variables can be local, too. If the optional assignment is present, it provides an initial value for the variable. Variables are usually made local to a subroutine, but they may be local to any block of statements enclosed in curly brackets, such as the body of a loop. The initializing expression is evaluated every time the local declaration is encountered.

Any variables used in a subroutine but not declared local with my are global[1] and may be accessed in the rest of the program. A subroutine may access global variables, either built in ones such as $ARG or user-defined ones. It may not, however, access any variables declared local to other subroutines, including those it has been called from. A local declaration will hide a global variable of the same name. In short, my implements static (or lexical) scoping.

    C programmers would say these variables belonged to the 'automatic' storage class.

---

[1]In fact they are only global to the module they are being used in, but since I have not yet described modules, the distinction is academic.

Although the use of globals, particularly those built in to Perl, is not considered total anathema in Perl, and may sometimes be preferable to passing arguments to and results out of subroutines, a programming style that relies heavily on them cannot be recommended. It is always best to constrain the interaction between different parts of a program, to make reasoning about what is going on—or going wrong—easier.

▷ There is an unfortunate legacy from earlier versions of Perl that may cause some terminological confusion. Before my was added to Perl, you could use a function called local to achieve a similar, but different, effect. Unlike my, which is evaluated at compile time, local is evaluated at run time. Its effect is to store the current values of any variables passed to it, restoring them on exit from the enclosing scope unit. It thus appears as if these variables were local to that unit. However, there is a big difference between variables localized in this way, and true local variables declared by my: the effect of local extends to any subroutines called from within the block to which the variables have been made local, since what you have done is give a local value to a variable whose scope is still global. These variables thus exhibit *dynamic scope*. Dynamic scoping makes thinking about your program more difficult, because it requires you to think about the chain of function calls, and not just the program text. Now that my and statically scoped variables are available, they should be preferred.

You may see the phrase 'local variables' being used in the Perl literature to refer to global variables that have been localized by the local function. I have consistently used the phrase to refer exclusively to statically scoped variables, declared within a block using my, since that is what the phrase means in most other programming languages I expect my readers to be familiar with, and there is no satisfactory
◁ alternative.

Results are returned from a subroutine in one of two ways. Either an explicit return statement, simply having the form

```
return ⟨expression⟩ ;
```

may be executed, with the effect of returning the value of the expression; or an expression to be returned may be evaluated as the last action in a subroutine, in the style of a do block. Your previous programming experience will dictate which of these mechanisms you consider the more natural. Neo-classical post-retropunks prefer explicit return statements, and I will always use them. A subroutine may include more than one return statement, perhaps on different branches of a conditional; similarly, different expressions may be the last thing evaluated, depending on the flow of control. Many programming theorists will tell you that every subroutine should have exactly one return statement, which should be at the end of the subroutine body, but not many programmers listen to those theorists.

A simple example of a subroutine with local variables that returns a value is this one, which counts the number of words in $ARG and returns the total. A word is loosely defined to mean a string consisting of letters, numbers, under-lines and apostrophes. While this may not conform to what you think a word is, it is adequate for estimating the length of manuscripts.

```
sub words_in_line {
  my $count = 0;
  ++$count while /[\w']+/g;
  return $count;
}
```

The local variable $count keeps track of the number of times we go round the while loop induced by the g qualifier on the pattern match. Since the pattern matches a word (as I have chosen to define it) each time, the final value of $count is the number of words in $ARG, so it is returned as the subroutine's result.

This subroutine can be used as if it was an expression, as it is here in a program which appends a running word count to each line of its input.

```
while (<>)
{
  chomp;
  $w += words_in_line();
  print "$ARG\t--$w\n";
}
```

Subroutine declarations can appear anywhere—there is no requirement that they be declared before use, and executable code may be interspersed freely with the declarations. However, for the sake of readability and to prevent some subtly strange behaviour, it is best to declare all your subroutines at the out-ermost scope level and to declare them before they are used unless you have a good reason not to do so.

A Small Compiler

Although we still cannot pass arguments to our subroutines, we are in a posi-tion to do some non-trivial computation in Perl. To demonstrate this, I will write a small compiler. Well, all right, perhaps 'extremely small translator' would be a better description, but I will structure it as a single pass recursive descent compiler. The purpose of this translator will be to assist with the production of syntax diagrams, such as the ones that decorate this book. The example is quite long, in order to show you a larger Perl script doing a relatively complex task, and at the same time, to illustrate the fact that conventional programming techniques can be used effectively in Perl, despite the superficial unconvention-ality of the language. It is also intended to consolidate the description so far, and to introduce a couple of minor language features.

I don't suppose many readers will give a moment's thought to how these diagrams are produced, and probably those few who do will assume that I use a graphics package to draw them. Some of us cannot even draw with a computer to help, though, so they are actually produced in quite a different way. If you are used to seeing what you are getting, the following description may horrify you.

Perl: The Programmer's Companion is typeset using LaTeX, which is a generic markup language. Typesetting commands, or 'tags', such as \chapter and \begin{table} are interspersed with the text, which is prepared with an ordinary text editor. Subsequently, the marked up file is processed by the TeX typesetting program, which produces output suitable for previewing and printing. LaTeX is extendible via a powerful macro facility, which has been used to produce many packages of extensions for setting particular sorts of material. One such package is Mark Wooding's syntax package, which includes a facility for setting syntax diagrams.

A diagram is introduced by the command \begin{syntdiag} and ended by \end{syntdiag}. Within it, symbols that stand for themselves may be written enclosed in double quote symbols (although backslashes must be doubled, since backslash is a special character in LaTeX, just as it is in Perl); those that represent syntactic categories, such as ⟨*expression*⟩, are enclosed in angle brackets. I will call these two sorts of symbol terminals and nonterminals, respectively, just to show I know something about grammars. A sequence of elements may be written one after the other. A collection of choices, which will appear as branches in the diagram, is introduced by \begin{stack}; individual choices are separated by \\; the collection is ended by \end{stack}. Elements to be repeated are enclosed between \begin{rep} and \end{rep}. If there is a separator between the repeated elements it follows a \\ before the \end{rep}; the separator will be set as a label on the backwards loop of the corresponding part of the diagram. All of these constructs may be nested within each other (although using anything complicated as a separator is complex and not advised). The package provides extra facilities and options, which need not concern us here.

Figure 4.1 shows a syntax diagram describing an element of a syntax diagram as written in LaTeX; below the diagram is the LaTeX source used to produce it. That isn't what I wrote, though. The syntax description was written in a modified form of extended BNF notation, and the code was generated from that by a simple Perl script.[2] Figure 4.2 shows the EBNF description for Figure 4.1.

In the EBNF notation I use, nonterminals are enclosed in angle brackets, as before, but terminals are enclosed in single quotes (simply to avoid the shift key); alternatives are separated by a vertical bar, as in Perl regular expressions; optional elements are enclosed in square brackets and repeated elements in curly brackets. If there is a separator between repeated items, it is written inside the curly brackets after an asterisk. The notation is neither standard nor particularly elegant, but it is somewhat easier to type than the raw LaTeX commands, and is easier to compose for someone used to thinking about grammars.

---

[2]Actually, the script does not do the indentation, since its output is not intended for humans.

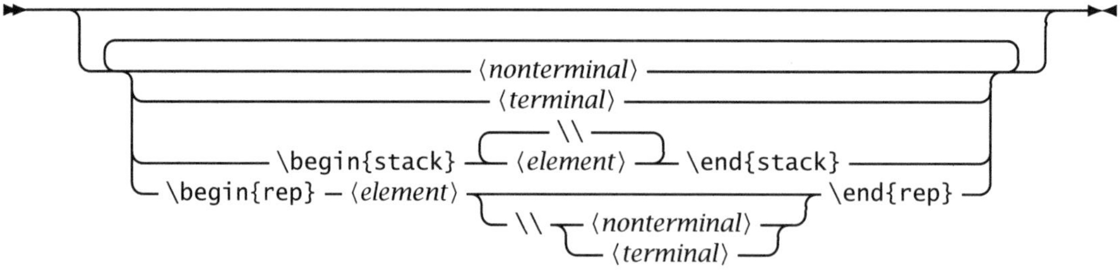

```
\begin{syntdiag}
\begin{stack} \\
  \begin{rep}
    \begin{stack}
      <nonterminal> \\ <terminal> \\ "\\begin{stack}"
        \begin{rep}
          <element> \\ "\\\\"
        \end{rep}
      "\\end{stack}" \\
      "\\begin{rep}"<element>
      \begin{stack} \\
        "\\\\"
        \begin{stack}
          <nonterminal> \\ <terminal>
        \end{stack}
      \end{stack}
      "\\end{rep}"
    \end{stack}
  \end{rep}
\end{stack}
\end{syntdiag}
```

Figure 4.1   A syntax diagram and its LaTeX source

```
[{<nonterminal> | <terminal> |
'\begin{stack}' {<element> * '\\' } '\end{stack}' |
'\begin{rep}' <element>
[ '\\' ( <nonterminal> | <terminal> ) ]
'\end{rep}' }]
```

Figure 4.2   Extended BNF description of a syntax diagram

EBNF	LaTeX
`'terminal'`	`"terminal"` (backslashes doubled)
`<nonterminal>`	`<nonterminal>` (backslashes doubled)
$EBNF_1$ `|` $EBNF_2$ `|` ...`|` $EBNF_n$	`\begin{stack}`
	LaTeX$_1$ `\\`
	LaTeX$_2$ `\\`
	...
	LaTeX$_n$
	`\end{stack}`
`[ ` *EBNF stuff* ` ]`	`\begin{stack} \\`
	LaTeX stuff
	`\end{stack}`
`{ ` *EBNF stuff* ` }`	`\begin{rep}`
	LaTeX stuff
	`\end{rep}`
`{ ` *EBNF stuff* ` * sep }`	`\begin{rep}`
	LaTeX stuff
	`\\ sep`
	`\end{rep}`

Table 4.1   Translation between EBNF and LaTeX notations

Once you have understood the two notations, the translation required becomes clear. It is summarized in table 4.1.

The first task that must be carried out by a translator is to take an EBNF description and separate it into its tokens—the individual lexical units such as brackets and nonterminals.[3] The decision as to what constitutes a token is a pragmatic one. I have chosen to treat each terminal or nonterminal as an indivisible symbol, rather than separate the delimiters and individual characters. At the same time as each token is picked out, white space can be discarded.

In compilers, this process is usually called lexical analysis, and it is customary to define the structure of tokens using regular expressions. In compilers written in mainstream programming languages, it is necessary to write (or automatically generate) a program to recognise tokens, usually by building a finite state machine from the regular expression describing their structure. In Perl, this is unnecessary, because the recognition of strings described by regular expressions is built into the language. Therefore, I can begin by writing a regular expression to describe my tokens. I will store it in a variable, for ease of modification, since I may need to use it in a pattern in more than one place.

---

[3]More correctly, these lexical units should be called *lexemes*, and token should be used for the integer codes customarily used to represent each class of lexeme in languages that have trouble dealing with anything more complicated than an integer. However, usage is casual, and lexeme is not a very happy word.

Comments and white space embedded in a regular expression are part of the expression, so I can embed such comments in my string, provided that any time I interpolate it into a pattern I add the x qualifier.

```
$tokens = q{\|           # vertical bar
          |\*            # separator separator
          |'[^']+'       # terminal
          |<[^>]+>       # nonterminal
          |\{|\}|\(|\)|\[|\] # various left and right brackets
};
```

I have used an explicit q to introduce a string delimited by curly brackets, in the hope that the result is more readable. I must put backslashes in front of all the regular expression metacharacters that occur within the string. The only interesting sub-expressions are those for nonterminals and terminals. I have described a nonterminal as a sequence of characters enclosed in angle brackets; I should have said, a sequence of characters other than a right angle bracket. The naïve pattern <.+>, which does, indeed, match any sequence of characters enclosed in angle brackets would lead to some surprises. Supposing my input included:

```
<a nonterminal> 'a terminal' <and another nonterminal>
```

<.+> would be matched by the entire line. This is because pattern matching is 'greedy'—a pattern is matched by the longest substring possible. This is usually what you want, but it means that you must be careful that your regular expressions say what you mean. For delimited strings, patterns such as <[^>]+> are required, which explicitly show that the closing delimiter cannot be part of the string.

▷ There is also a technological fix. The regular operators *?, +? and ?? mean exactly the same as *, + and ?, except that they match the shortest possible substring, not the longest. You can also put a ? after repeat counts in curly brackets. If you are worried that x*? was already a valid regular expression, you can prove some theorems to show that it was redundant.

You do not need these 'non-greedy' operators, and you may prefer to avoid them, because their use in a regular expression makes it necessary to think about the pattern matching process, rather than the set of strings described by the expression, in order to see what it does. However, sometimes, a greedy expression can be very clumsy compared to its non-greedy equivalent. Consider what you would need as a pattern to match nonterminals if they were enclosed between <# and #>, ◁ for some reason.

My lexical analyser is a subroutine next_token that returns...the next token. I will revert to my technique of stripping successive tokens out of the current line, until there is nothing left except, possibly, some white space. A global $the_line holds the current line while it is being taken apart. I thus know that if $the_line contains only white space, I need to read another line, either because I have a blank line or because I have used up the current line. I must, of course, take account of the possibility of multiple blank lines.

Since `$the_line` will be initialized to the null string by default, the first call to `next_token` will cause a line to be read. If, at any time, there is no line to read, the input operation will fail. In that case, I will return the otherwise illegal token EOF to indicate the fact.

```
sub next_token
{
  while ($the_line =~ /^\s*$/)
  {
    return 'EOF' unless defined($the_line = <>);
  }
```

Next, I must try and extract my token. I will strip out any preceding white space at the same time, for the sake of neatness.

```
if ($the_line =~ s/^\s*($tokens)//ox)
{
  return $1;
}
```

As advertised, I have appended the x qualifier to the substitution operation. You will also notice an o qualifier, which I have not mentioned before. The o stands for 'once' and refers to the number of times the pattern is compiled. Patterns which have interpolated variables in them may change over the course of a program's execution, so they have to be compiled into the internal form used by the pattern matcher every time they are used. The o qualifier tells `perl` that the compilation should only be done once. This is only a sensible optimization when, as here, the value of the variable never changes. There is no way for the compiler to check that the value of the pattern does not really change—you will just get wrong answers if it does.

Like most tasks in compiler writing, lexical analysis is easy as long as nothing goes wrong. It is necessary, though, to take account of the possibility of input that includes illegal tokens. If that happens, the substitution will fail. What should be done then?

A good strategy is to replace the offending symbols with a special error token, and pass that back as the result. When the error token is encountered later on in the compilation process it will trigger an error message the same way as a legitimate token in the wrong place would. This way, you can confine the error handling to one place. You must make sure that the input is cleaned up so that the offending symbol will not be read again. There are two cases to consider. If there is a legal token on the same line as the error, then everything up to that legal token should be discarded; I pack the discarded material into the error token to provide additional information. If there is no legal token left on the current line, the entire remaining line should be discarded. Hence, the remainder of the `next_token` subroutine looks like this:

```
else
{
```

Try matching against the token pattern. If the match succeeds, there is a token on the line; the built-in variable $PREMATCH ($`) will have been set to every-thing before it, $POSTMATCH ($') everything after it, since these two variables are always set to the substrings before and after $MATCH whenever a pattern matching operation succeeds.

```
if ($the_line =~ /($tokens)/ox)
{
  $the_line = $MATCH.$POSTMATCH;
  return "LEX_ERROR($PREMATCH)";
}
```

If the match fails, nothing on this line is any good, so I copy the entire line to put into the error token and set $the_line to the empty string, to force a read next time next_token is called.

```
else
{
  chomp($the_error =  $the_line);
  $the_line = '';
  return "LEX_ERROR($the_error)";
}
}
}
```

What is going to happen to the tokens returned by next_token? I will use them to determine whether the input is a correctly formed EBNF description, and, if it is, I will generate LaTeX commands to draw an equivalent syntax dia-gram. To do this, I need a grammar describing the form of legal EBNF descrip-tions. Such a grammar is shown in the form of (what else?) syntax diagrams, in Figure 4.3.

My compiler uses the recursive descent technique. This means that I must write a subroutine for each of ⟨*diagram*⟩, ⟨*diag*⟩, ⟨*alt*⟩, ⟨*item*⟩ and ⟨*prim*⟩, which recognizes and translates that construct. The structure of each sub-routine follows the structure of the corresponding syntax diagram, with while loops in the code corresponding to loops in the diagram, and conditionals to branches. The first token that has not been parsed so far (the lookahead to-ken) is used to control the loops and conditionals. It is important to ensure that each token is parsed exactly once. I do this by ensuring that, on entry to each subroutine, a global variable $the_token holds the lookahead. It is the responsibility of each subroutine to ensure that this invariant is maintained. The exception is the subroutine for diagram, which starts the whole process off by establishing the invariant.

For reasons which will become clear, every other subroutine returns a string holding the translation of the input which it, and any subroutines it called, has read. When diag finishes execution, we can print the string it returned, topping and tailing it appropriately. Before doing so, though, it is necessary to make

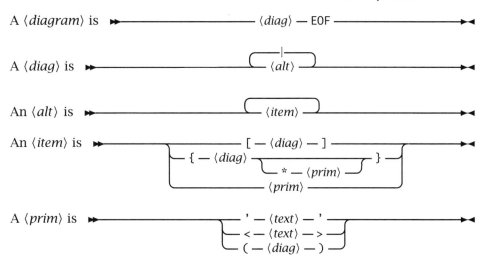

A ⟨*diagram*⟩ is

A ⟨*diag*⟩ is

An ⟨*alt*⟩ is

An ⟨*item*⟩ is

A ⟨*prim*⟩ is

Figure 4.3   Grammar for the EBNF notation

sure that the lookahead is EOF as it should be, and to protest otherwise. This translator stops whenever it finds an error in its input.

```
sub diagram
{
  $the_token = next_token();
  my $output = diag();
  unless ($the_token eq 'EOF')
  {  die "rubbish on end of input\n";  }
  print "\\begin{syntdiag}\n", $output, "\\end{syntdiag}\n";
}
```

As Table 4.1 shows, if we have a series of alternatives separated by vertical bars, we must generate instructions to draw each alternative, separated by \\, and enclosed in \begin{stack} and \end{stack}. The problem is that we don't know that we have such a series until we see the first vertical bar, *after* we have finished with the first alternative. It is for this reason that it is impossible to generate the output on the run; we need to hold on to the translation of the first ⟨*alt*⟩ until we know whether to generate a \begin{stack}. I count the number of times I have called the subroutine alt to see whether I need to do this. I know from the syntax diagram for ⟨*diag*⟩ in Figure 4.3 that I must keep on calling alt as long as the lookahead is |.

```
sub diag
{
  my $output = alt();
  my $alternatives = 1;
```

```
while ($the_token eq '|')
{
```

If I enter this loop, there is more than one alternative. I have to write the separators each time, flush the | to maintain the invariant, and then append the result of calling alt to $output.

```
$output .= "\\\\\n";
$the_token = next_token();
$output .= alt();
++$alternatives;
}
```

On exit from the loop, if I counted more than one alternative, I wrap the begin and end of the stack around the translated string.

```
if ($alternatives > 1)
{
  $output = "\\begin{stack}\n" . $output . "\\end{stack}\n";
}
return $output;
}
```

The subroutine alt must cope with a different problem. There is no explicit separator between items, corresponding to the |s between ⟨alt⟩s, so how do we know how long to keep looping, calling item? The answer is that we keep going until we find something that can legitimately follow an ⟨alt⟩. To discover the legitimate followers in general calls for some subtle mathematics and pretty algorithms, but for this simple grammar we can do it by looking at the diagrams—'by inspection' as they say. Checking for one of these legitimate following symbols is done by pattern matching, of course.

```
sub alt
{
  my $output = item();
  $output .= item() until $the_token =~ /^([])}|*]|EOF)$/;
  return $output;
}
```

Whereas the last two subroutines have been loops, item must deal with a set of alternatives. Inspection of the syntax diagram shows that two of these begin with distinctive tokens, so the lookahead can be used to choose between the alternatives. On returning from the recursive call to diag the lookahead should hold the closing bracket corresponding to the opening bracket used to identify the construct; this is checked for and an error message is issued if it is not found, otherwise the appropriate code is produced and returned.

```
sub item
{
  if ($the_token eq '[')
```

The enclosed element is optional, so generate a stack with an empty first alternative:

```
    {
      my $output = "\\begin{stack} \\\\\n";
      $the_token = next_token();
      $output .= diag();
      unless ($the_token eq ']') {  die "unmatched [\n";  }
      $the_token = next_token();
      return $output . "\\end{stack}\n";
    }
```

A curly bracket indicates the start of a repeated element. Produce the prefix for this, then call diag recursively to deal with it.

```
    elsif ($the_token eq '{')
    {
      my $output = "\\begin{rep}\n";
      $the_token = next_token();
      $output .= diag();
```

If the lookahead is a star, then there is a separator.

```
      if ($the_token eq '*')
      {
        $output .=  "\\\\";
        $the_token = next_token();
        $output .= prim();
      }
```

When we reach this point, the lookahead must be the closing curly bracket.

```
      unless ($the_token eq '}') {  die "unmatched {\n";  }
      $the_token = next_token();
      return $output . "\\end{rep}\n";
    }
```

For any other lookahead, we must look for a ⟨*prim*⟩. The lookahead is left alone, to preserve the invariant.

```
    else
    {
      return prim();
    }
  }
```

▷ A small point of style: I have used unless statements when I test for matching closing brackets, rather than qualifying the call to die with an unless clause, even though it requires two sets of extra brackets. I have done so because I want to stress the test; its failure and the consequent death ought to be rare and of lesser importance. Writing

```
    die "unmatched {\n" unless $the_token eq '}';
```

stresses the wrong thing. Conversely, I used until as a qualifier in the subroutine
◁ alt to stress the call of item.

The subroutine for ⟨*prim*⟩ begins with a similar case: if the lookahead is a bracket, we have a bracketed sub-expression, and must call diag recursively, then check for the matching closing bracket.

```
sub prim
{
  if ($the_token eq '(')
  {
    $the_token = next_token();
    my $output = diag();
    unless ($the_token eq ')') {  die "unmatched (\n";  }
    $the_token = next_token();
    return $output;
  }
```

The only other legitimate things we can have are nonterminals and terminals. We check the first character to make sure we have one or the other (this is sufficient, since the lexical analyser cannot return any other token beginning with either < or ').

```
  elsif ($the_token =~ /^['<]/)
```

If it is, change the single quotes to double ones, and double up the backslashes.

```
  {
    my $output;
    ($output = $the_token) =~ tr/'/"/;
    $output =~ s/\\/\\\\/g;
    $the_token = next_token();
    return $output;
  }
```

If all tests have failed, then the next token has no right being where it is.

```
  else
  {
    die "unexpected token <<$the_token>>\n";
  }
}
```

Note that this is where lexical errors will cause the program's death.

To set all this in motion we need to call diagram. It can only return if all goes well, which we may as well tell the user about.

```
diagram();
print STDERR "The EBNF was translated successfully\n";
```

Although the example I have just presented carries out a translation that is highly specific to one particular environment, I hope that it is obvious that other translators can be built using a similar framework: all you need to do is define the language that you are translating from, by providing a regular expression for its tokens and syntax diagrams for its structure, and define the translation of each structure into its equivalent in the language you are translating to. You should then be able to write the translator almost as fast as you can type. The only difficult bit is calculating the sets of tokens that can follow each construct, which you need to compare against the lookahead to determine when you have reached the end of a structure. For most small languages, these sets can be calculated just by looking at the syntax diagrams.

If you have ever read about, or written, recursive descent compilers in a more conventional programming language, you will recognize that the recursive descending is done in just the same way in Perl, but all the tedious and treacherous work of comparing strings, and building them and taking them apart, that takes so much effort in C or Pascal is done by native operators and functions in Perl. I could write a translator in C++ that looked just about as simple, but to make it work, I would have to construct—or find in a library—suitable classes to do the work that is done for me by Perl, with no effort on my part.

Exception Handling

The recursive descent translator illustrates a well-known computing fact: everything is easy until something goes wrong. When my program detects an error it just dies, because I know that attempting to recover from a syntax error without causing an avalanche of spurious error messages, skipping excessive amounts of input, or even crashing, is difficult. Often, giving up and dying in the face of erroneous input or other unforeseen events, such as failed attempts to open files, is not considered acceptable, and you have to try and do something about it. The trouble is that, often, it is not possible to do anything at the point where the error is detected. Instead you have to transfer control somewhere else, usually to a subroutine some way back in the chain of calls that led to the detection point.

Effecting such a transfer using conventional control structures is messy, and hard to get right. The best you can usually do is set some global error flag and return from the current subroutine, or return a special error value (often undef in Perl) trusting that your caller will check the flag or return value and take some appropriate action, such as propagating the error return, or fixing up the problem before trying again.

Error-checking code based on such a scheme can often overwhelm and obscure the code for doing the real job at hand, so many programmers prefer a different approach. In C, the functions setjmp and longjmp are used to allow you to make abrupt transfers of control out of the currently executing function, to a defined point from which recovery can begin. In more recent languages, the fashion is for more elaborate control structures designed specifically for handling exceptions, as unforeseen events are usually called. In C++, when an error is detected, you can 'throw an exception' of a particular type, which causes a transfer of control out of the currently executing function to an exception handler, designated to deal with exceptions of that type. Similar facilities are provided in Ada and Modula-3.

Perl, too, has exception handling, but as you might expect by now, without much in the way of elaborate linguistic machinery. In fact, exception handling falls out, almost as a side-effect, of a language feature apparently designed for a different purpose. We will approach exceptions obliquely, therefore, by looking first at the language feature on which it depends.

The eval Function

In its original form, the built-in function eval takes a string, and treats it as a Perl script, compiling it (at run-time) and then running it. Using eval you can construct parts of a program dynamically as it runs, perhaps on the basis of the input it receives. For a trivial example, consider a little guessing game. The program prompts for one of three words; only one of these is the correct answer. The start of the process is obvious.

```perl
$OUTPUT_AUTOFLUSH = 1;
print "this, that or tother? ";
chomp($guess = <STDIN>);
```

There are several obvious ways to proceed, but also a less obvious one. Suppose you define a subroutine for each possible answer, which prints a suitable response to the guesser:

```perl
sub this {
  print "not this\n";
}

sub that {
  print "yes, that\n";
}

sub tother {
  print "not tother\n";
}
```

What you want to do is call the subroutine whose name is in $guess. By passing $guess with a pair of empty brackets appended to eval that is exactly what you will do: the string is treated as Perl code. Since it has the form of a call to one of the subroutines, whose name is the input supplied by the user, the effect of eval will be to call that subroutine.

```perl
eval "$guess();";
```

If the user typed this, then the effect of this statement is to run a little Perl script comprising a call to the subroutine this. Since scripts run by eval execute in the environment in which `eval` was called, the declarations are in scope, and the correct effect is achieved.

In older versions of Perl, dynamic evaluation like this was needed to achieve certain computational effects which can now be achieved less deviously using new language features. Dynamic evaluation is only necessary if you need to construct your script on the basis of information that is not available until run time. Even then, it is well to look for alternative ways of achieving your goal, because `eval` can be very dangerous. Consider, for example, this run of the script just displayed.

```
this, that or tother? print "you win the jackpot\n"; exit
you win the jackpot
```

The wily guesser has cheated by typing a string which, when treated as Perl code, will cause a winning message. So what? This is a silly example, but in later chapters we will meet Perl functions which could do extreme damage to your files and other system resources. Constructing scripts dynamically out of user input could be asking for trouble.

What, then, is the point of `eval` if it is too dangerous to use for anything that cannot be achieved another way? It is its behaviour when something goes wrong that makes `eval` interesting.

Handling Exceptions

If a syntax error is detected, or a run time error occurs, during the execution of a call to `eval`, it immediately returns an undefined value and puts the error message into a built-in variable called $EVAL_ERROR, or $@. If no error occurs, $EVAL_ERROR will hold the empty string. That is, errors that would normally cause a program to terminate merely cause a transfer of control back to where `eval` was called from. In particular, a call to `die` does not cause death, but only an end of the current call to `eval`, with `die`'s argument being stored in $EVAL_ERROR. Isn't that more than a little like throwing and catching a named exception?

Real examples that require exception handling are too complicated for an introductory book like this, but the principle is easily illustrated. Suppose I modify one of my little subroutines like this:

```
sub tother {
  print "not tother\n";
  die "horrible death";
}
```

Now, if the user guesses `tother`, the message will be stored in $EVAL_ERROR when `eval` returns. The program will not cease, though. I could catch the exception by testing the value of $EVAL_ERROR, and recover from it, like this:

```
while()
{
  print "this, that or tother? ";
  chomp($guess = <STDIN>);
  eval "$guess();";
  $EVAL_ERROR or last;
  print "try again...\n";
}
```

In more realistic situations, a program might throw more than one sort of exception. That is, code executed from within a call to eval might call die in more than one place, with different arguments. By using pattern-matching on the value of $EVAL_ERROR, the calling program can discriminate between the different sorts of error, and take action appropriate to each.

▶ If you are familiar with C++'s exception handling facilities, you will see that a call to eval with an argument that may call die is like a try block; within it, die functions rather like throw; the effect of catch is achieved by pattern-matching on the error value. Exceptions cannot be grouped together using inheritance in Perl, but you could achieve a similar effect by using common prefixes in the strings passed to die, and arbitrary information can be encoded in those strings if necessary. You cannot, of course, call virtual functions through exception objects in Perl. ◀

Calls to eval can be dynamically nested, and exceptions that cannot be dealt with can be re-thrown:

```
sub main {
  eval 'the_code();';
  if ($EVAL_ERROR =~ /easy error/)
  {
    recover();
  }
  else
  {
    die $EVAL_ERROR;
  }
}

eval 'main();';
if ($EVAL_ERROR)
{
  print "Irrecoverable error\n";
}
else
{
  print "No problem\n";
}
```

But there is a problem with this: the argument to eval is being compiled expensively at run time, even though, in this case, we know all we need to know about it at compile-time. We are just using eval for its exception handling property. Under these circumstances, you can get the exceptions without the cost, by passing the code you want executed to `eval` in curly brackets, instead of as a string. The example just outlined would be better done with the calls to `eval` written as:

```
eval { the_code(); };
```

and

```
eval { main(); };
```

This form of `eval`, which is a purely compile-time construct, provides Perl with an efficient and simple exception-handling mechanism.

Dealing with unexpected events by throwing exceptions remains a controversial pastime, even though exceptions have been supported by mainstream programming languages for some time. One school of thought holds that it is a clean and effective technique, while another believes it to be a crude and dangerous way of escaping responsibility. In any language, effective exception handling requires more than just linguistic technology. Careful design and a consistent approach to exceptions is necessary if all the parts of a program are to work together, even when unforeseen events occur. This is especially true where libraries are being used. Thus, decisions about how to handle exceptions go beyond language issues, but if you need them, `eval` and `die` are there in Perl.

Lists and Hashes

5

Scalars are individual values. Often, you need to deal with a collection of values, such as the names of all the blues songs in a file of song titles, sometimes manipulating the collection as a whole. Even the crudest of programming languages provide some data types for representing such collections: at the very least, one dimensional arrays or vectors of a fixed size can be used to store an ordered sequence of values of the same type, with individual array elements being accessible using a numerical index into the array. More sophisticated languages provide dynamic arrays, which may grow or shrink as your program runs, and higher dimensional arrays or matrices. The highest level programming languages—particularly functional ones—provide sequence types, usually called lists, which, as well as behaving like dynamic arrays, can be taken apart, combined, and otherwise operated on by a collection of high level operators; at this level, lists become proper data types in their own right, rather than simply being containers for scalars.

Another way in which some higher level programming languages have extended the means of data aggregation provided by simple arrays is by allowing the indexes used to select individual elements to be strings—or even more complex objects—instead of numbers. The resulting data types are often called associative arrays, since they provide an association between a string, which you might think of as a key, and another data value. Associative arrays are also sometimes called tables, or dictionaries.

Perl provides dynamic arrays of scalars, with a good selection of operators for working on them, and associative arrays, which in Perl are called hashes, after the data structure most commonly used to implement associative arrays.

List Values and Arrays

Perl's arrays possess many of the features of lists, and a certain amount of terminological confusion between 'array' and 'list' pervades the Perl literature.

Making up my own terms would only add to this confusion, so I will try to stick with the 'official' usage, despite its occasional inconsistency. A list is an object consisting of a sequence of values; one way of writing down such a sequence is:

It is common to refer to this syntactic structure as a list, too. For example

```
1, 2, 3, 5, 7, 11, 13, 17, 19, 23
```

is a list (syntactically), or has as its value a list (semantically) consisting of the first ten prime numbers. It may help, in what follows, to imagine that whenever you write an expression that evaluates to a list, the resulting sequence of elements is then written in this form in place of the expression. Like any other expression, a list may be enclosed in brackets without changing its meaning; because of the low precedence of the list-forming comma, and other complications to be revealed later, it is almost always necessary to do so, although some idiomatic Perl uses unbracketed lists—notably the list of values in a print statement.

Lists which comprise a contiguous range of values can be generated using a shorthand notation:

⟨*expression₁*⟩ .. ⟨*expression₂*⟩

produces a list whose first value is ⟨*expression₁*⟩ and last value is ⟨*expression₂*⟩, with the elements in between differing by one, if the two expressions are numerical in value. For example, 1..10 produces the list 1, 2, 3, 4, 5, 6, 7, 8, 9, 10. If the limits of the range are not numerical, then the elements of the list will be generated by incrementing the initial value in the same way as the ++ operator works on strings. Hence 'Aa'..'Ak' is a shorthand for

```
'Aa', 'Ab', 'Ac', 'Ad', 'Ae', 'Af', 'Ag', 'Ah', 'Ai', 'Aj', 'Ak'
```

There is another shorthand for writing lists of single-quoted strings. The expression

```
qw(first second third fourth fifth sixth seventh)
```

is equivalent to

```
'first', 'second', 'third', 'fourth', 'fifth', 'sixth', 'seventh'
```

The qw operation is not a function but a quoting operator, like q and qq, so you do not have to use brackets around the words, you can use any delimiters, with the same rules as for the other quoting operators. Brackets are almost universally preferred here, though. It may not look as though the qw operator is of much use, but you will see it used extensively by experienced Perl programmers.

Just as you can store scalar values in scalar variables, you can store list values in variables. A list that has been given a name is called an array. To distinguish them from scalar variables, which are prefixed by a $, array variables are prefixed by an @, which you can read as 'the array'. An array variable can be used on the left hand side of an assignment operator; values to be stored in them can be generated in many ways, but we already know that one way is by writing a list.

```
@small_primes = (1, 2, 3, 5, 7, 11, 13, 17, 19, 23);
```

stores the first ten prime numbers into the array @small_primes. In the context of an assignment, the brackets around the list are necessary, because the comma has a lower precedence than the assignment operator. Without the brackets, the list consisting of the single element 1 would have been assigned to @small_primes, then the subsequent elements would have been evaluated and thrown away, since the comma would have been interpreted as the futile expression sequencing operator.

The individual elements of a list must be scalars—you cannot store a list as an element of an array, although you can copy an entire array by assignment:

```
@small_primes_copy = @small_primes;
```

This assignment produces a genuinely new array; subsequent changes to @small_primes_copy will not affect @small_primes or vice versa.

Lists within lists are flattened and the empty list, written () when you need to see it, just disappears. The list

```
0, 1, (2, 3, 5), (), (7, 11, (13, 17, 19, 23, 29))
```

has the same value as

```
0, 1, 2, 3, 5, 7, 11, 13, 17, 19, 23, 29
```

If you do use an array variable (or any other expression yielding a list value) as an element of a list, then in accordance with the idea that the resulting value is equivalent to a list, each of the (scalar) elements of the array is inserted into the list. For example, the list

```
0, @small_primes, 29
```

is no different from the one just displayed.

▶ Although Perl's behaviour is simple and consistent, it may surprise you in some contexts, particularly if you are used to C's arrays, whose length is fixed and determined at compile time, and the idea that an array's value is the address of its first element. In C, assignment of one array to another would not copy the elements, for example. Modern C++ programmers who use the vector class template from the standard library will find Perl's arrays more familiar. ◀

An array may be interpolated into a double-quoted string; an occurrence of its name is replaced by the string representation of each of its elements, in order, separated by whatever string is stored in the built-in variable $LIST_SEPARATOR ($"). By default, this is a space, so

```
print "The first ten primes are: <@small_primes>\n";
```

will produce the output

```
The first ten primes are: <1 2 3 5 7 11 13 17 19 23>
```

You may assign another string to $LIST_SEPARATOR to change the appearance of strings with arrays interpolated into them. After the assignment

```
$LIST_SEPARATOR = '><';
```

the same print statement would produce

```
The first ten primes are: <1><2><3><5><7><11><13><17><19><23>
```

Arrays may be interpolated into strings wherever a scalar variable can be interpolated, including in patterns and their replacements. If you wish to include a literal @ sign in a string, you must prefix it by a \ if it is followed by any character that could be the beginning of a name.

If you don't interpolate an array into a string, but just print it, for example, by writing:

```
print @small_primes;
```

the array's value is treated in just the same way it would be if you had written its elements out as a list, separated by commas, after print, so you would see

```
123571113171923
```

To be more precise, print always expects a list value to print. Usually, you write this value in the form of an explicit list, without brackets.

To refer to the individual elements of a list you index it by enclosing an expression that evaluates to an integer in square brackets after an expression that evaluates to a list (usually, but not always the name of an array). Indexes start at zero, like offsets into strings, and negative indexes count from the end of the list. The element you will access is a scalar, and scalars are prefixed with $, so the third element of the array @small_primes is written $small_primes[2]. I advised you to read $ as 'the scalar', now you see why; @small_primes[2] would be 'the array' small_primes[2], which is exactly what it means: an array of size one, consisting of the single element $small_primes[2].

You can use an indexed array anywhere you can use a scalar variable, including on the left hand side of an assignment operator, where it has the effect of updating the corresponding array element. If there is no corresponding element (that is, if the index value exceeds the highest subscript in the array), the array is extended as necessary. Any elements between the former highest element and the one being assigned to are given undefined values.

The following script constructs an array, whose elements are the first twenty-one terms in the Fibonacci series, in which each term is the sum of the two preceding terms. (The first two terms are both one, by definition.)

```
@fibs = (1, 1);
for ($i = 2; $i <= 20; ++$i)
{
  $fibs[$i] = $fibs[$i-1] + $fibs[$i-2];
}
```

If @an_array is an array, the scalar $#an_array holds the value of its highest subscript (which is one less than the number of elements, because subscripts start at 0). For example, on exit from the above loop $#fibs has the value 20. You can cause an array to stretch or shrink by assigning to this value. If you set it to a lower value, elements are chopped off the end of the array; if you increase its value, undefined elements are created. You might want to do this if you know that an array is going to grow to a large size; by assigning to its length, you force enough space to be allocated all at once; otherwise it would be allocated in smaller chunks as computation proceeded, which could slow down the execution of your program. If, for example, I wanted to compute the first thousand terms of the Fibonacci series, there might be some point in writing

```
$#fibs = 999;
```

before starting the loop. This would not fix an upper bound, it would just cause immediate allocation of enough room for all the terms.

You can iterate through the elements of an array using a for loop, with the loop variable being used as an index. Here is a script that computes a table of squares, for example:

```
@squares = (1..12);
for ($i = 0; $i < 12; ++$i)
{
  $squares[$i] *= $squares[$i];
}
```

However, loops that do something to each element of an array are so common that there is a special form of loop for such iterations.

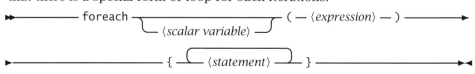

The ⟨*expression*⟩ should evaluate to a list.

In such a loop, the loop body is executed once for each element of the list in turn; on each iteration, the variable becomes a synonym for the list element.

Being a synonym, and not just a variable initialized to the element's value, it can be used on the left of an assignment to update an array. A more concise and idiomatic formulation of the program just given would be the following one:

```
@squares = (1..12);
foreach $s (@squares)
{
  $s *= $s;
}
```

If the loop variable is to be updated like this, the loop expression must have an l-value.

If no loop variable is specified, then $ARG is used.

▷ The keywords for and foreach are pure synonyms. Using for to introduce numerical iterations, and foreach to introduce iterations over lists is only a convention, ◁ but a widely used and perspicuous one.

You can use a foreach loop together with the range operator as a neat idiom for those common loops that iterate over numbers, as in

```
foreach $i (1..12)
{
  $s = $i * $i;
  print "$i squared is $s\n";
}
```

but you should be aware that the range operation creates a temporary array, and if the range is extensive this array may occupy a lot of memory.

An Example

Arrays' fundamental ability to hold an ordered collection of values can be put to use in many ways. The following example demonstrates several of them.

Do you ever get the feeling that the 13th of the month falls on a Friday more often than it should? Neither do I, but if you are plagued by certain sorts of computer virus, I guess it might feel that way sometimes. Don't worry, it doesn't, or at least, it hasn't over the course of the century up until now. A mathematician could probably prove that this was so, with the aid of a couple of arithmetical theorems. I prefer to demonstrate it with the aid of Perl.

My strategy will be to start from a known date and work backwards through the months until January 1901, tallying the day of the week on which the thirteenth falls. I want to use an array to hold the tallies, so I will map the days of the week to integers, representing Sunday as 0, Monday as 1, and so on. As I work back through time, I will need to keep track of the current month and year, as well as the day of the thirteenth. I could use the year itself, but I prefer to subtract 1900, so that my count goes down towards zero.[1] I will map months to integers, too, but unconventionally, I will map January to 0, February to 1, and so on, to fit the indexes of an array better.

These reflections on the thirteenth were prompted by the fact that the 13th of September 1996, when I was trying to think of things to do with arrays, was a Friday. Knowing that, I can deduce that the 13th of August was a Tuesday, because I know that there are 31 days in August, so the 13th of August was four full weeks and three days before the 13th of September, and three days before Friday is Tuesday. I can use similar reasoning to find out what day the 13th of July was, and so on backwards. How can I carry out similar reasoning in my program? I want to do it using arithmetic operations, since I have encoded my days of the week as numbers.

The key insight into how this can be done easily and neatly is that whenever I go back seven days, I get back to the same day of the week. Thus, I can ignore all multiples of seven in the number of days I subtract when I work back to the previous month. I just need to subtract the remainder I get from dividing the number of days in the month by seven. In the example I just gave, to get back to the day 31 days before Friday, I subtract three—the remainder from dividing 31 by 7—from five—the code for Friday—giving two, which represents Tuesday. Which is fine, until the result of my subtraction goes negative.

Suppose I do the subtraction as outlined, and end up with a value of -2. We can see that this means two days before Sunday, that is, Friday, with code value 5, which is the remainder you get after dividing -2 by 7. If you think a moment about how remainders work, you should be able to appreciate that we can therefore obtain the code for the day on which the thirteenth of last month fell by subtracting the number of days in that month from the code for the day of the thirteenth of this month, and *then* dividing the result by 7 and taking the remainder.

▷ This does work; Perl correctly defines the remainder of dividing a by b as the integer r satisfying $a = b \lfloor a/b \rfloor + r$, even if a is negative—unlike some other programming languages. The result is undefined if b is negative though, which is not ◁ unreasonable.

What all this means is that I need an array containing the number of days in each month: '30 days hath September...'

```
@days = (31, 28, 31, 30, 31, 30, 31, 31, 30, 31, 30, 31);
```

I will use another array, `@counts`, indexed by the code for day of the week to store the counts of thirteenths as I work back through time, and I will need to use scalar variables to keep track of the year and month, and the all-important day on which the thirteenth falls, as I travel back. I can initialize these from a known starting point.

---

[1]Yes, indeed, this program will fail if its range of investigation is extended by a few years. This is not a bug, it is a feature.

```
$year = 96;   $month = 8; $day = 5;
```

Now I loop backwards through the twentieth century, a month at a time. Every time I enter the loop body, $day holds the day of the week on which the 13th of $month falls in $year, so I begin by counting it.

```
while ($year > 0)
{
  ++$counts[$day];
```

The remainder of the loop ensures that the necessary relationship between $day, $month and $year is established for the next iteration. I decrement $month; if it goes negative, I have to wrap it round to 11 (December) and decrement the year.

```
if (--$month < 0)
{
  $month = 11;
  --$year;
}
```

Next, I use my table of days in the month to find out what day the thirteenth of this new month was. As always with any program dealing with dates, there is February's behaviour in leap years to contend with. I initialized $days[1] with 28; if the year is a leap year, I should subtract an extra day for February.

```
$day -= $days[$month];
--$day if $month == 1 && $year%4 == 0;
```

(Since I am only going back to the beginning of 1901 there is no need for the test for a leap year to deal correctly with centuries.) All I need to do before looping back for the previous month, is get the day into range ready for counting.

```
  $day %= 7;
}
```

Finally, I output the counts. To do this nicely, I set up an array containing the names of the days of the week to avoid the representation as integers polluting the output.

```
@day_names = qw(Sunday Monday Tuesday Wednesday
                Thursday Friday Saturday);
```

A loop just has to pick out each name and print it with the corresponding count.

```
foreach $i (0..6)
{
  print "$day_names[$i]: $counts[$i]\n";
}
```

And, in case you care, here are the results:

```
Sunday: 163
Monday: 165
Tuesday: 163
Wednesday: 166
Thursday: 163
Friday: 164
Saturday: 165
```

(Does this data really demonstrate anything?)

Lists as Structures

In the preceding program, you have seen lists and arrays used in four common ways. First, to tabulate the values of a function (@days), second, to accumulate a tally for a set of values (@counts), third, to map from an integer representation of something to a string (@day_names), fourth, to hold a range of values to control an iteration (0..6).

In addition to being used in these ways, lists in Perl are also used to perform some of the functions carried out by structures or records in other programming languages, since Perl has no direct equivalent of these. Instead, if you have some values that you wish to treat as the fields of a single record, you can put them into an array. If you are using an array for this purpose, it will typically neither grow nor shrink; you will just want to retrieve or update its elements. You must do this using their numerical indexes, since there is no way of defining a set of field names to use to select the individual elements.[2]

▷ Hashes, which we will meet near the end of this chapter, do allow you to select values by names, and are sometimes preferred to arrays for this reason, but hashes are not the same as structures or records, because their field names can be computed dynamically, whereas structures have a fixed set of names, and you can only ◁ select a field using a constant that it known at compile time.

Under these circumstances, it is often convenient to take your array apart and assign the individual elements to scalar variables. You can do this without having to use numerical indexing, by using a list of scalar variables on the left hand side of an assignment. The effect is to assign each element of the array or list on the right hand side to the variable in the corresponding position on the left. For example, if I had set up an array to represent a point in three dimensions, as follows:

```
@the_point = (100, 200, -200);
```

I could extract its coordinates like this:

---

[2]A facility for doing so is destined for a future release.

```
($x_coord, $y_coord, $z_coord) = @the_point;
```

I can use the list on both the left and the right of an assignment to update all these variables in parallel:

```
($x_coord, $y_coord, $z_coord) = (-$x_coord, -$y_coord, -$z_coord);
```

When I had finished playing with them, I could put them back in the array:

```
@the_point = ($x_coord, $y_coord, $z_coord);
```

▶ The effect is rather like a with statement in Pascal and its descendants, but it is up
◀ to the programmer to extract and restore the individual fields of the 'structure'.

Many of Perl's built-in functions return as their value a list which is working as a structure, and it is common to see that list immediately broken out into its fields by assigning it to a list of variables (or, to be precise, a list of expressions with l-values of any sort). For example, the function gmtime, if called without an argument, returns a list comprising the current second, minute and hour of the present time in the Greenwich Mean Time zone; today's day of the month, month (mapped to a small integer, starting at 0) and year; and the day of the week (also mapped to a small integer), the number of days since the first of January, and a flag indicating whether summer time is in force (according to your computer). A typical call would be:

```
($sec, $min, $hour, $month_day, $month,
 $year, $week_day, $year_day, $summer_time) = gmtime();
```

so that you could say:

```
++$month;
print "The date is $month_day/$month/$year\n";
```

and get today's date printed out in European format.

It is not an error for the list on the left hand side of the assignment to have fewer elements than the list value on the right. If I had only been interested in the time, I could have written:

```
($sec, $min, $hour) = gmtime();
```

If the values you are interested in are in the middle, though, you would have to assign intervening ones to dummy variables. If the left hand list is too long, trailing variables hold the undefined value after the assignment.

If the last element (or any other, in fact) of a list being assigned to is an array variable, all the unassigned elements of the right hand side will be stored into it. For example,

```
($sec, $min, $hour, @other_fields) = gmtime();
```

stores an array with the day of the month, month, and the other remaining fields, into @other_fields. So does,

```
    ($sec, $min, $hour, @other_fields, $year_day, $summer_time)
                                                     = gmtime();
```

The variables `$year_day` and `$summer_time` are undefined, they do not pick out the final two elements of the list.

When lists are assigned, the right hand side is completely evaluated before the assignments take place, so the following assignment exchanges the values of `$a` and `$b` without the need for a temporary variable:

```
($a, $b) = ($b, $a);
```

Operations on Lists

Context

If this book was padded out to twice its size with white space, and came in a lurid yellow cover, at about this point you would find a badly drawn cartoon of a person with eyes going round in opposite directions, crying 'Weirdness alert!!'. We prefer to be more dignified here, but there is a need for some sort of warning: Perl's rules for determining whether an expression has a scalar value or a list value are probably rather different from any approach to types you may have met in the past.

In brief, the type of result—scalar or list—returned by many expressions is determined by the context the expression occurs in. That is, many operators and functions can return either a list or a related scalar value. (Exactly how it is related depends on the operation.) To determine which, `perl` determines what sort of value could be used by the calling context. The most common example of a context which determines the type of an expression is an assignment: suppose I have written

```
$a_scalar = ⟨expression⟩;
```

where ⟨*expression*⟩ can return either a scalar or a list. Obviously, since I need a scalar to store in `$a_scalar`, that is what it should return, whereas in the context

```
@an_array = ⟨expression⟩;
```

it is the list value that I need, because arrays store lists.

In most other programming languages, context is used to restrict the permissible types of expressions. Every expression can return exactly one type of value, and this must match the type required by the context. The checks which the compiler makes to ensure this are said to improve program reliability. In Perl, *programmers* are supposed to ensure program reliability, and the language provides them with the maximum flexibility to do so.

One form of expression that may return either a list or a scalar does not even involve an operator: an array variable, when used in a context that requires a list, will evaluate to its stored value, as we have already seen. When it is used in a context requiring a scalar value, it will evaluate to the number of elements in that list. So, whereas

```
@small_primes_copy = @small_primes;
```

stored a copy of @small_primes into the array variable @small_primes_copy,

```
$number_of_small_primes = @small_primes;
```

sets the scalar variable $number_of_small_primes to the number of elements in that array (10, if it is initialized as it was earlier in the chapter).

Conversely, if you use a scalar where a list is needed, it will be converted to a list of length one. Looking at this another way, a list of length one is syntactically indistinguishable from a single scalar, so you *cannot* use a scalar where a list is needed.

You can force an operation to deliver a scalar where otherwise it would deliver a list, using the function `scalar`. The `print` operation normally requires a list, so

```
print @small_primes;
```

produces the output shown on page 87, but

```
print scalar(@small_primes);
```

prints 10.

A second example of context-dependency is the operation of reading from a filehandle. So far, I have only ever used a filehandle in angle brackets in a context where a scalar is required—assignment to a scalar variable or the condition of a while loop. The effect is to return the next line read from the filehandle (or an undefined value at the end of the file)—a scalar. If I use a filehandle in a context requiring a list, it will give me one, consisting of all the remaining lines of the associated file. So

```
$the_line = <INPUT>;
```

reads a single line into the scalar variable $the_line, but

```
@the_file = <INPUT>;
```

reads the entire file into an array, each element of which is a line. If you need the entire contents of a file in memory to work on, this is one way to do it, but beware of using a filehandle in the wrong context and inadvertently reading a whole huge file when you only wanted one line from it. The easiest way to do this is:

```
@lines[0] = <INPUT>;
```

Here, by confusing the array `@lines[0]` with the (scalar) array element `$lines[0]`, as newcomers to Perl are wont to do, I have caused the entire file to be read, when all I wanted to do was read the first line. Not only that, most of what was read was discarded, since `@lines[0]` can only hold one scalar; it would be set to the first line, almost as I expected, but the rest of my file would seem to have disappeared.

Another operation that we've seen before which returns a different value depending on the context in which it is used is pattern matching. As we know, if a scalar is required, it returns a true or false scalar value to indicate success or failure. If a list is required, it returns one consisting of the substrings which matched bracketed sub-expressions, that is, it returns (`$1`, `$2`,...). Often, you will immediately assign this value to a list of variables:

```
($protocol, $domainname, $discard, $pathname) =
                m!(http|ftp)://((\w+\.)*\w+)((/\w+)*/?)!;
print "$pathname on $domainname via $protocol\n";
```

As this example shows, one reason for doing so is to name parts of a string that you have dissected using a regular expression. Another good reason for performing such an assignment is to save the values of `$1`, `$2` and so on. These will be reset the next time any pattern matching is performed, so they cannot be used to store information; it is easier to assign the matched substrings immediately than to carefully copy the values of the transient variables.

If a pattern match fails, it returns the empty list; if it succeeds, but the pattern contained no brackets, it returns a list consisting of the single element 1.

▶ In C++ terms, some Perl operations are overloaded on their return types—something you cannot do at all in C++. There is some provision for user-defined operator overloading in Perl, but it is experimental and not really recommended. If you have seen the sort of knots the C++ standards committee have tied themselves in as a result of C++'s operator overloading rules, you may be glad that Perl does not ◀ encourage it.

Many of the operations which previously I have only applied to a single scalar argument can be applied to a list, when they operate on each of its elements. An example is the `chomp` function, introduced in chapter 3. When applied to a single scalar, it removes a trailing newline if it has one; when applied to a list, it chomps every member of the list; so

```
chomp(@the_file);
```

following the assignment above, would remove the newlines from every line that had been read into the array. You can now see that `chomp` was always applied to a list—until now, one with only a single element.

Some List Functions

A small but powerful collection of functions operating on list values is built in to Perl. The most straightforward (not coincidentally, the least useful) is reverse, which turns its argument back to front, returning a reversed list, if a list value is wanted:

```
@forwards = qw(first second third fourth fifth sixth seventh);
@backwards = reverse(@forwards);
```

leaves @backwards as the array

```
'seventh', 'sixth', 'fifth', 'fourth', 'third', 'second', 'first'
```

If a scalar is required, reverse will concatenate all its arguments as strings, and then reverse the result, character by character, so after

```
$backwards = reverse(@forwards);
```

$backwards holds 'htneveshtxishtfifhtruofdrihtdnocestsrif'.

The reverse function requires a list value as its argument; thus, the following code prints out a file with its lines in reverse order:

```
print reverse(<STDIN>);
```

If you provide a scalar (or, if you prefer to think of it that way, a list with only one element) and call reverse in a context requiring a scalar, though, the combination of its behaviours will reverse the argument, character by character. Hence,

```
$palindrome = 'able was i ere i saw elba';
$palindrome = reverse($palindrome);
```

...presents an interesting challenge to an optimizer.

Before describing the rest of Perl's list processing functions, it is time to clarify the syntax of function calls. Previously, I stated that when you call a built-in function, you enclose its arguments in brackets, as in log($x) or reverse(@forwards). Some functions, such as open, print and die seem to be anomalous: their arguments are not usually enclosed in brackets.

The anomaly is explained by the fact that a collection of arguments separated by commas is syntactically a list. As in other contexts where you use a list, brackets may be necessary to delimit the argument because of precedence. The precedence works so that most of the time you don't need the brackets, and from now on I shall usually leave them out. Function application has a lower precedence than a list forming comma following it, so a function will take all the elements of a list after it to be its argument, up to the end of the expression, or a closing bracket. On the other hand, function application has a higher precedence than a comma preceding it, so that functions can be called within a list without bracketing the call. For example,

```
@up_down = ('first', 'second', 'third', reverse 'first', 'second',
                                                           'third');
print "@up_down\n";
```

prints

```
first second third third second first
```

The list being assigned is parsed as

```
'first', 'second', 'third', (reverse 'first', 'second', 'third')
```

You could resolve all potential precedence conflicts resulting from function application by bracketing functions with their arguments as I have just done, in the manner beloved of logicians and Lisp programmers. In case of doubt, it is probably the best thing to do, but Perl also lets you resolve the conflict by bracketing the argument list, adding the extra rule that if a function name is followed by a left bracket, then everything up to a matching right bracket, but no further, is its argument, giving the normal programming language style of function call as I have been using up until now. The rule can hold some surprises if you think you are using an argument without brackets, but you have to put in some brackets for precedence anyway:

```
print (2 + 2)*3;
```

prints 4 (the space before the bracket makes no difference to `perl`). If you compare this to

```
log(2 + 2)*3
```

perhaps it should not be a surprise. If you activate compiler warnings, this is another potential problem you will be warned about. You can fix it with some brackets, or, if you insist, by putting a unary plus in front of the expression.

```
print +(2 + 2)*3;
```

prints 12.

Some built-in functions can take a special first argument before the list. For example, as we have seen, `print` may take a filehandle before the values to be printed. This extra argument is not considered part of the argument list, so it is not followed by a comma: we write

```
print STDOUT "the value is ", $value, "\n";
```

not

    `print STDOUT, "the value is ", $value, "\n";`

Several of the list functions to be described in this section take a first argument in the form of a block of code, or a subroutine name. In those cases, too, there is no comma separating this argument from the main argument list.

A function to sort a list is built in to Perl, so you will never need to write a sort routine again if you don't want to. In its full generality, it is quite complex, although for simple use it could hardly be simpler.

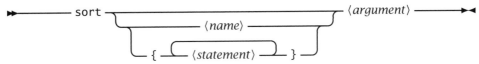

If you leave out the optional parts, `sort` returns a list consisting of the elements of its argument sorted in ascending lexicographical order.

```
@sorted = sort qw(first second third fourth fifth sixth seventh);
print "@sorted\n";
```

prints

```
fifth first fourth second seventh sixth third
```

An easy way to sort in descending order is to reverse the result of `sort`. Function application associates to the right, so functions can be composed in a comfortable way without brackets:

```
@r_sorted = reverse sort qw(first second third fourth
                            fifth sixth seventh);
```

However, the optional elements of a `sort` are there to give you control over the sorting order. If the ⟨*name*⟩ is present, it should be the name of a subroutine to be used to compare a pair of elements. Within the subroutine, the names $a and $b must be used to denote two elements being compared. This is not Perl's normal way of passing arguments to subroutines, but then, `sort` does not call its subroutine in Perl's normal way, it does something more efficient. This subroutine must return a negative value if $a is less than $b, zero if they are equal, and a positive value if $a is greater than $b according to the definitions of less, equal and greater you want to hold when your list is sorted. To sort it in reverse order, less than must be interpreted as the conventional greater than, and vice versa, so a suitable definition of a subroutine to use would be

```
sub rev_cmp {
  $b cmp $a;
}
```

which you would use as:

```
@r_sorted = sort rev_cmp qw(first second third fourth
                            fifth sixth seventh);
```

to achieve the same effect as the composition of `reverse` and `sort`. Here, the effort can hardly be justified, but the general mechanism allows you to define a variety of orderings for your sorts, such as one that ignores spaces or the case of letters, or a telephone book ordering, with Mac and Mc, Saint and St prefixes appearing together.

If you prefer, instead of defining a subroutine, you may insert its body directly into the call to `sort`:

```
@r_sorted_2 = sort {
  $b cmp $a;
} qw(first second third fourth fifth sixth seventh);
```

A pair of functions map and grep[3] can be used to apply a computation to every element of an array. Each can be followed by a series of statements, enclosed in curly brackets, culminating in an expression (like a do-block) and then its argument:

The effect is to evaluate this block once for each element of the argument; during each evaluation, $ARG is set to the value of the current element. The two functions differ in what they return: map returns a list consisting of the results of these evaluations; grep returns a list of the elements for which the evaluation produces a true value.

For example, suppose that the array @urls contains URLs. The following code would extract the Web page URLs into @web_pages.

```
@web_pages = grep { m<^http://> } @urls;
```

and the following would set @domain_names to an array consisting of the domain names from the URLs. (Compare this with the example on page 23.)

```
@domain_names = map
              { m<(http|ftp)://((\w+\.)*\w+)((/\w+)*/?)> ; $2 }
              @urls;
```

Since the argument of map or grep must be a list value, a concise way of extracting lines satisfying a certain condition from a file into an array is to use a filehandle as the argument of grep—providing your file is not too large to fit into memory all at once. I could do this with my blues titles:

```
@blue_lines = grep { /[Bb]lues$/ } <>;
```

▷ If you just want to evaluate a single expression for each list element, you may omit
  the curly brackets, but then you must put a comma between the expression and the
◁ array argument.

The effect of grep and map could be achieved using a loop, but the functions permit a more concise and elegant programming style, somewhat resembling that used in functional languages.

The function split allows you to write in another style, one based on the processing of variable-length records, divided into fields. Small scale databases

---

[3]If you have never unixed, this name will be totally inscrutable. The function is named after a Unix utility which searches files for lines matching a pattern.

are often constructed in this form: each line of a file is considered to be a record; a special string serves to separate individual fields of each record. For example, I might construct a database to record information about digitized video sequences, or 'clips'. For each clip, I could record a name, the duration, the compression method used when it was made, and the file size in kilobytes. I could separate these fields with a vertical bar. A typical record would be the line

```
Rainy Days|00:03:10|Miro MJPG|1985
```

The duration is in the form $mm : ss : ff$, where mm is the number of minutes, ss is seconds and ff the number of frames. (We don't have enough disk space to make it necessary to allow for hours.) This timecode format can be considered a record with fields itself.

The `split` function may take a list of zero, one, two or three arguments; the simplest case is when it takes two. The first will be a pattern and the second an expression that evaluates to a string. The pattern defines a set of possible field separators; the string will be split into fields separated by any of these, and a list with the resulting fields as its elements will be returned, if a list is what the context requires, otherwise the number of fields will be returned. Where you are processing a file of records all of which have the same structure, assigning the result of `split` to a list of expressions with l-values is often a sensible way to proceed. For example, if the record just shown was in the string `$the_record`, I might break out its fields like this:

```
($title, $duration, $compressor, $size) = split /\|/, $the_record;
```

and then separate out the individual components of the duration:

```
($mins, $secs, $frames) = split /:/, $duration;
```

Alternatively, I could extract all the fields and sub-fields in one operation:

```
($title, $mins, $secs, $frames, $compressor, $size) =
                                 split /:|\|/, $the_record;
```

If the string is omitted, `split` splits $ARG (which should come as no surprise by now). A common idiom for record processing (based, as we will see in chapter 11, on the execution model of the programming language Awk) has the form:

For example, I might wish to compute the total size and duration of a collection of clips:

```
$total_size = $total_duration = 0;
while (<>)
{
```

```
   ($title, $mins, $secs, $frames, $compressor, $size)
                                          = split /:|\|/;
   $total_size += $size;
   $total_duration += (60*$mins+$secs)*25 + $frames;
}
print "The total space occupied is ", $total_size/1024, " Mbytes\n";
print "The total duration is ", $total_duration/25, " seconds\n";
```

(European video standards use 25 frames per second.)

▷ In case you are tempted (as I was), you cannot do this:

✗   ($total_size, $total_duration) +=
                ($size, (60*$mins+$secs)*25 + $frames);

◁ It doesn't parse that way.

Often the processing will select records based on properties of certain fields, or it will extract selected fields. If you know about relational databases, you will see that you could easily achieve the effect of selection and projection operations in this idiom. For example, to print the name and duration of all clips occupying more than a megabyte, you could use the following Perl script:

```
while (<>)
{
  ($title, $duration, $compressor, $size) = split /\|/;
  print "$title, $duration\n" if $size > 1024;
}
```

▶ In SQL, you would write something like

```
SELECT TITLE, DURATION
FROM CLIPS
WHERE SIZE > 1024
```
◀

Because split is so useful, Perl furnishes it with special cases to suit all needs. If you omit the pattern as well as the string, split on its own splits $ARG on white space (although any white space at the beginning of the line is discarded, whereas if any other separator appears at the beginning of a record, an empty field is assumed to be before it), so it will separate a line of text into words. If you specify // as the pattern, the string will be split into individual characters. If you add a third argument, it is taken to be a limit on the number of fields to split into; the last ones are concatenated, retaining their separators, so

```
($title, $duration, $rest) = split /\|/, $the_record, 3;
```

sets the variables $title and $duration as before, and assigns the string
'Miro MJPG|1985' to $the_rest.[4]

If you want your program to generate records with field separators, you
can use the function join. This takes two arguments, a string and an array,
and produces a string made by joining together all the elements of the array,
separated by the string. For example,

```
print join '|', $title, $duration, $compressor, $size;
```

will print a reconstituted clip database record. Nothing very exciting there, but
you may like to note that joining with a null string is said to be the fastest way
of concatenating several strings.

Although the final set of list functions is arguably the most important, it
will only be described briefly here, because it is more instructive to see these
functions working in context than in isolation. They perform traditional list
processing, and between them provide operations to support the full range of
linear abstract datatypes.

The function shift returns the first element of its array argument, and as a
side effect, removes it from the array. Because of this side-effect, the argument
must be a named array, not just any list. If the array is empty, shift returns
an undefined value. If @numbers is set to (1..5), shift @numbers returns
1, leaving @numbers set to 2, 3, 4, 5. However, shift (1..5) is an error.
Putting elements onto the front of an array is achieved using unshift. It may
take any number of further arguments, and inserts them at the beginning of
the array. For example, after the shift just performed,

```
unshift @numbers, 0, 1;
```

will change @numbers to 0, 1, 2, 3, 4, 5. With a single argument after the
array, unshift is the inverse of shift. That is,

```
unshift @A, (shift @A);
```

does nothing. In any context, unshift returns the number of elements of the
new array, never the array itself.

The pair of functions pop and push operate like shift and unshift, but on
the end of an array. So pop removes the last element from an array and returns
it, and push appends elements to the end of an array.

It should be clear that if you operate on an array with either push and pop
or shift and unshift exclusively, the array will behave as a stack. Equally, if
you use either push and shift or unshift and pop, it will behave as a queue,
and if you use all four, it will behave as a double-ended queue, or deque.

The most general list processing function is splice, which takes an array,
an offset, a length, and a list as its arguments, for example

---

[4]Even this does not fully exhaust the subtleties of split. Consult the documentation for the
ultimate details.

```
splice @numbers, 1, 2, 'two', 'three', 'whoops!';
```

The effect of the general case

```
splice ⟨array⟩, ⟨offset⟩, ⟨length⟩, ⟨list⟩;
```

is to remove ⟨*length*⟩ elements from the array, starting at ⟨*offset*⟩, and replace them with ⟨*list*⟩, which need not be ⟨*length*⟩ elements long. The elements removed are returned by `splice`. In the specific example given, the offset is 1 and the length 2, so the second and third elements of `@numbers` are removed and replaced by the elements of the list `'two'`, `'three'`, `'whoops!'`, so, if `@numbers` had its original value of `1, 2, 3, 4, 5`, it would be updated to `1, 'two', 'three', whoops!, 4, 5`, and the list `2, 3` would be returned.

If you omit the replacement list, `splice` operates as a function to delete elements from an array. If you also omit the length argument, it deletes everything from the offset onwards. It is easy to write expressions defining `push`, `pop`, `shift` and `unshift` in terms of `splice`, if you like that sort of reductionism. The simpler functions are used more often, but `splice` can be used to pick apart data that has been stored in a single array, although logically it consists of several sets of elements.

Suppose, for example, I had been given a data file consisting of a series of blocks, each one consisting of a number, say *n*, followed by *n* records. Assuming both *n* and each record occupied a single line, and that I knew how many blocks were in the file, I could easily read each block into an array, by reading the length and then building up the array with `push` operations in a loop. Or I could do this:

```
@all_data = <ALLDATA>;
chomp @all_data;
$n1 = shift @all_data;
@data1 = splice @all_data, 0, $n1;
$n2 = shift @all_data;
@data2 = splice @all_data, 0, $n2;
```

and so on. I assume the filehandle `ALLDATA` has been opened on the file in question; the assignment to `@all_data` reads all its lines into the array. Each `shift` operation then extracts a count, and the following `splice` pulls out a block of data of the right length. True, it wasn't a very good file format to start with, but you often cannot choose what you start with, and Perl is there to sort this kind of thing out for you painlessly.

Arguments

Lists are used to pass arguments to subroutines in Perl. All subroutines take a list of arguments, which may be of any length, including zero;[5] you do not even

---

[5]Unless you use the recently-introduced subroutine prototypes, which are described on page 154.

necessarily have to provide a subroutine with the same number of arguments every time you call it. Provided your subroutine has been declared before you use it, you can use the same calling syntax as you do for built-in functions, just following the subroutine's name with the list of argument values. If you cannot provide a definition of your subroutine before you use it (because of mutual recursion, say), you can just provide a declaration of its name:

```
sub ⟨name⟩;
```

and define it in the usual way later. If you like to use subroutines before declaring them, though, `perl` needs some way of determining that you are calling a subroutine. Long ago, this was done by prefixing a subroutine's name with an &, the way scalars are prefixed with $ and arrays with @, and you can still do this, if you like, but it has become more usual to take advantage of recent versions of Perl's more mellow mature nature: if you enclose the argument list in brackets, `perl` has enough information to identify a subroutine call from its syntactical form.

Subroutines in Perl do not have named arguments; a subroutine with arguments is declared no differently from one without. The list of arguments is available within the subroutine's body as an array called @ARG (or @_). It is almost as if, just before calling the subroutine, the list of arguments was assigned to @ARG. Almost, but not exactly, because arguments are passed by reference (but not *as* references, in Perl's terms) meaning that the elements of @ARG become synonyms for the actual arguments, they do not just acquire copies of their values. Updating an element of @ARG will change the value of the actual argument supplied to the call—so this had better have an l-value if you want to do so.

Mostly, you will not want to do so. Updating arguments that have been passed by reference is usually done in other programming languages in order to achieve the effect of returning more than one result from a function, or to return an elaborate data structure when the language does not allow you to do so any other way. In Perl, you can do both these things directly, so updating elements of @ARG is unnecessary and usually unwise.

To simulate both named arguments and call by value—where updating the argument in the subroutine body does not affect the actual argument in the caller—you can assign @ARG, or elements of it, to local variables, declared with my.

In the simplest case of a subroutine with a single scalar argument, the idiom used is

```
my $⟨arg name⟩ = shift;
```

which means the same as

```
my $⟨arg name⟩ = shift @ARG;
```

because, inside a subroutine, if you omit the argument to `shift`, it defaults to @ARG. For example, I could make my code for extracting the first letters of phrases into a subroutine that took the phrase as its argument and returned the first letters as its result. To add a little extra interest, I will do the extraction this time in a brazenly functional way, using some of the functions described in the last section.

```
sub first_letters {
  my $phrase = shift;
  my @words = split /\s+/, $phrase;
  return join '', map { substr($ARG, 0, 1) } @words;
}
```

This subroutine could be called as follows, assuming its declaration preceded the call:

```
while (<>)
{
  chomp;
  $initials = first_letters $ARG;
  print "$ARG -> \U$initials\E\n";
}
```

Notice that the idiom of shifting @ARG means that supernumerary arguments are simply ignored, which you might regard as a convenience, or as an act of criminal negligence on the part of Perl, depending on your view of programming. If you fail to provide any argument to `first_letters`, so that @ARG is empty, the shift will leave `$phrase` undefined—it does not default to $ARG, as you might have hoped, unless you make it do so yourself. This will not cause any error message until and unless you try to use `$phrase`, at which point you would get a warning if you had turned on compiler warnings.

For several scalar arguments, you would usually use an extended form of the my construct. You may have a list of variables and a list of initializing values, so that the construct following the my keyword looks like an assignment, in general. This is illustrated in the following example, a subroutine to compare the domain names of two URLs, returning true if they are the same, and false otherwise.

```
sub equal_domains {
  my ($url1, $url2) = ($ARG[0], $ARG[1]);
  my ($protocol1, $domain_name1) =
          ($url1 =~ m!(http|ftp)://((\w+\.)*\w+)((/\w+)*/?)!);
  my ($protocol2, $domain_name2) =
          ($url2 =~ m!(http|ftp)://((\w+\.)*\w+)((/\w+)*/?)!);
  return $domain_name1 eq $domain_name2;
}
```

Initialization of locals not only looks like an assignment, it works like one, so if you include an array among your locals, it will absorb any trailing elements of @ARG. Hence, you can only easily have one list argument, and it must follow all the scalar arguments. The following subroutine performs the action of putting brackets round section numbers at the beginning of lines, first done by the script on page 22. This time, the left and right brackets are passed as scalar arguments to the subroutine, allowing for a variety of styles, and the lines to be bracketed are passed all together in a list.

```
sub insert_brackets {
  my $left = shift;
  my $right = shift;
  my @strings = @ARG;
  return map { s/^[\d.]+/$left$MATCH$right/; $ARG; } @strings;
}
```

A typical call would be:

```
@bracketed_lines = insert_brackets '[', ']', @lines;
```

Passing two or more lists as arguments is clearly not possible, although it can easily be done. The best way is probably to pass references, and we will see how to do that once we have found out what references are in chapter 7. Alternatively, if you pass the length of each list explicitly as an argument, you can use splice to take apart @ARG, just as I used it to extract blocks of data from a file at the end of the previous section. The following subroutine compares two arrays of strings to see whether they are the same length and contain the same elements; it assumes that, when it is called, each of the two arrays is preceded by its length, like this:

```
if (equal_arrays $#a1+1, @a1, $#a2+1, @a2)
```

The subroutine does nothing clever once it has disentangled its argument list.

```
sub equal_arrays {
  my $len1 = shift;
  my @array1 = splice @ARG, 0, $len1;
  my $len2 = shift;
  my @array2 = splice @ARG, 0, $len2;
  my $i;
  return 0 unless ($len1 == $len2);
  for ($i = 0; $i < $len1; ++$i)
  {   return 0 unless $array1[$i] eq $array2[$i]; }
  return 1;
}
```

▷ Although the Perl language does not force you into defensive programming, there is nothing to stop you inserting code to check the integrity of the actual arguments supplied to your subroutine. For example,

```
sub equal_arrays {
  my $len1 = shift;
  defined($len1) && $len1 =~ /^\d+$/ ||
```

```
        die "inappropriate first length argument to equal_arrays\n";
my @array1 = splice @ARG, 0, $len1;
my $len2 = shift;
defined($len2) && $len2 =~ /^\d+$/ ||
  die "inappropriate second length argument to equal_arrays\n";
my @array2 = splice @ARG, 0, $len2;
@ARG == 0 ||
    die "inconsistent length arguments passed to equal_arrays\n";
```

This will catch most errors in the arguments, although it might still be tripped up
◁ if the strings in the arrays were numeric in form.

Sometimes, if your subroutine takes a single list argument and is not complex, you could demonstrate your lack of inhibitions by using @ARG directly.
This little subroutine returns a random element from its argument list:

```
sub random_element
{
  return $ARG[int(rand()*($#ARG)+0.5)];
}
```

As several of the preceding examples have shown, a subroutine can return
a list as its result. What happens if you call such a subroutine in a context
where a scalar is required? Unless you do something about it, the length of the
list will be used. You may wish to emulate the behaviour of built-in functions,
and have your subroutine return a different scalar value, which provides more
information. For example, if the subroutine insert_brackets was called in a
context requiring a scalar, it would not be very helpful to return the length of
the list that would be returned when a list was required—you know it already,
after all. Perhaps it would be better to return a string built out of the elements
of the list. In order to arrange to return different values depending on the
calling context, the subroutine must be able to discover what the caller requires.
The built-in function wantarray, which returns true if a list is required, false
if a scalar is required, is provided for this purpose. I would use it to make
insert_brackets behave in the way I just described.

```
sub insert_brackets {
  my $left = shift;
  my $right = shift;
  my @strings = @ARG;
  my @result =
      map { s/^[\d.]+/$left$MATCH$right/; $ARG; } @strings;
  return wantarray? @result: join "\n", @result;
}
```

A widespread Perl convention is that when an operation fails, it should return an undefined scalar value, or an empty list. Hence the idiom:

```
return wantarray? (): undef;
```

Here, always returning `undef` would be wrong, since the list consisting of a single undefined value is not empty.

Your Perl script itself has arguments—the command line arguments, which, so far, we have always treated as the names of input files. In fact, it is only the helpful behaviour of the `<>` operator that lets you interpret the arguments in this way; they themselves are just strings, which you can use in any way you like. They are available in your program as the elements of the array @ARGV (not to be confused with @ARG). We will see in chapter 6 how to exert finer control over the use of command line arguments as file names, but you should also realize that they can be used in other ways. Quite how useful this is to you depends on whether you (and the people who use your Perl scripts) consider a command line an acceptable interface to a computer system.

As a simple example, consider writing a script to search a collection of files for a given string. A command line interface to such a script could allow you to specify the string as the first argument, and the filename as the second. The code would then look like this:

```
$string = $ARGV[0];
$file = $ARGV[1];
open FILE, $file or die "unable to open $file ($OS_ERROR)\n";
while (<FILE>)
{
  print if /$string/;
}
```

The restriction to a single file is tiresome; command line users would probably expect to be able to provide a list of files to search. You could quite easily cope with this, by opening each element of @ARGV in turn, but there is an easier way. The operator `<>` does exactly this for you; the only trouble here is that the first element will be the target string. The solution is to shift it out of the way. Happily, outside a subroutine, if you omit the argument to `shift`, it defaults to @ARGV. Hence, the following script is not only more general than the previous one, it is shorter:

```
$string = shift;
while (<>)
{
  print if /$string/;
}
```

Hashes

If you know about hash tables, symbol tables or associative arrays, then you already know what Perl's hashes are. If not, there are several ways you can think about them. In the abstract, a hash is a way of storing a finite partial function as a collection of pairs of scalar values. If that's too abstract, think of it as being like a table with two columns, headed *key* and *value*. If I give you some scalar value, you can look in the key column and, if this particular key is there, you can tell me the associated value. Or you might prefer to think of a hash as a generalization of an array; instead of indexing it using a positive integer less than the number of elements in the array, you can index it with any scalar value you like. It is probably best to think of hashes in all of these ways at once, since each contributes something to your understanding.

Whichever way you look at a hash, one thing is pretty certain: you need some way of referring to it and its elements. Like scalars and arrays, hashes are identified by a special character prefixing their names; in the case of hashes it is %, so a hash storing the capitals of some countries might be `%capital`. An individual value, say the capital of Venezuela, is accessed by using the country's name as a key. The result is a scalar, so like an array element, it is prefixed by a $; to show that it is a hash value, and to identify which value it is, you follow the hash's name with the key in curly brackets, as in `$capital{'Venezuela'}`, whose value is presumably `'Caracas'`. You can use such an expression anywhere you could use any other scalar, including interpolated in strings and patterns, but how would that value have got there?

The expression `$capital{'Venezuela'}` has an l-value. In tabular terms, it is the entry in the value column opposite the key `'Venezuela'`, and assigning to this expression fills in or updates that value. In other words, the assignment

```
$capital{'Venezuela'} = 'Caracas';
```

adds the pair (`'Venezuela'`, `'Caracas'`) to the hash `%capital`, replacing any other pair with key `'Venezuela'`. In other words, it looks up `'Venezuela'` in the table `%capital` and, if it finds it, updates the entry to `'Caracas'`; otherwise, it creates a new table entry for this key and value.

Alternatively, you can set up all the key and value pairs at once. There is no special form for writing down a hash literal. Instead, if you assign a list to a hash, consecutive pairs of the list are treated as a key and a value to be inserted into the hash. I could set up a small table of capitals like this:

```
%capital = ('Venezuela', 'Caracas', 'Scotland', 'Edinburgh',
            'Australia', 'Canberra', 'Kenya', 'Nairobi',
            'Belgium', 'Brussels');
```

As you can see, initializers of this form are not very readable; judicious layout—one pair per line, for example—can improve their readability somewhat. A further improvement—to most eyes—comes from using the composite symbol =>, which looks a bit as if it might mean 'maps to', to separate the key and value of each pair. Here is an example of its intended use:

```
%capital = ('Venezuela' => 'Caracas',
            'Scotland'  => 'Edinburgh',
            'Australia' => 'Canberra',
            'Kenya'     => 'Nairobi',
```

```
        'Belgium'    => 'Brussels');
```

▷ => is just a lexical synonym for a comma (which means that creative programmers
    can use it just as effectively to make their programs harder to read), except that it
    lets you write strings as bare words to the left of it, provided they do not clash with
    the names of any built-in function or subroutine, without triggering any compiler
    warnings. A leading minus sign is also permitted. You can do the same thing inside
    the curly brackets used to select an element of a hash, as in `$capital{Venezuela}`,
    so you do not need to put single quotes around your hash keys if they only consist
◁ of a single word. Which they often do, so this is quite a convenience.

There are several ways of iterating over every pair in a hash. One idiom uses
a while loop, and a special function, called each:

▶▶──── while ─ (─ (─ ⟨*key*⟩ ─ , ─ ⟨*value*⟩ ─) ── = ─ each ─ ⟨*hash*⟩ ─) ────▶

▶──────────────────────── { ── ⟨*statement*⟩ ── } ────────────────────◀

where ⟨*key*⟩ and ⟨*value*⟩ are scalar variables. Every time it is called with the
same hash argument, the function each returns a list of length two, consisting
of the next pair from the hash; this is immediately assigned to be used in the
loop body. For example, I might print out everything I know about geography
in the following way:

```
while (($country, $capital) = each %capital)
{
   print "The capital of $country is $capital\n";
}
```

Pairs are returned by each in an arbitrary order, not the order in which they
were inserted nor the lexicographic order of the keys.

The ability to interpolate hash elements into a pattern means that it is possible to build a table of pattern and replacement pairs dynamically, and use it
in a loop as an alternative to a sequence of replacements. This facility finally
enables me to do something useful with the first letters of phrases.

The following script takes the name of a file of phrases as its first command
line argument. The remaining arguments are supposed to be the names of files
containing messages, in which it is feared abbreviations for these phrases might
occur. The program will replace any abbreviations it finds by the corresponding
phrase, in the hope of making the message intelligible. We need a definition of
the subroutine first_letters, but we have seen several of those, so I will not
repeat it here.

A small subroutine does the hard work of reading the phrases and building
up a table with the first letter abbreviations as its keys and the full phrases as
its values. First, it extracts the name of the file of phrases from @ARGV (using a
shift, so that subsequently <> can be used to read all the remaining files). It
then tries to open the file in the usual way.

```
sub read_phrases {
  my $phrases_file = shift @ARGV;
  open PHRASES, $phrases_file or
      die "Unable to open $phrases_file ($OS_ERROR)\n";
```

If that works, it reads a phrase at a time, and calls `first_letters` to build the key, so it can insert it and its phrase into a hash called %phrase_book, which is global, because there is no point making it local.

```
while (<PHRASES>)
{
  chomp;
  $phrase_book{first_letters($ARG)} = $ARG;
}
}
```

The main program is an example of the file processing idiom. It starts by calling `read_phrases`, and then enters its loop.

```
read_phrases;
while (<>)
{
```

The loop body starts with an inner loop, which works its way through the phrase book, substituting each value for every occurrence of its key in $ARG.

```
while (($abbreviation, $phrase) = each %phrase_book)
{
  s/\b$abbreviation\b/$phrase/gi;
}
```

The \bs in the pattern ensure that the abbreviation is not substituted when it occurs within a word; the g and i qualifiers ensure that all occurrences are replaced and that case is ignored—people who use these abbreviations may not have much respect for the shift key.

The outer loop finishes off in the usual way.

```
  print;
}
```

Functions on Hashes

The selection of functions operating on hashes built into Perl is much less than that of functions on arrays. This is more a reflection on the underlying abstract datatype than on Perl.

The functions `keys` and `values` each return a list, comprising...the keys and the values, respectively, of their hash argument. You don't see `values` used very often, but `keys` is used in several Perl idioms. The usual idea is to extract all the keys, manipulate the list of keys somehow, perhaps selecting some of them, or sorting it, and then iterate over the resulting list, using each element as a key back into the original hash, to get an image, as it were, of the transformation you have applied to the keys.

That may sound abstract and peculiar, but it is really straightforward. For example, you may want to retrieve the pairs from a hash in some order, such as ascending key order. The each function just returns them in random order; to achieve your goal, you can sort the keys and then retrieve each key's value, like this:

```
foreach $country (sort keys %capital)
{
  print "The capital of $country is $capital{$country}\n";
}
```

That loop will print the information in alphabetical order of country.

The question may arise: How do I get rid of an entry in a hash? Simply assigning an undefined value does not do so:

```
$capital{'Belgium'} = undef;
```

will leave Belgium with an undefined capital, but it will not eliminate Belgium. It is as if I had crossed out Brussels in the values column of a table: Belgium is still there in the keys column. To get rid of it entirely, you must use the function delete, which takes a key and removes it and its value from the table:

```
delete $capital{'Belgium'};
```

Once you realize the difference between a key being present in the hash, but with an undefined value associated, and a key not being present at all, you may well want to be able to find out which of these situations prevails. You can use defined on a hash element, just as on any other scalar, but it fails to distinguish between the two situations: defined $capital{'Belgium'} is false after either of the two operations above. A separate function, exists, is used to find out whether a key is present: exists $capital{'Belgium'} is still true if $capital{'Belgium'} has been set to undef, but false if it has been deleted. You often use exists to check whether you have already created a hash entry for a particular key, in the cases where it is meaningless to have more than one entry for the same key.

An Example

The use of hashes is limited only by your imagination. (I think I've got that the right way round.) They are at their most effective when used in conjunction with Perl's other data structures, as we will see in later chapters. To consolidate this introduction, the next example shows hashes being used in conjunction with arrays, and various operations on both.

This is another script based on my database of records of video clips. A clip of full frame video of any substantial length will be a big file—hundreds of megabytes is normal. If you do much work with digital video, the four gigabyte hard disk that seemed so huge once will be barely enough to hold a few days' work. You will have to archive. Recordable CDs are a good archiving medium, being relatively cheap and robust. However, you only have one chance to write a CD,[6] and you would like to fill as much of it as possible. If you have enough clips to fill several CDs, you need to decide how to allocate files to disks in order to leave as little unused space on your CDs as possible.

We know (or think we know) from theory that the only way to determine the best allocation is to try all the possible combinations, which is not a feasible computation for any non-trivial number of files. Hence, we have to use some heuristic strategy that will provide a good allocation, most of the time. An effective heuristic is to fill up disks using the biggest file that will fill the available space at each step. This is what my script does.

First, having opened a filehandle CLIPDATA in the usual way, it reads the data and builds a hash called %filesizes, whose keys, somewhat unusually, are the sizes of the files, and whose values are their names. In case there are several files of the same size, it checks first whether the key exists in the hash; if it does, it adds one (kilobyte) to the size and tries again. It thus errs on the safe side. The extra recorded size does not really matter, though, given how big the files are expected to be.

```
while (<CLIPDATA>)
{
  chomp;
  ($title, $mins, $secs, $frames, $compressor, $size)
                                          = split /:|\|/;
  ++$size while exists $filesizes{$size};
  $filesizes{$size} = $title;
}
```

Next, the keys are ordered in descending sizes, ready for the allocation.

```
@ordered_sizes = sort { $b <=> $a } keys %filesizes;
```

I will generate names for the disks as I go along, so I initialize a variable with a suitable starting name; I also initialize the size of a disk.

```
$disk = 'DISKa';
$disk_size = 640*1024;
```

I have assumed a 74 minute CD and allowed for some overhead. If this was a production script, I would have allowed the user to specify the size and also the names of the disks, as command line arguments or via a dialogue, according to their expectations.

---

[6]Yes, it is possible to record over several sessions, but it is clumsy and not very satisfactory.

Before starting to allocate, I have to make sure that there are not any files too big to fit on a disk at all. Because I have sorted @ordered_sizes with the largest at the beginning, I just have to scan it from the top, shifting away any files I cannot possibly allocate. Of course, I do mention the fact to the user.

```
while (($size = shift @ordered_sizes) > $disk_size)
{
  print "File $filesizes{$size} is too big -- ignoring it\n";
}
unshift @ordered_sizes, $size;
```

Now I am ready to allocate files to disks. Whenever I allocate a file to a disk, I will splice its size out of the @ordered_sizes array, so when the length of that array reaches zero, I know that all the files have been allocated to some disk. I can test the length by using the array name in the context of the loop test, where a scalar is required.

```
while (@ordered_sizes)
{
```

This outer loop is executed once for every disk I write. During its execution, I need to keep track of the amount of available space remaining on the current CD, and the index of the next file to look at in @ordered_sizes. I need to reset these on entry to the loop.

```
$available = $disk_size;
$i = 0;
```

The inner loop scans @ordered_sizes, from largest to the smallest, allocating a file to the current disk if it fits. It is conceivable that I will be able to fill the disk up exactly, so that the available space becomes zero, at which point I can quit this loop and go on to the next disk. More likely, though, I will exit the inner loop after I have tried every file. The loop test takes account of both possibilities.

```
while ($available && $i < @ordered_sizes)
{
```

I find out how big the next file under consideration is and compare it with the space left on this CD. If it fits, I record the fact by appending it to the entry for this CD in a hash called %allocations. I also subtract its size from the space remaining, and splice @ordered_sizes so this file will not be considered again.

```
$file_size = $ordered_sizes[$i];
if ($file_size < $available)
{
  $allocations{$disk} .= " $filesizes{$file_size}";
  $available -= $file_size;
  splice @ordered_sizes, $i, 1;
}
```

If I removed an element from the array, then the index $i will pick out the next element on the next iteration, so it does not need adjusting. However, if this file did not fit, I need to add one to $i for the next time round.

```
    else  {  ++$i; }
  }
```

When I fall out of the inner loop, I have done all I can with the current CD, so I generate a new name and go round the outer loop again, if necessary.

```
  ++$disk;
}
```

When the outer loop terminates, all files have been allocated to some disk, and the allocations have been recorded in the %allocations hash, so I just have to write out what it contains.

```
foreach $d (sort keys %allocations)
{
  print "$d: $allocations{$d}\n";
}
```

As we will see in later chapters, Perl could have automated more of this process, if that was desired. It could easily have discovered the file sizes for itself, and, on some systems, it could probably have set the writing of the CD archives in motion, too.

Input, Output and Files

6

There is more to input and output than reading from files and writing to the standard output stream. There is writing to files, for a start, and 'random access' i/o, as well as output formatting. Perl has got it all, as well as facilities for manipulating files and directories themselves: renaming and deleting files, and finding out useful things about them, such as how big they are and whether you can write to them.

The subject of this chapter is necessarily system-dependent. The structure of file systems and the meaning of access privileges and other attributes of files are things that the operating system dictates, and given the present diversity of operating system designs, there can be no portable specification of such features. Even the existence of files and directories is not something that should necessarily be taken for granted.

Perl adopts an unsatisfactory solution: it assumes that every operating system is Unix, leaving the programmers who port Perl to other systems to interpret Unix's view of the world as best they can. For the other two major platforms (MacOS and Wintel), many of the concepts can be mapped across fairly cleanly. I will concentrate on those; for features that are native to your particular system, you will have to consult your documentation—even if your system really is Unix.

More About Filehandles

Opening Files

We know how to open a file for input or output and associate it with a filehandle: you call the **open** function. The first character of its second argument is used to determine whether to prepare the filehandle for input or output. To open a filehandle for output instead of input, prefix the filename argument to **open** with a > character, like this:

```
open OUT, ">Results" or
    die "couldn't open Results file ($OS_ERROR)\n";
```

If you like to be explicit, you can prefix a file name with < to open it for input, although this is what will happen anyway if you omit any prefix, as I have done so far.

The second argument to open can be any expression that evaluates to a suitable string; double-quoted strings with interpolated variables are common. Here, for example, is a program that takes two filenames as command line arguments, and copies the contents of the first to the second. You could substitute any other processing for this straight copy.

```
open FROM, "<$ARGV[0]" or
    die "Couldn't open $ARGV[0] for input ($OS_ERROR)\n";
open TO, ">$ARGV[1]" or
    die "Couldn't open $ARGV[1] for output ($OS_ERROR)\n";
print TO <FROM>;
```

Since print expects a list, the last statement copies the entire file—although it could fail if the file was large and your memory allocation small.

▷ On systems that support i/o redirection, you would be more likely to write a script that read from STDIN and wrote to STDOUT—which are opened for you by perl— and provide a suitable command line to tell the operating system to associate these with your chosen files. For example, on Unix, you might type something like:

```
perl processfiles <input.dat >results
```

if you wanted to process the contents of input.dat and write the results to ◁ results.

You might want to associate the standard input or output with some file-handle other than the customary ones, STDIN and STDOUT. You can do so by opening a filehandle on the special pseudofiles >- and <-, representing standard input and output, respectively. The following fragment will open the file-handle INPUT on the file whose name is in $ARGV[0], if one has been supplied, and on the standard input otherwise.

```
open INPUT, $ARGV[0] || '<-' or
    die "Couldn't open input file ($OS_ERROR)\n";
```

Opening a file for output has the effect of destroying its old contents, if it had any. If you want to add new material on the end of a file, without damaging the old version, you can prefix the file with >> when you open it. This might be a suitable thing to do if you wish to record some information in a log file every time your script is run.

```
open LOG, '>>db.log' or
    die "Unable to open the log file ($OS_ERROR)\n";
($sec, $min, $hour, $month_day, $month, $year) = gmtime();
```

```
print LOG
  "DB archived at $hour:$min:$sec on $month_day/$month/$year\n";
```

If you need to open a file for reading *and* writing, you can prefix its name with either +< or +>. You might be tempted to think that it would not make any difference which you used (read and write, or write and read?), so be warned: if you use +>, the file is first opened as if for writing, which means its old contents are discarded. Generally, you will want to use +<. For example,

```
open DBFILE, "+<mydb.txt" or
    die "couldn't open database file ($OS_ERROR)\n";
```

To make sensible use of a file for both reading and writing requires Perl's random access facilities, to be described later in this chapter.

▷ If your system implements 'pipes'—communication channels that behave like files, but pass information between different processes, instead of between a process and a disk—you can open them from within a Perl script, both for writing and for reading. You do so by using a | (vertical bar) as the first or last character of the second argument to open. The rest of the argument is taken to be an operating system command line, which is executed, usually creating a new process. If the | occurs first, then anything written to the filehandle is passed to the standard input of the command; if it occurs last, then the standard output of the command is passed to the filehandle for reading. For example, assuming Unix, for simplicity,

```
open STDIN, 'ls -lR|' or
    die "Unable to open pipe from ls command ($OS_ERROR)\n";
```

If the open was successful, subsequent reads from STDIN will return a line of output from the ls command.

```
open STDOUT, '|lpr -Ppsc' or
    die "Unable to open pipe to lpr command ($OS_ERROR)\n";
```

Anything written to STDOUT will be passed to the lpr command, which will print it on the device psc.

If your system does support pipes, you will know when to use them; if it does not, you probably will not miss them, even though people with pipes will tell you ◁ that you cannot possibly live without them.

The Null Filehandle

The null filehandle has been used since the first example in this book, but I still have not given a full account of its behaviour. In particular, you should know that ARGV is a synonym for the null filehandle, and that the variable $ARGV (which is different from both @ARGV and the filehandle ARGV) holds the name of the file which is currently associated with it. Here is an improved version of an earlier script (see page 109) that searches for its first command line argument in all its others. This time, when it finds a matching line, it prints the name of the file it found it in, as well as the line itself.

```
$string = shift;
while (<>)
{
   print "$ARGV: $ARG" if /$string/;
}
```

You can even keep track of the line number as you read from a filehandle: the variable $INPUT_LINE_NUMBER ($.) holds the number of the line that was last read from a filehandle. In the case of the null filehandle, it counts from the beginning of the first file, not resetting itself when a new file is opened. This behaviour makes sense, but is often not what you want. To get line numbering to reset, you must close each file (see below).

▷ As you can see, Perl's model of file opening is firmly rooted in command lines and the tradition of users typing filenames. Such an interface is unlikely to find wide acceptance on systems whose users are accustomed to graphical and manipulative interaction. System-dependent facilities do exist for providing some of the elements of a graphical interface to Perl scripts. On MacOS systems, for example, compiled scripts can be saved as 'droplets', small executables which can be run by dragging and dropping the icons of files onto them. The names of the files thus dropped appear in the @ARGV array, as if they had been specified as command line arguments. Additionally, on that system (only) it is possible to prompt the user to select a file for opening via the standard MacOS open dialogue, by calling the function StandardFile::GetFile (the StandardFile:: notation will be explained in chapter 9), which takes a prompt string and a list of file types as its argument. Typically, a MacPerl script with a single input file might include code like this:

```
$source = shift || StandardFile::GetFile('Data file?', 'TEXT');
open SOURCE, $source or
      die "I can't open $source ($OS_ERROR)\n";
```

◁ Other functions allow you to open files for output, or open directories. MacPerl users should consult their local documentation for full details.

Closing Files

A filehandle remains associated with the file (or files, in the case of the null filehandle) it was opened on until it is closed. Files are implicitly closed when your program terminates or when you open the same filehandle on a different file. Explicit closing of a filehandle is done with the close function, which just takes a filehandle as its argument: close ARGV would close the currently opened file associated with the (null) filehandle ARGV. If you only wanted to close it in order to reset the line numbers, you need some way of determining when you have reached the end of a file. The function eof is supplied for this purpose. You can use it in three ways:

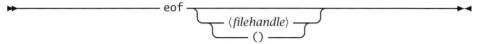

With a filehandle argument, it checks whether the last line of the associated file has been read (i.e. whether the next attempt to read will fail). It is rarely necessary to use this form, since the behaviour of the <> operator in a test usually tells you the same thing at the time you need to know it. Similarly, eof() returns true if all the files associated with the null filehandle have been read to the end; again, explicitly testing this condition is rarely necessary. Calling eof with no arguments and no empty brackets will check the current file from several associated with the null filehandle. This is what you need to do if you want to explicitly close each one yourself to reset the line numbers. To get a search program to print out the line number within each file where it found a string, you would have to do so, like this:

```
$string = shift;
while (<>)
{
  print "$ARGV:$INPUT_LINE_NUMBER: $ARG" if /$string/;
  close ARGV if eof;
}
```

Input and output is clumsily handled in almost all programming languages. Although Perl's filehandles provide a convenient mechanism for simple operations, they have some regrettable anomalies. In particular, passing a filehandle to a subroutine involves some subterfuge and an obscure language feature. Filehandles do not really constitute a proper datatype in Perl, unlike, say, C++'s streams. Fortunately, the object-oriented features of Perl have made it possible to provide an interface to filehandles that hides much of their nonsense. For this reason, further description of the operations on filehandles will be deferred until chapter 9.

Line Ranges

It is occasionally useful to specify that some operations be applied only to a selected range of lines. To do this, use the range operator as the condition in an if statement:

if (⟨*left expression*⟩ .. ⟨*right expression*⟩)
{ ⟨*statements*⟩ }

or as a statement qualifier:

⟨*statement*⟩ if ⟨*left expression*⟩ .. ⟨*right expression*⟩ ;

In this context, a scalar value is expected so, instead of producing a list of consecutive numbers, the range operator behaves in a quite different way. The left and right expressions are each interpreted as conditions. The range operator combines them in a strange-sounding but, in practice, quite natural way. The range expression is false until its left sub-expression becomes true; at that point, the whole expression becomes true and remains so until the right sub-expression becomes true. A range thus only makes much sense inside some sort of loop with side-effects that alter the conditions being tested.

▷ Each time the range expression is true, it returns as its value a sequence number, starting from one, which is incremented by one each time the expression is evaluated. All these numbers are true in a context where a Boolean value is needed. The final number in the sequence has the characters E0 appended; this does not affect its numerical or Boolean value, but provides a way of identifying the last element in the range, should you need to do so. ◁

The simplest case is a special one, as is often the way. If the sub-expressions are numbers, they are compared with $INPUT_LINE_NUMBER, so that the expression specifies a range of lines by number. This script will print the first ten lines of its input.

```
while (<>)
{
  print if 1..10;
}
```

Another useful idiom makes use of patterns to specify a range. The next script prints everything between a line containing the word 'Limited' or its abbreviation 'Ltd' and the next blank line, inclusive. If there is more than one block of lines satisfying that description, each one will be printed. You might wish to perform this operation if you had a file of addresses, separated by blank lines, some of which were for limited companies.

```
while (<>)
{
  print if /(Limited|Ltd\.?)/../^$/;
}
```

If you want to specify everything from a certain line to the end of the file, eof can be used:

```
while (<>)
{
  print if /^$/..eof;
}
```

This script prints everything after the first blank line; it might be useful for throwing away header information of one sort and another.

Multi-line Records

In all this description I have led you to believe that the <> operator always reads a line at a time (or a list of lines, if that is what the context requires). So it does, usually, but you can change this behaviour so that it reads arbitrarily delimited chunks of data each time. This is done by assigning to the variable $INPUT_RECORD_SEPARATOR, which has two other names, $/ for fans of symbols, and $RS. The second of these names is taken from the programming language Awk, where it serves a similar function. The value of this variable is a string, which is taken to denote the end of an input record—the unit of input that <> reads each time it is used. By default, the value is "\n", so a record is a line, as you thought. Sometimes the format of your data means that it is better to treat several lines as a single record; in that case, you need something to show where each record ends, and you can assign a suitable value to $INPUT_RECORD_SEPARATOR so that your input operations will reflect this.

The most common case occurs when records consist of several lines, and each record is separated from the next by a blank line. Examples of such data include address lists and bibliographical databases. It is also common for the paragraphs of text files to be separated by blank lines, when the text is stored as plain ASCII, not formatted by a word processor. You can arrange to read such data a record or paragraph at a time by assigning "\n\n" to $INPUT_RECORD_SEPARATOR, but then you need to make sure that there is exactly one blank line between records, otherwise subsequent ones may become part of the following record. If, instead, you assign the null string to $INPUT_RECORD_SEPARATOR, any sequence of consecutive blank lines is treated as a record separator, which is probably what you want.

Suppose I have a file called `address.book`, which contains a collection of names and addresses, laid out more or less conventionally (by UK standards), with each entry separated from the next by a blank line, like this:

```
Orinoco Womble,
The Burrow,
Wimbledon Common
London SW19 0MB

Scott Monument,
Prince's Street,
Edinburgh EH1 1WW
```

and so on, for many entries. I might want to construct a hash, with the names of my correspondents as the keys and their addresses as the values. Because the number of lines in the address is not the same for each record, building up the value a line at a time is clumsy, since I have to keep checking for the blank line. Instead, I can set $INPUT_RECORD_SEPARATOR to the null string, read an entire entry at a time, and just strip off the first line to use as a key. The following script reads such an address book and prints it out in alphabetical order of name. First, it arranges to read entire entries at once, and opens the file.

```
$INPUT_RECORD_SEPARATOR = '';
open ADDRESSES, 'address.book' or
    die "Unable to open address book ($OS_ERROR)\n";
```

The main loop reads each entry and builds up a hash as previously described. The chomp function understands about $INPUT_RECORD_SEPARATOR, and will chomp off the appropriate string; even if the separator is the null string, chomp does the right thing, removing as many trailing newlines as it finds.

```
while (<ADDRESSES>)
{
  chomp;
  s/(.*)\n//;
  $addresses{$1} = $ARG;
}
```

Now the names and addresses can be written out in order. I am being simpleminded here, by just sorting the keys of %addresses using the default ordering. To do this properly, you would have to supply a comparison function that, at the very least, compared the last words of the names (assuming they were written according to Western conventions), but preferably dealt with Jr, von, d' and all the other complications.

```
for $name (sort keys %addresses)
{
  print "$name\n$addresses{$name}\n\n";
}
```

Another nifty move is to set $INPUT_RECORD_SEPARATOR to an undefined value, using undef. If you do that, no string is treated as a record separator, so a single input operation will read an entire file into a scalar, assuming you have room for it.

▷ The variable $INPUT_LINE_NUMBER counts the number of records you read, whatever you have set $INPUT_RECORD_SEPARATOR to. Hence, despite what it appears to say, the following code actually numbers the *paragraphs* read from the filehandle SOURCE.

```
$INPUT_RECORD_SEPARATOR = '';
while (<SOURCE>)
{
  print $INPUT_LINE_NUMBER, ".  ", $ARG;
}
```

◁

You will have noticed that when I stripped off the first line from each address record just now, I made use of the fact that a dot is not matched by a newline. Sometimes, when you are reading entire files or paragraphs at once, it is easier for you if it does match, so that you can treat the whole record as a single string for searching and substitution. By appending the qualifier s to a pattern or a substitution operation, this effect can be achieved. At the same time, you might still want ∧ and $ to match the beginning and end of each line within the record. To do this, you use the m qualifier. This leaves you the problem of what to do when you want to match the beginning and end of the entire string. Two new regular expression elements \A and \Z are provided for this purpose.

For example, suppose my address book contains some entries for private individuals and some for limited companies. We have seen one way to pick out the latter by using a range operator. Another, more flamboyant, way is to read the entire address book in one and remove everything except the entries we are interested in.

Assuming the filehandle ADDRESSES has been opened on the file containing the address book, we begin by reading its entire contents into a scalar variable.

```
undef $INPUT_RECORD_SEPARATOR;
$address_book = <ADDRESSES>;
```

The pattern for entries that are not limited companies is quite complicated, so I will build it up a piece at a time. First, a regular expression that matches a line ending in Limited or its abbreviated form, followed by a comma (since the first line of an address will end with a comma).

```
$ltd_line = '(∧[∧\n]*(Limited|Ltd\.?),$)';
```

Next a pattern to match one or more blank lines.

```
$blank_line = '\n\n+';
```

Now we can do the actual substitution. I want to remove everything from either the beginning of the file or a blank line up until a line including Limited. I do this by matching up to and including such a line, and using the matched line as the replacement text. I also put back the blank lines, if there were any, to maintain the format of the file. (This is why I defined $blank_line the way I have.) I need the m and s qualifiers so that my big string is treated as a buffer of lines, the g qualifier to make sure all occurrences are replaced, and the o qualifier to prevent recompilation of the pattern each time it is used. Furthermore, I have to use the non-greedy repetition operator *? (see page 72) to stop the pattern matching as many entries as possible: I only want to match up to the first line with Limited on.

```
$address_book =~ s/(\A|$blank_line).*?($ltd_line|\Z)/$1$2/ogms;
print $address_book;
```

Formatted Output

The print function prints strings as it finds them, and numbers in a default format, which is usually acceptable, if not always aesthetically delightful. Sometimes you will find it necessary to exercise more control over the appearance of your output. You might need to tabulate numerical data, justify paragraphs of text, or print floating point values to a specific precision. Perl offers several complementary ways of exercising this control.

Certain built-in variables provide a very coarse mechanism for altering the appearance of printed output. We have already seen (on page 87) that assigning to $LIST_SEPARATOR will alter the way arrays are interpolated into strings, and consequently the way they are printed. Two other variables directly affect the behaviour of print. Normally, if you provide more than one argument, all of them are concatenated; $OUTPUT_FIELD_SEPARATOR can be assigned a string, which will be printed between the arguments to print (in the places corresponding to the commas in the call). $OUTPUT_RECORD_SEPARATOR can be used similarly to hold a string to be printed after each record is output. Both of these variables are normally null, however...

```
$OUTPUT_RECORD_SEPARATOR = "!!\n******\n";
$OUTPUT_FIELD_SEPARATOR = '! ';
print "This", "is", "the", "life";
print "It really", "is";
```

will print

```
This! is! the! life!!
******
It really! is!!
******
```

If you don't like the long names for built-in variables use $, or $OFS for $OUTPUT_FIELD_SEPARATOR, and $\ or $ORS for $OUTPUT_RECORD_SEPARATOR.

Clearly, the potential of this mechanism is limited. When you need to have tight control over how your output is formatted you need to resort to a more traditional way of doing things.

Formatting Strings with sprintf

Everything you see printed is a string. The way in which a value appears when you print it is determined by how it is been converted to a string representation. This conversion is the fundamental operation that you need to take control of when you want to format your output in a special way. The function sprintf lets you do so.

▶ Perl's sprintf is almost exactly the same as C's function of the same name, so if
◀ you know C you need only skim this section.

The first argument to `sprintf` is a string; its result is built out of this argument by replacing special formatting control sequences with string representations of the remaining arguments. The formatting control sequences determine how the representation is constructed. Its operation is equivalent to the following Perl code, assuming that the string `$control_seq` holds a pattern that matches any formatting control sequence, and that the subroutine `formatify` will return a string representation of its first argument in a style specified by its second argument.

```
sub pseudo_sprintf  {
  my $fmt = shift;
  do { $ARG = shift }
      while $fmt =~ s/($control_seq)/formatify($ARG, $1)/ex;
  return $fmt;
}
```

A suitable pattern for `$control_seq` would be the following (note that I used the x qualifier on my substitution):

```
q{
   %                      # All sequences are introduced by %
   (\-|\+|\ |\#|0)?        # Optional flags
   \d*                    # Optional minimum width
   (\.\d+)?                # Optional precision width
   [diouxXfeEgGcs]         # Style key letter
}
```

Some examples of strings matching this pattern are %d, %-6d and %+3.4G.

The first symbol is always a % character, which just indicates the presence of the control sequence. (If you actually want to include a % character in your string, you must use %%.) The only necessary component of the sequence is the key letter, which appears at the end. This specifies how the bits of the argument should be interpreted when it is converted to a string. The meaning of the available letters is given in Table 6.1. Preceding the key letter may be some flags, which control detailed attributes of the conversion specified by the letter, such as whether a value should be left or right justified. The possible flags and their meanings are given in Table 6.2. The minimum width, which may follow the flags, specifies exactly that: if the string produced by the conversion is smaller than this minimum width, it will be padded out to fit it; exactly how is determined by the flags, if any. If the string is larger than the minimum width, it is printed in its fullness. If the 'precision width' is present, it has the form of a dot (decimal point, if you like) followed by another number. For floating point numbers, this specifies the number of digits to print after the point; for strings, it specifies a maximum width.

This all sounds complicated, because it is, but you can get by quite well with just a few control sequences. For most programmers, %d, %g and %s, with widths and a few flags, are adequate. Some examples will make it clear what is going on.

Letter	Conversion
d	signed decimal integer representation
i	signed decimal integer representation
o	unsigned octal representation
X	unsigned hexadecimal representation; upper case letters are used for the digits A–F
x	unsigned hexadecimal representation; lower case letters are used for the digits a–f
f	decimal representation ($xx.yyyyyy$) of a floating point number
e	'scientific' representation of a floating point number, using e to separate mantissa and exponent ($x.yyyyyy$ennn)
E	'scientific' representation of a floating point number, using E to separate mantissa and exponent ($x.yyyyyy$Ennn)
g	'automatic' floating point representation: if the exponent is less than 4, uses f, otherwise e
G	'automatic' floating point representation: if the exponent is less than 4, uses F, otherwise E
c	value is treated as a character code
s	a string

Table 6.1   Key letters for `sprintf` conversions

Flag character	Effect
–	left justify in the specified minimum width
+	for numeric arguments, insert a + sign if the value is positive
⟨*space*⟩	for numeric arguments, insert a space in front of positive values, unless + is specified (so they line up nicely with the negative ones)
#	prefix octal numbers by 0, hexadecimal ones by 0x; always insert a decimal point in floating point numbers, and do not remove trailing zeroes
0	pad numbers with leading zeroes

Table 6.2   Flags for `sprintf` conversions

```
$a_third = 1/3;
print "$a_third\n";
```

prints

```
0.333333333333333
```

but

```
print sprintf "%3.2G\n", $a_third;
```

prints

```
0.33
```

The %s sequence may seem redundant—aren't we always printing strings?—but with a minimum width specification, it goes some way towards letting you tabulate data.

```
$a_string = 'Hooray for Captain Spalding';
$another_string = 'The African explorer!';
print "$a_string\n$another_string\n";
```

prints the strings left aligned:

```
Hooray for Captain Spalding
The African explorer!
```

but

```
print sprintf "%30s\n%30s\n", $a_string, $another_string;
```

right aligns them in a field 30 characters wide:

```
   Hooray for Captain Spalding
         The African explorer!
```

Finally, suppose I have computed the duration of a video clip in minutes, seconds and frames, and stored the values in scalar variables. If I try to output the duration in standard time code format (mm:ss:ff), like this:

```
print "$mins:$secs:$frames\n";
```

components with values less than 10 come out wrong (or, at least, unconventionally):

```
4:2:9
```

It is easy to obtain the right format with `sprintf`:

```
print sprintf "%02d:%02d:%02d\n", $mins, $secs, $frames;
```

gives

```
04:02:09
```

If you find video timecodes esoteric, consider how you would like to see times and dates appear in your output.

Although the formatting facilities of `sprintf` are useful in many contexts, you often want to print a string as soon as you have formatted it. For convenience, the function `printf`, which is just the composition of `print` and `sprintf`, is provided. Although it is strictly redundant, you will come to appreciate `printf` when you are reading your Perl scripts out loud to your circle of admirers.

Formats

With a certain amount of effort on your part, `sprintf` can do any formatting of ASCII text you can reasonably expect, but for more than a few values it becomes clumsy. Perl provides a complementary formatting mechanism, which requires somewhat less effort when all you want to do is tabulate data or produce simple report summaries. Even if some of what follows reminds you of Fortran and Cobol, try to think of it as retro, not old-fashioned.

The idea is to separate a description of the output—its appearance and any variables whose value it includes—from the output operation itself. The latter becomes especially simple: it is just a call to the function `write`, which may optionally be followed by the name of a filehandle to which the data should be written. The description of what and how to write to that filehandle is given by a construct called a format.

A format is declared using the following syntax:

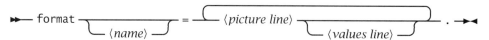

The ⟨*name*⟩ is usually the name of the filehandle with which you want the format to be associated. (You can associate arbitrarily named formats with filehandles, but it is best done using the object-oriented form of filehandle manipulation, which will be described in chapter 9.) If you omit the name, it defaults to `STDOUT`. Format declarations are line-oriented; unlike other Perl constructs, the newlines within a format matter. Each ⟨*picture line*⟩ and ⟨*value line*⟩ must, indeed, occupy a line on its own. So must the dot which terminates the format.

As you can probably guess, the picture lines describe the appearance of the output, while the value lines specify what should be output. The two sorts of lines come in pairs: each picture line specifies how the following value line should be printed. A picture line consists of literal text and spacing characters, which will be printed the same every time the format is used, interspersed with special value fields, so it is similar to the first argument of `sprintf`, although the value fields work differently from the formatting control sequences. On output, the values from the following line are inserted in place of these value fields, so there should be as many values on a value line as there are value fields on the preceding picture line. The possibility that a picture line contains no value fields is not ruled out; you can use such lines to insert dividers or headings.

The simplest value fields consist of an @ sign, followed by several <, >, | or # symbols. The number of symbols indicates the width of the field, the choice of symbol determines whether the corresponding value will be inserted into the field left justified (<), right justified (>), centred (|) or, for numeric fields, lined up on decimal points (#). In the last case, you can insert a dot among the # symbols, to indicate where the decimal point lies.

Each value line consists of a list of expressions to insert in the preceding picture line. When the expressions are evaluated, a list is expected, so there may be fewer expressions than value fields, but the number of elements finally produced must match the number of fields to be filled in. If a value is too long to fit into the field allocated for it, it is truncated. Contrast this behaviour with that of `sprintf`, where fields stretch to accommodate values.

As a simple but typical example, consider again my video clips database. For compactness and ease of splitting, the records, you will recall, are stored in this form:

```
Red1|00:09:10|Cinepak|985
Red2|00:05:14|Miro MJPG|1455
Red3|00:10:23|Miro MJPG|3150
Blue1|00:09:00|Apple Animation|2850
Blue2|00:01:01|Miro MJPG|2500
Yellow1|00:03:10|Miro MJPG|1250
Yellow2|00:03:22|Miro MJPG|1250
Yellow3|00:05:00|Cinepak|650
```

If I wanted a printed list, I would prefer it to look like this:

```
Red1        00:09:10 Cinepak            985
Red2        00:05:14 Miro MJPG         1455
Red3        00:10:23 Miro MJPG         3150
Blue1       00:09:00 Apple Animation   2850
Blue2       00:01:01 Miro MJPG         2500
Yellow1     00:03:10 Miro MJPG         1250
Yellow2     00:03:22 Miro MJPG         1250
Yellow3     00:05:00 Cinepak            650
```

The transformation can be achieved very simply using a format:

```
format STDOUT =
@<<<<<<<<< @||||||| @<<<<<<<<<<<<<< @>>>
$title, $duration, $compressor, $size
.
```

This stipulates that whenever I `write` to STDOUT, the value of the variable $title will be printed left justified in a field 10 characters wide (the @ is counted in as part of the field), followed by a space, then the value of $duration centred in 8 characters, another space and $compressor on the left of a 16 character field, one more space and then the value of $size right justified in four spaces. The table above was produced by adding the following trivial loop to that format declaration.

```
while (<>)
{
  ($title, $duration, $compressor, $size) = split /\|/;
  write;
}
```

Some column headings would be nice. You can associate a header format with a filehandle by declaring a format whose name consists of the filehandle's name with _TOP on the end. (Again, you really have more flexibility than this, but you will have to wait until chapter 9.) Such headers often consist of nothing but picture lines. For example,

```
format STDOUT_TOP =
title       duration compressor       kbytes
-------------------------------------------
  .
```

changes the output to

```
title       duration compressor       kbytes
-------------------------------------------
Red1        00:09:10 Cinepak             985
Red2        00:05:14 Miro MJPG          1455
```

and so on.

Formats are particularly useful if you need to tabulate data that covers more than one page. You can set the variable $FORMAT_LINES_PER_PAGE ($=)to the number of lines you want on each page. perl will ensure that a new page is thrown after that many lines have been printed, and also that the header, if any, will be printed at the top of each page.

Suppose for a moment that you are working in digital video production. You will find that most of the time durations of clips and positions within a clip are best expressed in timecode form; other times, you may know, or need to know, a number of frames, and want to find out how it would be expressed as a timecode. For example, I might know I had just made a clip of 70 frames, when what I needed to know was that its last frame had timecode 00:02:19. The conversion does not involve a difficult calculation, but as the numbers get large, it is not something you would necessarily want to do in your head. And then there is always the problem of remembering that you have to start counting at 0 to get a frame number, but at 1 to get a duration. You would not necessarily want to run a program every time you needed the answer. It would be far more convenient to have a printed table you could look it up in.

The following little script produces such a table, formatted with four seconds' worth of codes per page (I assume, as ever, that we are using European video standards with 25 frames per second), in a nice columnar format.

The script shows that formats and `sprintf` are not mutually exclusive approaches to formatting, but can be used together. Formats can deal gracefully with some aspects that `sprintf` cannot—for example, page throws and headers—and vice versa—for example, inserting leading zeroes into numeric fields. The following subroutine takes a frame count as its argument, and computes and returns a properly formatted timecode corresponding to it.

```
sub timecode
{
  my $n = shift @ARG;
  my ($s, $f) = ($n/25, $n%25);
  my $m = $s/60;
  $s %= 60;
  return sprintf("%02d:%02d:%02d",  $m, $s, $f);
}
```

The following format produces column headers on the top of each page.

```
format STDOUT_TOP =
frames     duration    last frame    |  frames     duration    last frame
-----------------------------------+-----------------------------------
                                   |
.
```

The vertical bars will separate two columns, each of which has three sub-columns: a number of frames, the timecode representing the duration of a clip of that many frames, and the timecode for that frame, which will be one less than the column to its left, because codes start at zero. I will get `perl` to make sure that I get that right, by embedding the fact in the expression used to compute the values in the format:

```
format STDOUT =
@>>>>      @|||||||||   @|||||||||   |  @>>>      @|||||||||  @|||||||||
{$i+$k, timecode($i+$k), timecode($i+$k-1), $i+$k+50,
timecode($i+$k+50), timecode($i+$k+49)}
.
```

I have had to split the value 'line' across two lines to fit it on the page. Perl allows you to do this if you enclose the entire list of values in curly brackets, making sure that the opening bracket is the very first character on a line.

I need 50 rows plus three lines of header on every page.

```
$FORMAT_LINES_PER_PAGE = 53;
```

All I need to do to produce the tables is open a file and loop through 16 pages (a fairly arbitrary, but practically useful number), writing my 50 lines on each page.

```
open STDOUT, '>timecode.sheets' or
    die "Unable to open output file ($OS_ERROR)\n";
for ($j = 0; $j < 16; ++$j)
{
  $k = $j*100;
  for ($i= 1; $i <= 50; ++$i)
  { write; }
}
```

Formats using @ value fields are fine for tabulating numerical data and short strings, but not much good if you want to format paragraphs of text. Suppose, for example, I wanted to add a comment of arbitrary length to each video clip record, and have it printed out along with the other data, like this:

```
Red1        00:09:10 Cinepak          985 This took ages to
                                          compress! Do it
                                          another way if
                                          possible
Red2        00:05:14 Miro MJPG        1455 Good take.
Red3        00:10:23 Miro MJPG        3150 Some problems with
                                          quality.  Need to
                                          try again.
```

To achieve this effect, you need to use a different sort of value field, one that begins with a ∧ character, instead of a @. The fields may contain the same characters as before, but the way they are filled up when a `write` occurs is slightly different. The corresponding value from the next value line must be a scalar variable holding a string. As much of it as will fit is inserted into the field and stripped off the front of the string, leaving the variable holding whatever is left over. The string will only be broken at a space or hyphen character. If a sequence of identical picture lines with a ∧ field appears in a format, with the same variable appearing in the corresponding place in the following value line, then the value of that variable will be printed as a filled paragraph (with ragged left or right margin, or both, depending on whether left or right justification or centring was specified). For the above example, I could almost use the following format:

✘
```
format STDOUT =
@<<<<<<<<< @|||||||| @<<<<<<<<<<<<<< @>>> ∧<<<<<<<<<<<<<<<<<<<
$title, $duration, $compressor, $size, $comment
~                                        ∧<<<<<<<<<<<<<<<<<<<
$comment
~                                        ∧<<<<<<<<<<<<<<<<<<<
$comment
~                                        ∧<<<<<<<<<<<<<<<<<<<
$comment
```
✘
```
.
```

with the following loop:

```
while (<>)
{
  ($title, $duration, $compressor, $size, $comment) = split /\|/;
  write;
}
```

However, that would use four lines for every entry, no matter how short the comment was. To suppress lines that would be blank because a ^ field had exhausted its variable, you only need to put a ~ anywhere in the picture line, so to produce the output above, the last three picture lines of the format looked like this:

```
~                                                    ^<<<<<<<<<<<<<<<<<<<
```

That is fine if you can put an upper bound on the number of lines in a paragraph, but if you need to be able to accommodate arbitrarily long ones, this approach would become unsatisfactory. Fortunately, you have an alternative. If you include a pair of ~ characters in a picture line, then that line will be used as often as necessary to eat up all the strings in the following line corresponding to ^ fields. For example, the following script will typeset a document as numbered indented paragraphs.

```
format STDOUT =
@>. ^<<<<<<<<<<<<<<<<<<<<<<<<<<<<<<<<<<<<<<<<<<<<<<<<<<<<<<
$the_number, $the_paragraph
~~  ^<<<<<<<<<<<<<<<<<<<<<<<<<<<<<<<<<<<<<<<<<<<<<<<<<<<<<<
$the_paragraph
.

$INPUT_RECORD_SEPARATOR = '';
while (<DATA>)
{
  $the_number = $INPUT_LINE_NUMBER;
  $the_paragraph = $ARG;
  write;
}
```

It transforms this:

```
The party of the first part will hereinafter be referred to
as the party of the first part.

The party of the second part will hereinafter be referred to
as the party of the second part.

The party of the third part will hereinafter be referred to
as the party of the third part.
```

into this:

1. The party of the first part will hereinafter be
   referred to as the party of the first part.
2. The party of the second part will hereinafter be
   referred to as the party of the second part.
3. The party of the third part will hereinafter be
   referred to as the party of the third part.

Formats are global; any variables used in a format must be in scope at the point the format is declared. This tends to encourage you to use global variables with formats; there is something to be said for the practice of keeping the variables you use in a format reserved for that purpose, and assigning the values you want to print to them just before you call `write`.

Although Perl's formats are among the ugliest language features this side of HTML, they make producing tabular data and reports nice and easy. If you need more sophisticated formatting than is offered by straightforward use of formats and `sprintf`, rather than try to push them to their limits, you will often be better off generating output including LaTeX or SGML tags, and offloading the actual formatting to a more powerful program. You could even consider generating your own PostScript.

Binary Data

All data is binary, of course, but the bits of the data we have been using so far are interpreted as characters, so we can treat the data as text. But there is all the other stuff that makes you wish you hadn't when you try to edit it with a text editor: sound and graphics files, video, executables, databases, even word-processor files. Since these files do not contain text, you cannot expect to use Perl's text processing facilities, but you can still carry out useful processing on binary data in Perl.

You open binary files the same way as text files, associating them with filehandles using `open`. On some operating systems, newlines present a problem with binary files. Although \n is used in Perl to represent a 'newline character', the actual character is not always the same; it is not even always a single character. Whereas on Unix systems, newline is a linefeed character, on MacOS it is a carriage return, and on MS-DOS and its descendants, it is the pair consisting of both. It is this last possibility that can cause problems, since, normally, library routines translate the pair into a single newline. You do not want this to happen when you are reading a binary file, because there the combination has no special significance, and you want to read every character as it appears in the file. You can call the function `binmode`, with the filehandle as its argument, to suppress newline translation. Even on systems where no translation actually takes place, it is good practice to call `binmode` (which does nothing on those systems), in case your program ever gets ported to a system where it matters.

You cannot sensibly use the <> operation to read from a binary file, since it is not divided into records. Instead, you can use the function `read`, which takes

byte number

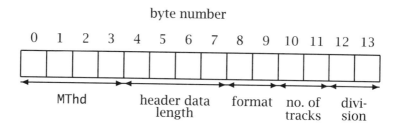

Figure 6.1   Standard MIDI File header

a filehandle, a scalar and an integer and attempts to read the specified number of bytes from the filehandle into the scalar. It returns the actual number of bytes read (which may be fewer than you specified if there are not that many bytes left in the file). For example:

```
$bytes_read = read INFILE, $next_block, 512;
```

will attempt to read 512 bytes and store them as a string in the variable `$next_block`. The actual number read is remembered in `$bytes_read`. If you need to write binary data to a file, you can just use `print` with a string of arbitrary bytes.

Although not organized as lines of text, binary files almost always possess some structure. Consider, for example, a Standard MIDI File (SMF). MIDI is the Musical Instruments Digital Interface, a simple protocol used to communicate between computers, synthesizers, samplers and other digital musical instruments and controllers. SMF is a file format used to store sequences of MIDI instructions, so they can be edited or played back. A SMF is a bit like a digital pianola roll. It has a very simple format.

A SMF comprises several tracks, each one recording the performance instructions for one 'voice' of an instrument. At the beginning of the file is a header consisting of four bytes, which must hold the characters `MThd`, followed by four bytes which are interpreted as a 32 bit integer, giving the number of data bytes in the header chunk. (This is slightly odd, since there are always exactly six data bytes, but the format *was* designed for extensibility.) The data bytes consist of a two byte format code, a two byte integer giving the number of MIDI tracks in the file, and finally two bytes (called the division) which specify the way in which times are recorded in the file. (See Figure 6.1.)

If the variable `$midi` holds the name of a standard MIDI file, I can easily open the file and read the header:

```
open MIDI, $midi or die "I can't open $midi ($OS_ERROR)\n";
binmode MIDI;
```

```
$header_size = 14;
(read MIDI, $header, $header_size) == $header_size or
  die "Unable to read track header\n";
```

To examine the fields of the header in most programming languages would
now require me to extract the individual bytes, and recombine them using shifts
and bit operations. As usual, Perl makes life easier. The function unpack takes
two arguments; the second is a string, which will be treated as a sequence of
bytes; the first is a template describing the structure you wish to impose on
this string of bytes (e.g. two characters, followed by an integer, followed by a
floating point number); the function returns a list consisting of the elements
of the structure obtained by interpreting the bytes of the string in accordance
with the template.

Templates are brutally simple. The type of each element of your intended
structure is signified by a single letter, which may be followed by a count. The
template is just a string of these letters and counts. Unpacking bytes into
strings and numbers is complicated by the different conventions regarding
byte ordering employed by systems and networks. Perl tries to provide sufficient options in its templates to accommodate all possibilities; you will need
to determine the exact way bytes are packed in the files you need to work with
before you can unpack them. Table 6.3 lists the principal types that can be
specified in a template; they are defined in terms of C's numerical types, which
reflect the different numerical formats provided by the hardware. Note that
for most characters, a following number is a repeat count (e.g. n4 denotes four
short integers in big-endian format) but for a and A it denotes the length of the
string. (For example, a4 is a string of length 4, not 4 strings.) A means that
trailing null characters will be stripped off the string as found, a means they
will be included in the unpacked string. If you put a * instead of a count, all
the remaining values will be unpacked according to the preceding letter.

I need to break apart the header of my SMF into a four byte ASCII string,
for the identifying MThd, a long integer for the header data length, two short
integers for the format code and number of tracks; according to the SMF specification, these are stored high byte first, so I need to use N and n specifiers to
unpack them. I could handle the remaining two bytes in several different ways,
but since I know that I need to look at the most significant bit of the division, I
will unpack it into a 16 element string of bits. Hence, the following assignment
separates out all the components of the header:

```
($id, $header_data_length, $format, $number_of_tracks, $division)
                          = unpack "a4NnnB16", $header;
```

Presumably, I would next verify the integrity of the file by checking that $id
was indeed 'MThd' and that the header data length was right. If I intended
to analyse the file further, I would need to look more closely at the division.
The most significant bit tells me how time is represented in this SMF; if it is
0, then the remaining bits give the number of MIDI clock ticks per quarter
note (an electronic equivalent of a metronome setting); if it is 1, then the file

Letter	Type
a	ASCII string with nulls
A	ASCII string
b	bit string, low to high order
B	bit string, high to low order
c	signed char (byte)
C	unsigned char (byte)
d	double precision float
f	float
h	hexadecimal string, low to high characters in a byte
H	hexadecimal string, high to low characters in a byte
i	signed integer, native machine format
I	unsigned integer, native machine format
l	signed long integer, native machine format
L	unsigned long integer, native machine format
s	signed short integer, native machine format
S	unsigned short integer, native machine format
N	four-byte integer, high byte first (big-endian format)
n	two-byte integer, high byte first (big-endian format)
V	four-byte integer, low byte first (little-endian format)
v	two-byte integer, low byte first (little-endian format)

Table 6.3   Common type specifiers for templates

uses SMPTE timecode. I have unpacked the division into a string of bits, most significant first, so the bit I need to look at is the first element of this string. SMPTE timecode is nasty stuff to deal with, so I would proceed as follows:

```
$div_type = substr($division, 0, 1)?
            die "Can't handle SMPTE format\n":
            'ticks per quarter note';
```

But now I need to turn the bits of the division into a short integer. There is no built-in function to do this in Perl; an easy way is to pack it back up and then unpack it again as a short. To pack it, I use the function `pack`, which undoes the work of `unpack`.

```
$resolution = unpack "s", pack "B16", $division;
```

The call to `pack` puts my 16 bits back together, producing a string of two bytes; `unpack` then takes these out as a short integer in my machine's format. I know the most significant bit is zero, so it is all right to include it in the packing.

I now know enough about my SMF to read the track data. Each track begins with a header, consisting of the four characters `'MTrk'` and a four byte integer specifying the number of data bytes for this track. The data bytes consist of instructions for starting a note, finishing a note, changing pitch, applying effects, and so on. We will not go into the internal structure of the track; the technique of reading bytes and unpacking them is adequate to extract all the data. Here is a loop that would work through every track, calling a subroutine to process the data from each.

```
$track_header_size = 8;
for ($i = 0; $i < $number_of_tracks; ++$i)
{
   read MIDI, $track_header, $track_header_size;
   ($tid, $track_data_length) = unpack "a4N", $track_header;
   $tid eq 'MTrk' or die "Corrupt SMF; track id was $tid\n";
   read MIDI, $the_track, $track_data_length;
   process_track($the_track);
}
```

It is usually possible, when dealing with binary data, to determine the position within a file at which each component of the file begins. For example, since each track of a SMF records its own length, I can work out where the next track begins. In some files, particularly database files, each component of the file is a fixed length record, so, knowing the length of a record, I know where the nth record is. Processing such records is often helped by the ability to go directly to a particular position within the file and start reading from there.

The function seek (taken from the C function of the same name) is provided for such 'random access' positioning. It takes three arguments: a filehandle, an offset and a code indicating how the offset is to be interpreted. If the code is 0, it is an absolute number of bytes from the beginning of the file; if it is 1, the offset is relative to the current position; if it is 2, it is relative to the end of the file. The offset may be negative to move backwards relative to the current position, or a specified distance from the end of the file.

Suppose that we wished to skip certain tracks in a SMF. If an array @skips was set up so that $skips[$i] was 1 for those tracks which should be skipped, and 0 for the ones to process, then the body of above loop could be replaced by:

```
read MIDI, $track_header, $track_header_size;
($tid, $track_data_length) = unpack "a4N", $track_header;
$tid eq 'MTrk' or die "Corrupt SMF; track id was $tid\n";
if ($skips[$i])
{
   print "skipping track $i\n";
   seek MIDI, $track_data_length, 1;
}
else
{
   read MIDI, $the_track, $track_data_length;
   process_track($the_track);
}
```

With fixed-length records, `seek` can be used to implement an indexed sequential file. There are, however, more sophisticated ways of storing databases to be accessed by `perl`, as we will see.

▷ If you ever need to remember whereabouts in a file you are, you can call the function `tell`, giving it your filehandle as an argument. It will return a value that can subsequently be used as an argument to `seek`, with a code of 0, to get back to the
◁ same place in the file.

Files and Directories

The Perl scripts we have seen so far have been concerned with the contents of files as data. Perl also lets you manipulate files themselves, and directories (or folders, or drawers, or whatever they are called on your system). Operations such as deleting and renaming files, finding out which files are in a directory, discovering whether a file is readable, or what its size is, are available via Perl functions and operators.

The questions it is meaningful to ask about your files and directories depend on your operating system. Perl is based on the belief that all operating systems are Unix, so you can find out whether a file has its `setgid` bit set, and what its `inode` number is. This is little comfort on systems without `setgid` bits or `inode`s. In practice, some of the operations provided by Perl will be meaningless on many systems, while others will have a different interpretation. I will try to concentrate on those operations which are independent of particular systems, but you will have to consult your local documentation to find out about specific details on your system. Unless you actually know what a `setgid` bit is.

File Tests

A collection of operators with the form -⟨*letter*⟩ is provided for discovering properties of files. You can apply these operators to either a filehandle or a string, which is taken to be a filename. Most of the operations are Boolean, returning 1 or the null string, indicating whether the predicate they test is true or false. Table 6.4 lists those file test operators that you can expect to be meaningful on most systems.

The meaning of most of the operators should be clear. -T and -B are really just guessing; they read the beginning of the file, and look for characters that cannot be printed. If there is a high enough proportion of such characters, the file is classified as binary, otherwise it is text. -M and -A return a floating point value, so they can be used meaningfully on files newer than yesterday.

Operator	Meaning
-r	program can read this file
-w	program can write this file
-x	file is executable
-o	you own this file
-e	file exists
-z	file has size 0
-s	file has size > 0, returns the size
-d	'file' is actually a directory
-t	filehandle is attached to a terminal
-T	text file
-B	binary file
-M	days between file's last modification and start of program
-A	days between last access to the file and start of program

Table 6.4   Common file test operators

▷   Note that the -r, -w, -x and -o operations on a Unix system refer to the effective
uid of the program; for the real uid, use the same letters in upper case.

MacPerl users will be disappointed to learn that -s and -z only look at the size
of a file's data fork, and do not take account of its resource fork, so they can provide
some surprises—the MacPerl executable has size zero, for example, on my machine.

◁

Here is an excessively cautious way of opening a file for reading.

```
-e $filename or die "$filename does not exist\n";
-r $filename or die "you cannot read $filename\n";
-s $filename or die "there is nothing in $filename\n";
-T $filename or die "$filename is a binary file\n";

open FILE, $filename or
     die "some other problem ($OS_ERROR) opening $filename\n";
```

▷   Each file test operation may involve a system call; it may well be that the same system call is used for each one—the Unix stat call, for example, returns most of the
information in a single structure. To minimize the overhead of these calls when you
apply a sequence of operations to the same file, you may use an underline symbol,
on its own, as the argument to any of them. It means 'the last file I tested'. The
system call results are cached, and when you use the underline, the cached value
is examined, without any additional call being made. If efficiency was considered
important, the tests in the program just given should probably be written like this:

```
-e $filename or die "$filename does not exist\n";
-r _ or die "you cannot read $filename\n";
```

```
-s _ or die "there is nothing in $filename\n";
-T _ or die "$filename is a binary file\n";
```

◁

Operations on Directories and Files

One of the things that makes Perl so handy is the ability it gives you to automate tasks that you normally perform from the command line or desktop. A small number of functions that work on directories and files, coupled with Perl's programming and pattern matching facilities, are sufficient to make disk housekeeping tasks simple. The only drawback—and I'm sorry if I seem to be repeating myself here—is that the operations are images of Unix commands, with suitably enigmatic names, that do not always make complete sense on other systems.

Most of these functions are dangerous. For example, `rename` takes two arguments, the old and new names for a file, and changes the name from the old to the new. If there was already a file with the new name, it will be destroyed. You can deliberately destroy files by calling `unlink`, which takes a list of file names and deletes them all. Goodbye, files.

What makes the file operations especially useful is that they can be used in conjunction with operations on directories, to apply tests and functions to all the files in a directory and, possibly, its sub-directories. The directory operations work with objects called directory handles, which are analogous to file handles, but are attached to directories instead of files. You attach them using `opendir`, which is analogous to `open`; it takes a directory handle and a directory name and tries to open the directory. If it is successful, the handle is attached to the directory for subsequent use by a function called `readdir`. Depending on the context it is called in, `readdir` will return a list of directory entries from its directory handle argument, or the next entry if a single scalar is needed.

On hierarchical file systems, each file has a full path name consisting of the names of all the directories and sub-directories leading from the root of the hierarchy down to the file itself, which is the last element of the path name. Usually, there is also a concept of a 'current directory'; if a filename is given with no directories, the pathname of the current directory is prefixed to the file. Perl implements a current directory. The function `chdir` is used to change the current directory; it takes a pathname to use as the new current directory as its argument. It is often easiest to carry out your file operations within a current directory.

Here is one of the scripts I alluded to in chapter 1. The problem that led to it is one of those maddeningly stupid things that make computers so much less useful than they could be. Single frames of video are being captured for stop-frame animation. The program that is used to capture them automatically names them in sequence, as `picture1`, `picture2`, and so on. The individual frames have to be put together into a video sequence. The editing program that can do that insists that the files it imports are numbered as `picture.001`, `picture.002`, and so on. Without the dot and the leading zeroes, chaos will result. Perl to the rescue:

```
opendir DIR, $folder or die "I can't open $folder ($OS_ERROR)\n";
chdir $folder or die "couldn't change directory to $folder";

@files = readdir DIR;

foreach (@files)
{
  /(\d+)$/ &&
  (rename($ARG, $name.sprintf(".%03d", $1)) or
    die "couldn't rename $ARG\n");
}
```

Before this sequence of code, `$folder` is set to the directory in which the captured pictures reside, and `$name` is set to the desired prefix for the new sequence of names. The call of `readdir` puts all the file names into `@files`. Within the loop, each file name is matched against a pattern ending in a sequence of digits; if the match succeeds, `$1` is set to the number as a side-effect, and its value is used to construct the new filename, by reformatting it with `sprintf`. Evidently, this script makes some assumptions about the files that may be in the directory to begin with; in the environment it is used in, these assumptions will always be valid. Honest.

Often, you want to traverse a directory and all its sub-directories and all their sub-directories, and so on, performing some operation. It can be awkward or expensive to do so from the desktop or command line, but in Perl you can map the naturally recursive nature of the traversal on to a recursive subroutine. The following script looks at a hierarchy and identifies all those directories which contain any files larger than a specified size. The work is done by a subroutine called `lookin`. It takes the full path name of a directory as its argument, and begins by opening and reading that directory.

```
sub lookin
{
  my $dir = shift;
  opendir DIR, $dir or die "I can't open $dir ($OS_ERROR)\n";
  my @files = readdir DIR;
```

I now loop through the list of directory entries. Some of these will be the names of sub-directories, others the names of files. In either case, I construct the full path name by appending the directory entry to the directory's path name. The two are separated by a symbol recorded in the variable `$pathsep`. For a Unix system, this would be a slash, for MacOS a colon, and for MS-whatever, a backslash.[1]

---

[1] VMS users are left out in the cold, as usual, and would have to use a more elaborate approach to cope with their form of directory specification.

```
foreach $f (@files)
{
  my $p = $dir . $pathsep . $f;
```

I use the file test operator -d to determine whether I have a sub-directory. If so, I call `lookin` recursively. Otherwise, I find out the file's size, using -s on the cached value, and compare it with the specified limit `$size_in_bytes`, which is computed in the main program, in a way to be described shortly. If I find a file larger than the limit, I increment a count of big files in a hash called `%big_directories`, under the key of the directory's path name, since what I am looking for is not the big files, but the directories containing them.

```
    if (-d $p) {  lookin($p); }
    elsif (-s _ > $size_in_bytes)
    {  ++$big_directories{$dir};  }
  }
}
```

A simple subroutine is needed to summarize the results of the traversal. It just lists the directories, if any, that contain big files, with a note of how many such files there are in each.

```
sub report
{
  my @bigs = keys %big_directories;
  if (@bigs)
  {
    print "These folders had files bigger than ${size}bytes:\n" ;
    foreach $d (sort keys %big_directories)
    {
      print "$d ($big_directories{$d})\n";
    }
  }
  else
  {  print "No folder had any file bigger than ${size}bytes\n"; }
}
```

The variable `$size` is a bit of finesse. In the main program, the user is prompted for a size; this may be a number, optionally followed by K or M, for kilobytes or megabytes, respectively. The program computes the size in bytes required for comparison with the result of -s.

```
$size_in_bytes = $size;
if ($size_in_bytes =~ s/M$//i)   {  $size_in_bytes *= 1024*1024; }
elsif ($size_in_bytes =~ s/K$//i)   {  $size_in_bytes *= 1024;  }
```

The value of `$size` is obtained from the user before this computation, as is `$root`, the root of the directory hierarchy to be traversed. The rest of the main program just calls the two subroutines.

```
lookin($root);
report;
```

References and Data Structures

Data structures hold a special place in the hearts of computer programmers of the old school. Much of their—*our*—time was spent implementing linked lists, trees, hash tables, and the other structures that provide the material for a host of data structures books and courses. Of late, we have learned to use abstract datatypes, and to separate the interface to a type from its implementation as a concrete data structure, but hacking pointer-based data structures is what we still spend a lot of time doing.

But Perl has done it for us. Lists and the functions operating on them give us sequences, stacks, queues and deques. Hashes give us symbol tables and sets. Do we have to throw out our copies of *The Art of Computer Programming* now that we have learned Perl? Perhaps that would not be such a bad idea; after all, just how many functions to delete an element from a circular two-way linked list do you want to write? However, it never pays to be too hasty, especially about throwing away good books.

What I just said about data structures in Perl is true, with one important qualification: lists and hashes can only contain scalars. Hence, you cannot have lists of lists, or hashes of lists, or any other hierarchical data structure. You can work round this restriction, as any Fortran programmer will tell you, but the work-rounds are often cumbersome and error-prone. Older releases of the Perl language forced you into them, but Perl5 incorporates a simple facility which allows you to build complex data structures directly: references. And once you start using references, the old tricks will turn out to have some life left in them, after all.

References

When I assign one variable to another, as in

```
$x = $y;
```

we would describe the effect by saying that the value currently held in $y is stored in $x. But $x is just a scalar variable, a piece of text in a Perl script; we really mean that the value held in a storage location associated with $y at run-time is copied into a location associated with $x. References allow us to manipulate those storage locations themselves: not just read and change the values stored in them, but store them in other locations. Store a location? To understand this process properly, it helps to have a better idea about what we mean by a 'value'. By clarifying the relationship between a variable, the storage location associated with it, and the value stored in it, you will be able to appreciate not just what a reference is, but also why the particular notation used to manipulate references in Perl has been chosen.

> ▶ If you are used to programming languages with pointers, then you can simply think of references as domesticated pointers, and you will have a good idea of what they can be used for, but the notation will seem peculiar unless you take a more abstract view. C++ programmers should note that Perl's references are different in some important ways from C++'s. In particular, you have to create references explicitly in ◀ Perl.

A Brief Excursion into Semantics

To appreciate references, we have first to take a closer look at variables.

I have spoken of variables and expressions 'having an l-value', as a coded way of saying that they can be assigned to. It is time to explain the expression more fully. It comes from consideration of an assignment statement such as:

```
$var = $var + 1;
```

(I have eschewed the shorthand assigning operators to make what is happening more explicit.) The scalar variable $var is being used in two distinct ways in this statement: on the left of the = it is being used to denote a storage location in which the result of the expression on the right is to be stored; on the right, it is being used to denote the value stored in that location. In other words, on the right of an assignment, we take the contents of a variable before using it.

Because the mapping between variable names and machine addresses may be complex, the terms l-value and r-value were coined[1] to distinguish between the two uses of variables in imperative programming languages. The l-value is the one used on the left of a simple assignment; it corresponds to the storage location associated with the variable. The r-value is the one used on the right of a simple assignment; it is the value stored in the l-value. Hence the names: the l and r in l-value and r-value stand for left and right. However, it is not the case that the only place you use an r-value is on the right of an assignment—think about

---

[1]In the 1960s, by Christopher Strachey.

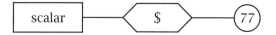

Figure 7.1   A scalar variable

```
$array[$i] = $i;
```

It is helpful to refer to the contexts where an r-value is used as *r-contexts*, and those where an l-value is used as *l-contexts*. R-contexts include the right hand side of an assignment, an array subscript, and an argument to a subroutine call. L-contexts are not restricted to the left of assignments, but we have not yet met any others. Any expression has an r-value, but only some have an l-value, the most common being simple variables and array and hash elements.

The distinction between l-values and r-values holds in any programming language with an assignment statement (or something equivalent). In Perl it also helps clarify the way in which names work. Figure 7.1 is a schematic representation of the relationship between a name and its l- and r-values. The hexagonal lozenge represents the l-value of the name in the box on the left of the picture; the circle attached to it represents the value stored in it—its current r-value. If you like to think in terms of the possible implementation, you can consider the name in a box to be a symbol table entry, pointing to a storage location, the lozenge, which contains a value. I have put a $ sign in the l-value to indicate that putting a $ in front of a name takes you from the name to a scalar l-value; using the name prefixed by a $ in an r-context causes a contents-taking operation, usually called de-referencing, which yields the r-value.

Arrays and hashes are only slightly more complicated. For an array, the l-value can be thought of as containing the elements of the array, each of which has its own l- and r-value (see Figure 7.2). Here, I have put an @ in the lozenge, since putting @ in front of the name takes me to the array. The act of subscripting an array implicitly de-references the l-value and then selects the appropriate element. Hashes and % work similarly.

The same name can be associated with more than one l-value, since Perl allows you to give the same name to a scalar, an array, a hash and a subroutine (at least); Figure 7.3 shows the association between a name and several l-values. The character you prefix the name with when you use it chooses between the several available values. For subscripted expressions, the presence and form of the brackets round the subscript selects either an array or a hash to apply the subscripting operation to. The prefix in that case (usually $) selects the l-value associated with the subscripted expression.

▷ You can refer to the complete set of l-values associated with a name by prefixing it with a *, an operation with the pretty name of 'typeglobbing'. This is the key to several underhand operations that are less necessary in the current (Perl5) version of Perl than in previous versions of the language. One legitimate use is to create

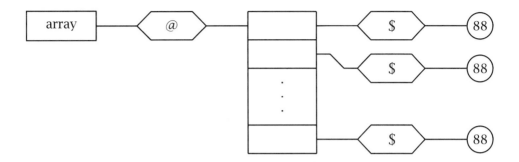

Figure 7.2   An array variable

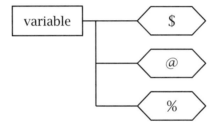

Figure 7.3   A name associated with several l-values

synonyms. For example, the module that implements the long form of names for built-in variables is full of lines like:

```
*ARG = *_;
```

which makes $ARG into a synonym for $_, @ARG for @_, and so on. (Although you never use the 'and so on'.)

The relevance of the preceding discussion to references is this: *a reference is an l-value that can be used like a scalar r-value.* A reference can be stored anywhere a scalar can, which means that you can have arrays of references and hashes of references; and those references can hold arrays or hashes, which might themselves hold references to arrays or hashes. So references allow you to construct arbitrarily complex data structures.

Figures 7.4 and 7.5 show a scalar variable holding a reference to a scalar, and a scalar variable holding a reference to an array. Again, to get from the name to its value, we prefix it with a $; this gives us the reference, and to get from

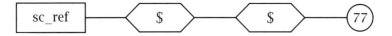

Figure 7.4   A reference to a scalar

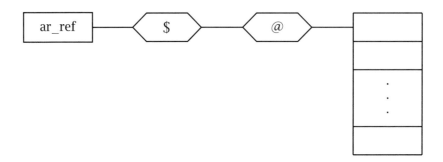

Figure 7.5   A reference to an array

there to *its* value, we prefix the prefixed name with either a $ or @, depending on the type of value referred to. In the first case, $$sc_ref is the l-value which contains the r-value 77; in the second, @$ar_ref is the array value. To reach its elements, you use subscripting, which, as before, implicitly has the effect of an @ prefix followed by de-referencing, so the second element of the array referred to by ar_ref is $$ar_ref[1].

▷ You may wonder what happens if you write an expression like $$womble, but $womble does not hold a reference. This is not, by default, considered to be an error; instead, the value of $womble is taken to be the name of another variable, and its value is used. So, if $womble held the string 'orinoco', the expression $$womble would mean the same as $orinoco. A variable holding the name of another variable is called a *soft reference*.

Soft references can be used to build reference-based structures dynamically, but they are generally unnecessary. The fact that you can de-reference something that is not a reference can lead to accidents. If you want to prevent such accidents, you can put

```
use strict 'refs';
```

at the head of your program, and any attempts (deliberate or not) to use soft references will be treated as compile-time errors. ◁

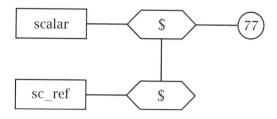

Figure 7.6   A reference to a scalar variable

Making References

From the preceding section, you will be able to see how references can be used to put together elaborate data structures, once you can actually create some references to store. There are several ways of doing so.

You can create a reference to a scalar by putting a \ in front of any expression with a scalar value. The situation depicted in Figure 7.4 could have been brought about in any of the following three ways:

```
$sc_ref = \77;
```

```
$sc_ref = \(7*11);
```

```
$scalar = 77;
$sc_ref = \$scalar;
```

The brackets in the second case are needed for precedence reasons. The third case, in which I am, as it were, re-using a reference I already have, is the most typical and the most dangerous. It is illustrated in Figure 7.6. The storage occupied by the value 77 is accessible either as $scalar or as $$sc_ref, in either r-context or l-context, which means that you can update it through either. Thus, after the initialization just shown,

```
$$sc_ref = 99;
print "scalar is $scalar\n";
```

prints

```
scalar is 99
```

even though I have not apparently assigned a new value to $scalar.

Putting a \ in front of a scalar variable creates a synonym for the variable, which is rarely a sensible move. Creating a reference from an array or hash variable is sometimes slightly more sensible. It is done the same way, with a \, and the result is similar (see Figure 7.7) and holds the same potential for

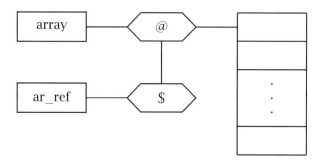

Figure 7.7   A reference to an array variable

confusion. To offset this, though, is the fact that the reference you have created can be used wherever a scalar can.

In general, it is probably unwise to put references to named arrays into data structures, because you create the possibility of changing the value of the same storage in more than one way—never an aid to program comprehensibility and maintenance. References to named arrays can be put to good effect, though, for passing arguments to subroutines.

You will recall that if you pass two arrays to a subroutine their elements are concatenated into a single list which appears in the subroutine as @ARG. If you really want to pass two separate lists, you have to pass their lengths, too, and unravel @ARG using `splice`, as I did on page 107. Alternatively, you can pass references to the arrays.

Here is a revised version of `equal_arrays` that takes two arguments, which must be references to the two arrays being compared.

```
sub equal_arrays {
   my $ref1 = shift;
   my $ref2 = shift;
```

The local variables `$ref1` and `$ref2` now hold copies of the references passed as arguments; they refer to the same lists as those arguments did. By de-referencing where I need a scalar, I can obtain the lengths of the two lists.

```
   my $len1 = @$ref1 + 1;
   my $len2 = @$ref2 + 1;
```

The actual comparison proceeds as in the original subroutine, but a level of de-referencing is needed to obtain the values of the list elements.

```
   my $i;
   return 0 unless ($len1 == $len2);
```

```
   for ($i = 0; $i < $len1; ++$i)
   {  return 0 unless $$ref1[$i] eq $$ref2[$i]; }
   return 1;
}
```

Notice that I did not create local array variables; I could have done so, like this:

```
   my @array1 = @$ref1;
   my @array2 = @$ref2;
```

This would have had the effect of creating local copies of all the elements of the two lists. Sometimes, you would want to do this, but more often, it is preferable to work with array references inside the subroutine and avoid the overhead of copying all the elements.

A call to a subroutine expecting reference arguments must create the references. A possible call to `equal_arrays` would look like this:

```
   equal_arrays \@a1, \@a2
```

where I have created references to two existing arrays `@a1` and `@a2`.

Notice that, in the body of `equal_arrays`, a reference was returned as the result of a call to `shift`. There are many forms of expression whose r-value can be a reference; so far, I have only ever de-referenced scalar variables holding references, but there is no reason why I should not wish to de-reference other expressions. For example, when creating local arrays in the second version of `equal_arrays`, there is no real reason to use the variables `$ref1` and `$ref2` to hold the references. You can, in fact, de-reference any expression by putting a `$` or `@` in front of it, but you have to enclose it in curly brackets, too. I could have created my local arrays like this:

```
   my @array1 = @{shift()};
   my @array2 = @{shift()};
```

▷ There is a slightly unpleasant complication here, though. There is nothing in Perl to stop me calling an array `@shift`. You will remember that if I wish to interpolate `@shift` into a string, but it is followed immediately by a character that could be part of a name, I can use curly brackets to delimit the extent of the array's name, as in `@{shift}` (compare the example on page 42). You can put brackets around the name in any other context, too, so if I had just written

        ```
        my @array1 = @{shift};
        ```

`@array1` would have been initialized with a copy of the (undefined) array `@shift`. To avoid this interpretation, I put the empty brackets after `shift`, forcing it to be parsed as a function call with no arguments. ◁

References to named hashes are produced by a \ prefix, just like references to scalars and arrays; \%capital is a reference to the hash %capital. It can be passed to a subroutine in the same way as a reference to an array can.

▷ Being able to pass references to subroutines can make programming easier and your programs more efficient, but it requires the caller of your subroutine to create the references. This is rather like the situation in C, where, to achieve the effect of passing an argument to a function by reference, the caller must explicitly take the argument's address. In contrast, in C++ or Pascal, the function's declaration indicates whether a reference or a value is being passed, and the caller does not need to know; the call looks the same, whichever mechanism is being used.

Some of Perl's built-in functions behave more like Pascal than C. For example, when I call splice like this:

    my @array1 = splice @ARG, 0, $len1;

its arguments are not combined into a single list; the first argument is the array being spliced. It is as if a reference to @ARG was being passed. Why cannot user-defined subroutines behave in the same way?

In short, because trying to make things defined by programmers behave like their built-in equivalents is the start of a long slippery slope that leads to C++. Nevertheless, the first tentative steps have been taken. From version 5.002 of Perl, you can provide a *prototype* for your subroutines. Syntactically, a subroutine declaration with a prototype has roughly the following form.

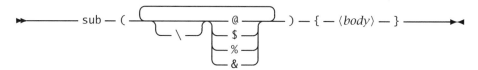

That is, in brackets following the keyword sub you can have a sequence of the prefix characters used to identify the different types of variable, each optionally preceded by a \. If the \ is present, then the actual argument must be a variable of the appropriate type (i.e. it must begin with the character after the \), and a reference will be created and passed as the argument. If the \ is not there, then the character defines the context in which the argument will be interpreted (e.g. a $ will force the next argument to evaluate to a scalar).

If I had declared my subroutine with the following prototype:

    sub equal_arrays(\@\@)

(and the same body), then it could have been called simply like this:

    equal_arrays @a1, @a2

On the other hand, if I had used the following prototype:

    sub equal_arrays(@)

I would have got the behaviour of the first version from chapter 5, since the argument would have been interpreted as a single list.

Subroutine prototypes are a very new addition to the Perl language. In some ways, they are extremely radical, since they introduce something resembling type checking, and the notion that user-defined entities should behave like built-in ones. It remains to be seen whether prototypes will gain wide acceptance among Perl programmers, and how they will develop. In the meantime, for a full description, ◁ consult the latest version of the Perl on-line documentation.

If you are going to build data structures out of references to arrays and hashes, without creating synonyms and confusion, you need some way of getting a reference to a value that has not been assigned to a variable. For array references, you do this by enclosing an expression that yields a list in square brackets. The result is a reference that can be assigned to a *scalar* variable, or stored anywhere a scalar value can be.

In the simplest case, you can enclose a syntactic list in square brackets to produce a reference. You may find it helpful to think of the brackets as manufacturing an anonymous array. For example:

```
$ar_ref = [ 'an', 'anonymous', 'array' ];
print "ar_ref is $ar_ref\nand points to @$ar_ref\n";
```

produces the output:

```
ar_ref is ARRAY(0xe2f5b8)
and points to an anonymous array
```

The second time the variable is interpolated into the argument to `print`, it is de-referenced and the value of the array it points to is therefore printed. The first time, though, it is not de-referenced. This is not an error, and as you can see, meaningful output is produced. Whenever you interpolate a reference into a string without de-referencing it, a string comprising an indication of the type of value the reference refers to, together with the actual address it points to, is produced. The first part of this string can also be obtained by passing a reference to the function `ref`, which returns false if it is passed anything but a reference. It thus provides a rudimentary runtime type identification facility.

More useful effects can be achieved by creating anonymous arrays from the lists returned by functions. The following example shows the kind of effect that can be achieved by doing so, and then storing the resulting references into a hash or two.

Once again, the example concerns my database of video clips. This time, I want to build an indexed data structure to the information in the database. It will take the form of two hashes, one whose keys are the names of the clips, the other whose keys are their sizes. Notionally, the values of both hashes will be lists comprising the fields of the records, but in fact, they will be references to them, because I cannot store lists in a hash.

Things begin in a familiar way.

```
while (<>)
{
  chomp;
```

Next I call `split` to break the record into a list; I put the call inside square brackets to obtain a reference to the resulting list, and I assign that reference to a scalar variable.

```
$record = [ split /\|/ ];
```

Next, I extract the title and size fields, by de-referencing and subscripting.

```
($title, $size) = ($$record[0], $$record[3]);
```

I want to use the title and size as hash keys; for this, I need to have unique values. It is reasonable to suppose that the names are unique (although I could easily check and issue a warning if duplicates were found), but not that the sizes are. I am not particularly proud of the trick used to ensure unique keys for the size index: keys are strings, so I insert leading zeroes to generate a unique string if needs be, without affecting its numerical value.

```
$size = '0' . $size while exists $sizes{$size};
```

Now I can create entries in two hashes `%titles` and `%sizes` with these keys. The value for both is the reference in `$record`.

```
$titles{$title} = $sizes{$size} = $record;
}
```

Having constructed these hashes, I could use them in several ways, for example, to look up the details of a clip, given its name, or to sort the records by size. To do the latter, it is necessary to supply a collating function, to force a numerical comparison on the keys, which would otherwise be sorted lexicographically.

```
foreach $size (sort { $a <=> $b; } keys %sizes)
{
  print "@{$sizes{$size}}\n";
}
```

Notice the curly brackets in the argument to `print`: `$sizes{$size}` is the expression returning the reference to an array; I need to de-reference this entire expression, so I write `@{$sizes{$size}}`. Had I omitted the outer pair of brackets, and written `@$sizes{$size}`, only `$sizes` would have been taken to be the reference, and the value of the expression would have been undefined.

▷ An alternative way of looking at de-referencing comes from reflecting that you can use an expression yielding a reference anywhere that you can use a name. Thus, if `$orinoco` is a variable containing a reference, I can write `$$orinoco`, just as I could write `$womble`. Under this interpretation, curly brackets may be necessary to delimit the extent of the reference expression, in just the same way as they are sometimes necessary to delimit the extent of a name (e.g. when it is interpolated ◁ into a string).

Lists of references to hashes are as useful as hashes of references to lists, and just as easy to build. Many Perl programmers like to use hashes rather than lists in place of the records and structures of other programming languages. The hash keys can be treated like field names, allowing the individual elements of the structure to be looked up by name. In the following example, I build such a hash for each record in my clips database, and insert a reference to it into a list.

Within the usual loop, I split each record as I read it into a hash %record, using suitable strings as the hash keys, that is, field names.

```
while (<>)
{
    chomp;
    ($record{'title'}, $record{'duration'}, $record{'compressor'},
                                $record{'size'}) = split /\|/;
```

I need to create an anonymous hash from %record to store in the list @records. If I just stored a reference to %record, next time around the loop the stored values would be overwritten by the next record. (Look at Figure 7.7 again, if you cannot see the problem.) Anonymous hash references are created by enclosing an expression yielding a hash in curly brackets.[2]

```
    $records[$n++] = { %record };
}
```

To print out the database when it is stored in this form, I need to explicitly extract all the fields. Each element of @records is a reference to a hash, so the loop variable in the following code must be de-referenced to get at each record structure.

```
foreach $r (@records)
{
    while (($field, $value) = each %$r)
    { print "$field => $value\n"; }
    print "\n";
}
```

This loop produces output like this:

```
title => Red1
size => 1985
compressor => Cinepak
duration => 00:09:10
```

Lists of (references to) lists and hashes of (references to) hashes can be used in much the same way. If the occasion demands, so can lists of lists of lists,

---

[2]Had I been more concerned with efficiency than with demonstrating how to create anonymous hashes, I would probably have started with a reference to an empty hash, and added the elements to it, thereby avoiding the overhead of constructing the hash twice.

and lists of hashes of lists, and the other six possibilities, as well as the sixteen at the next level of nesting, and... It is also possible to build lists containing a mixture of references to lists and to hashes, and so on. Hugely elaborate data structures are rarely necessary, though, and can lead you into trouble. You must take considerable care when copying structures built out of references, to avoid inadvertently sharing storage between copies; if you always copy sub-structures and their sub-structures recursively, you must take care not to get caught out by circular data structures. It is often better not to try and stuff all your data into one complex structure, but to use several parallel simpler structures.

Accessing individual elements of a list of hashes or one of the other combinations is awkward in itself. For example, to get at the title of the third element of the list built in the preceding script, I would have to use the expression `${$records[2]}{'title'}`. To get at the duration of the clip called Red2 from the earlier hash of lists would require `${$titles{'Red2'}}[1]`. Neither of these expression is very easy to read—although if you keep calm and work from the inside out, their meaning is clear—and things get more complex as you nest your structures more deeply. To alleviate the complexity, Perl provides an alternative notation for subscripting array and hash references.

If ⟨*a-ref-expr*⟩ is any expression yielding a reference to an array, and ⟨*subscript*⟩ is any expression yielding a number, then

  `${` ⟨*a-ref-expr*⟩ `}` `[` ⟨*subscript*⟩ `]`

can be written as

  ⟨*a-ref-expr*⟩ `->` `[` ⟨*subscript*⟩ `]`

Similarly, if ⟨*h-ref-expr*⟩ is any expression yielding a reference to a hash, and ⟨*key*⟩ is any expression yielding a string, then

  `${` ⟨*h-ref-expr*⟩ `}` `{` ⟨*subscript*⟩ `}`

can be written as

  ⟨*h-ref-expr*⟩ `->` `{` ⟨*subscript*⟩ `}`

In the first expression given above, `$records[2]` is an expression yielding a reference to a hash, so I could have obtained the same value using the simpler expression `$records[2]->{'title'}`. The duration of the clip Red2 could have been extracted from the hash of lists as `$titles{'Red2'}->[1]`. Even better, if the `->` occurs between a right and a left subscript bracket of either kind, you can leave it out, so these two examples could have been written as `$records[2]{'title'}`, and `$titles{'Red2'}[1]`. This last abbreviation is especially comfortable to use with lists of lists, since it lets you write double subscripts in the form `$matrix[$i][$j]`.

Using Data Structures

Although references are the most powerful data structuring facility Perl offers, you should not neglect the more straightforward lists and hashes. Most complicated Perl scripts will employ a mixture of structures. This section presents an example showing how different data structures can work together.

Perhaps fittingly, it is an implementation of an algorithm that appears in volume 1 of *The Art of Computer Programming*: topological sorting. The problem it solves can be explained in several ways. Figure 7.8 illustrates it in abstract graphical terms. The data for the algorithm is some representation of a directed graph—a collection of labelled circles (nodes) connected by arrows (edges)—and the output is a list of the nodes such that, if you draw them from left to right in the order they appear in the list, then the arrows corresponding to the edges in the original data will all run from left to right.

Why would anybody want to carry out such an apparently futile exercise in draughtsmanship?

If the labels on the nodes represented sub-tasks for some project, and an arrow from node A to node B meant that task A had to be performed before task B, then the output of the topological sort algorithm would be a schedule for performing tasks one at a time, which guaranteed that no task would be attempted before all its prerequisite tasks had been finished.

Suppose, for example, that the graph in Figure 7.8 represented the project of connecting your home computer to the Internet in order to browse some World-Wide Web pages. The letters on the nodes might correspond to necessary sub-tasks, in the following manner:

A. discover some interesting URLs;

B. choose an Internet Service Provider (ISP);

C. sign up with your chosen ISP;

D. obtain a modem;

E. connect up your modem;

F. obtain some basic communications software;

G. install the basic communications software;

H. make a connection to the Internet;

I. download a Web client program;

J. browse web sites.

The graph expresses constraints on the order of these tasks: you must obtain a modem before you can connect it up, and so on. Because some of the tasks are independent, it does not specify an order for carrying out all the tasks to achieve the goal. However, the topologically sorted graph output by the algorithm does, and you can check that it respects the given constraints,

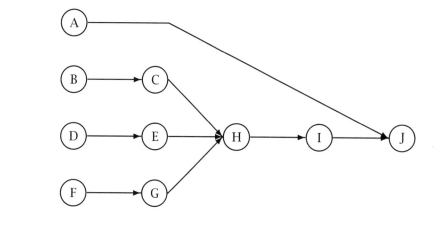

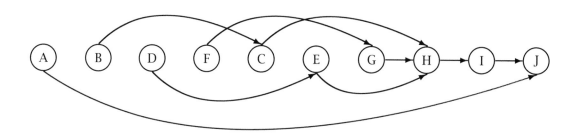

Figure 7.8 Topological sorting

and therefore provides a possible sequence in which the tasks can be carried out one after another.

In this example, you could produce the required ordering just by looking at the input—or by using your common sense—but for a manufacturing project with hundreds of sub-tasks, you would not find it so easy. The algorithm I am about to describe automates the production of a task schedule; it can also be applied to similar jobs that must be carried out by a program, such as instruction scheduling on pipelined processors.

The algorithm for producing the sequence begins by constructing a table containing a count of the prerequisites for each task. It then chooses a task with no prerequisites and writes it to the output sequence. Every task for which that task was a prerequisite then has its count decremented by one; another task with no unscheduled prerequisites is then chosen to be performed next, and so on, until all the tasks have been scheduled. To avoid repeated checks for tasks with no prerequisites, whenever a count falls to zero, the task is placed in a queue. At each step, the first element of the queue is selected.

There is one massive flaw in this algorithm: if the prerequisites graph contains a loop (some task must be performed before itself), no ordering is possible. What will happen is that the prerequisite count of such a task will never fall to zero, so it will never enter the queue. Eventually, the queue will become empty, and a schedule will seem to have been produced, even though one or more tasks will be missing from it. This must not be allowed to happen without warning, so it is necessary to ensure that every task has been scheduled.

Since this is a fairly complicated algorithm, I have broken my script down into subroutines. I have also chosen to avoid global variables, by passing structures into and out of subroutines as references, as much to demonstrate how easy it is to do so, as from any methodological imperative.

Before beginning, it is necessary to decide on a representation of the data. I have chosen to represent the prerequisites graph by a file containing a collection of pairs of tasks, one pair per line, with the two elements separated by a < (a mnemonic for 'precedes'). The data thus corresponds directly to the arrows in the diagram. The set of tasks can be deduced from the arrows, and is not specified separately.

The first subroutine in my script reads the data, stores a representation of the graph, and initializes the counts of each task's predecessors. I need three hashes, each of which uses the task names as keys.

```perl
sub read_data {
  my %arrows;
  my %tasks;
  my %predecessor_count;
```

The hash `%tasks` is just acting as a set; there will be a non-zero value for each task, indicating its existence. The counts of predecessors will be built up as the data is read: we know that the first element of each pair is a prerequisite for the second, so we can count it then and there. This hash is operating as a map, holding a value for each key. The `%arrows` hash is what is sometimes called a 'multi-map'; for each task it holds a set of tasks that can be reached from it by following arrows. The obvious representation of a multi-map in Perl is a hash of references to lists.

The main loop that reads the data begins by splitting out the two elements of the pair, recording their existence, and updating the correct predecessor count.

```perl
while (<>)
{
  chomp;
  ($before, $after) = split /</;
  ++$tasks{$before};
  ++$tasks{$after};
  ++$predecessor_count{$after};
```

Next comes the only tricky bit of data structure manipulation. If there have already been any arrows with `$before` at their tail, then `$arrows{$before}` will hold a reference to a list; $after must be added to that list. Otherwise, a reference to a list consisting of $after alone must be created and stored in %arrows.

```
    if (exists $arrows{$before})
    {
      push @{$arrows{$before}}, $after;
    }
    else
    {
      $arrows{$before} = [ $after ];
    }
}
```

The three hashes must be returned as the result of the subroutine. This is simply achieved by returning a list of references to them.

```
    return (\%arrows, \%tasks, \%predecessor_count);
}
```

▶ A gasp of horror goes up from experienced C and C++ programmers. 'Those references to local variables are dangling!' No they're not. Storage allocation in Perl is not the same as it is in those languages. Values continue to exist as long as they can be reached, either from a variable, or via a reference. (In other words, the l-value of a local variable in a subroutine is not an address on the run-time stack, which might get overwritten.) A garbage collector disposes of memory when it is no longer reachable.

◀ So that's another thing you don't need to worry about.

The next little subroutine sets up the queue of tasks with no prerequisites. It needs the set of tasks as well as the predecessor counts, since the tasks with no predecessor will not be among the keys of the predecessor count map. The arguments are passed as references, and are de-referenced as necessary. I am going to use an array as the queue, and the convention that tasks are added to the queue using push, so they must be removed with shift, if a first in, first out discipline is to be maintained.[3]

```
sub init_queue {
  my $tasks_ref = shift;
  my $predecessor_count_ref = shift;
  my @queue;
```

---

[3]Which is not actually necessary to the correct functioning of the algorithm—although the ordering that you produce if you do use a queue has some claim to be canonical—but it is always done that way, and I see no reason to be different this time.

```
foreach $task (keys %$tasks_ref)
{
  push @queue, $task unless $predecessor_count_ref->{$task};
}
return \@queue;
}
```

These two subroutines are called in turn from the main program, with the references they return being stored in scalar variables.

```
($arrows_ref, $tasks_ref, $predecessor_count_ref) = read_data;
$queue_ref = init_queue $tasks_ref, $predecessor_count_ref;
```

Now we are in a position to do the actual work. I want the output to look vaguely like a set of instructions for carrying out the tasks, so I begin by printing an opening.

```
print "First,\n";
```

The tasks are written out in a loop that continues as long as the queue is not empty. Evaluating @$queue_ref where a scalar is required returns the number of elements in the array referred to by $queue_ref, just as using a simple array variable would.

```
while (@$queue_ref)
{
```

The first element is removed from the queue and printed. A hash %done is used to hold the set of tasks that have been dealt with; the value corresponding to this task is incremented, to record the fact that it has been done.

```
my $x = pop @$queue_ref;
++$done{$x};
print "$x then \n";
```

Now decrement all the predecessor counts of tasks that depended on the one that has just been done, and queue up any with no remaining predecessors. To find all the dependent tasks, it is necessary to use the reference to a list originally stored in the %arrows hash. Now we only have a reference to it, so some extra de-referencing is needed; I use the -> notation to make this easier to read.

```
foreach $after (@{$arrows_ref->{$x}})
{
  push @$queue_ref, $after
    unless --$predecessor_count_ref->{$after};
}
}
```

When we drop out of this loop, the queue has emptied, but have all the tasks been scheduled? The following slick assignment sets the array @not_done to any tasks that have not been recorded as being done in %done.

```
@not_done = grep { !$done{$ARG}} keys %$tasks_ref;
```

Here, the second argument I have given to `grep` will be a list of every task; the expression causes `grep` to look up each one of these in `%done` and return those that are not there. It thus computes the set of all tasks minus (in the set-theoretic sense) the set of done tasks, that is, the set of all tasks that did not get done, as required.[4] I could have used a similar call to `grep` to set up the queue, as an alternative to the loop in `init_queue`.

If `@not_done` is empty all is well; otherwise, it was not possible to schedule the tasks it contains. As a consolation, we let the user know which ones were left over.

```
unless (@not_done)
{
  print "you are done\n";
}
else
{
  print "\nAlas! you can go no further",
        " -- the prerequisites graph has a loop.\n";
  print "The following tasks could not be scheduled:\n";
  $LIST_SEPARATOR = "\n";
  print "@not_done";
}
```

If you provide this program with data corresponding to the graph in Figure 7.8, with the nodes interpreted as the tasks involved in setting up an Internet connection to browse some World-Wide Web pages, it produces the following output:

```
First,
obtain a modem then
choose an Internet Service Provider then
discover some interesting URLs then
obtain some basic communications software then
connect up your modem then
sign up with your chosen ISP then
install the basic communications software then
make a connection to the Internet then
download a Web client program then
browse web sites then
you are done
```

The assumption is that the 'basic communications software' includes an FTP client. What if it does not? If you add the following extra data:

```
download an FTP client<install an FTP client
```

---

[4]I didn't make this technique up; it appears in the first edition of the 'Camel Book'—see page 249.

```
install an FTP client<make a connection to the Internet
make a connection to the Internet<download an FTP client
```

the output changes to this:

```
First,
obtain some basic communications software then
install the basic communications software then
discover some interesting URLs then
choose an Internet Service Provider then
sign up with your chosen ISP then
obtain a modem then
connect up your modem then

Alas! you can go no further -- the prerequisites graph has a loop.
The following tasks could not be scheduled:
download an FTP client
browse web sites
make a connection to the Internet
download a Web client program
install an FTP client
```

References to Subroutines

We don't usually think of subroutines as values that can be stored, so the idea of a reference to a subroutine might seem to be a rather unlikely one. Since subroutines are named entities, it must be possible to store a reference to them in a symbol table, so why not permit references to subroutines to be manipulated like any other references? Perhaps you will reply, 'Because it is not useful'; to which I would respond, 'You are mistaken'. Once you have a reference to a subroutine, you can use it like any other reference; in particular, you can pass it into and out of subroutines, and store it in data structures. Most programming languages let you pass functions as arguments to other functions, and many let you construct data structures containing functions (or pointers to them). Unfortunately, too many books and programming courses treat this facility as an obscure and useless feature, whereas it can, if used properly, provide a powerful alternative to conventional control structures, and gives you another form of abstraction to help you structure and understand your programs.

Subroutines as Arguments

There are programming languages—called *functional* or *applicative* languages— in which pretty much all computation is performed by applying functions to arguments. These languages rely heavily on 'higher order' functions: ones which take other functions as arguments or return them as results. By making functions into arguments, we abstract away from a particular computation to get a higher order function that captures a pattern of computation. In Perl, some built-in functions, such as map and grep behave much like higher-order functions; they both capture variations on the pattern of applying a function to every element of a list. By defining subroutines that take references to subroutines as their arguments, you can define your own abstractions of computational patterns.

For example, consider the script beginning on page 144, which recursively traverses a directory and its sub-directories, recording which ones contain files bigger than a certain size. Here is a pattern I would like to re-use: visiting a directory and all its sub-directories and doing something to each file I encounter. Whenever I do such a traversal, the code for opening the directory, reading its entries and traversing sub-directories recursively will be the same. Only the actions I perform on each file that is not a directory will be different. By making these actions into subroutines and passing them as arguments to a higher-order traversal subroutine, I can generate a whole family of computations. Before I can do so, I need to know how to create references to subroutines, and how to call a subroutine through a reference.

As with scalars, lists and hashes, the simplest way to create a reference is using a backslash prefix, in this case to a named subroutine. When you do this, you must identify the subroutine as a subroutine by putting an ampersand in front of its name. (Recall from chapter 5 that you *may* do this whenever you call a subroutine, but it is not usually necessary. When you create a reference, it is always necessary.) Thus, if I had defined a subroutine called find_big (as I will very shortly), I could create a reference to it by writing \&find_big. The resulting reference can be used anywhere a scalar can. If I assign it to a scalar variable, $find_big_ref, say, I can call the subroutine as &$find_big_ref, passing it arguments in the usual way, if that is appropriate. In general, if ⟨*sub-ref-expr*⟩ is any expression that yields a reference to a subroutine, you can call that subroutine by writing &{⟨*sub-ref-expr*⟩}. The operation is really no different from that of de-referencing a reference to a scalar or list.

As a first step in creating a higher-order version of the directory traversal, consider simply wrapping up the part that checks the size of a file and makes a hash entry if necessary, as a subroutine. It will have to take both the file and directory names as arguments, so it would look like this:

```
sub find_big {
  my ($file, $dir) = @ARG;
  if (-s $file > $size_in_bytes)
  {  ++$big_directories{$dir};  }
}
```

I could substitute a call to find_big in place of the in-line code that does the same thing in my original version of the subroutine lookin without altering its effect. However, I want to be able to carry out arbitrary actions at that point, so I want the subroutine I call to be passed into lookin as an argument. Assuming I do that, the subroutine can be rewritten as follows:

```
sub lookin
{
```

Begin by picking up the arguments; the second is a reference to a subroutine.

```
my ($dir, $function_ref) = @ARG;
```

Most of the rest of this subroutine is unchanged; open the directory and loop through the entries, calling lookin recursively for sub-directories. The subroutine reference has to be passed as an argument to the recursive call.

```
opendir DIR, $dir or die "I can't open $dir: $OS_ERROR\n";
my @files = readdir DIR;

foreach $f (@files)
{
  my $p = $dir . $pathsep . $f;
  if (-d $p) {  lookin($p, $function_ref); }
  else
```

The else branch now calls the subroutine which was passed as an argument, giving it the file and directory as arguments.

```
  {
    &$function_ref($p, $dir);
  }
}
}
```

I can call this new version of lookin with a reference to find_big to achieve the original effect.

```
lookin($root, \&find_big);
```

I can also use the same lookin subroutine to perform some other action during a recursive directory traversal, by defining a suitable subroutine and passing a reference to it as an argument. For example, if I wanted to delete every file that ended in the characters .log, I could define this subroutine:

```
sub delete_logs {
  my $file = shift;
  if ($file =~ /\.log$/)
  { unlink $file;  }
}
```

and use the following call:

```
lookin($root, \&delete_logs);
```

Note that `delete_logs` ignores the directory name which it will be passed as an argument. To provide a framework general enough to accommodate traversals like the one to find the big folders, `lookin` must pass this argument to whatever subroutine is plugged in to it; because of the way Perl passes arguments in `@ARG`, it is easy for a subroutine that does not need the second argument to behave as if it was not there.

Creating references to named subroutines is not harmful in the same way that creating references to named scalars, arrays or hashes is; since you cannot update a subroutine, creating a synonym for one does not create the same potential problems. However, you may consider it inelegant to have to declare a named subroutine, merely to be able to create a reference to it. You do not have to do so; references to anonymous subroutines can be created. They are produced by expressions of the form:

```
sub { ⟨body⟩ }
```

which may be used anywhere a reference to a subroutine is required. For example, instead of declaring `delete_logs` as I just did, I could simply have called `lookin` as follows, to achieve the same effect:

```
lookin($root, sub {
    my $file = shift;
    if ($file =~ /\.log$/)
    { unlink $file; }
  }
);
```

The previous version is easier to read, but references to anonymous subroutines can be more usefully employed in another context, as the next section will demonstrate.

Closures

There is a level of generality lacking in the previous example. Just suppose that I find my directories are cluttered not only with log files, with names ending in `.log`, but also with auxiliary files, with names ending in `.aux`, and perhaps other sorts of temporary file, each with its own distinctive form of name. For each sort of file I wished to delete, I would have to write a little subroutine, which would be almost identical to `delete_logs`, except for the pattern identifying the offending files. Normally, I would only write a single subroutine and would make the pattern into an argument to it. Here, I cannot do that in an obvious way: my subroutines are being called (via references) from within `lookin`, but `lookin` cannot pass the pattern to them. (Well, it could, but only if I passed the pattern as an extra argument to `lookin`, which then passed it on to every subroutine it called, even though the pattern would be irrelevant to most of them.) I need some way of, as it were, passing that argument to my deleting subroutine at the point I create a reference to it, not at the point it is eventually called.

I can do almost exactly that, because of the way anonymous subroutines interact with local variables in Perl. Within the body of an anonymous subroutine, you can refer to local variables of an enclosing block. In particular, if your anonymous subroutine occurs inside the body of a subroutine, it can refer to the locals of that subroutine. Furthermore, if that anonymous subroutine is passed out of the enclosing routine, as its result, when it runs and uses those locals, they will have the values they had when the anonymous subroutine was created. An anonymous subroutine behaving in this way is called a *closure*.

▷ It is worth re-emphasizing that I am using the expression 'local variables' to mean statically scoped variables, declared using `my`. Variables localized by the `local` function are, despite appearances, global, and will not behave as described with ◁ closures—another reason to avoid `local`.

As a simple example, consider the following:

```
sub multiplier {
  my $x = shift;
  return sub {
          return $x * shift;
  };
}
```

The subroutine `multiplier` takes a number as its argument; it returns as its result a reference to a closure, which is a subroutine taking a single numerical argument and returning the product of its argument with `$x`. The `$x` used inside this closure is bound to the value which the local variable has when the closure is created, that is, the argument passed to `multiplier`. So, if I call `multiplier` with an argument whose value is some number n, it gives me back (a reference to) a subroutine that multiplies things by n. Thus,

```
$doubler = multiplier(2);
$tripler = multiplier(3);
```

set `$doubler` to a subroutine that doubles things, and `$tripler` to one that multiplies them by three; `&$doubler(2)` is 4, and `&$tripler(2)` is 6.

Returning to my original example, if I want to delete files whose names match a certain pattern, I can define a subroutine that, in effect, generates subroutines that delete files matching its argument.

```
sub delete_files {
  my $pattern = shift;
  return sub {
    my $file = shift;
    if ($file =~ /$pattern/)
```

```
        { unlink $file;  }
      };
  }
```

The logic of `delete_files` follows the same pattern as that of `multiplier`; it returns a closure which refers to a local variable whose value is supplied as an argument. I can use it to achieve my goal in the following way:

```
lookin($root, delete_files('\.log$'));
lookin($root, delete_files('\.aux$'));
```

The first call to `delete_files` generates a subroutine that deletes log files, the second, one that deletes auxiliary files. Both of these can be passed to `lookin`, which is expecting a reference to a subroutine as its second argument.

▷ Although you can declare named subroutines nested inside other subroutines, and return references to them, they do not behave as closures. Only anonymous subroutines can do this, because they are, in effect, created at run time, whereas named ◁ subroutines are created and stored in a symbol table at compile time.

If you have not come across this style of programming before, closures will probably look tricky and a bit obscure, but once you get used to them, they provide a powerful mechanism for constructing programs.

Subroutines in Data Structures

You can store a reference to a subroutine in a hash or array, just as you can a reference to anything else. Before support for object-oriented programming was provided by programming languages, imaginative programmers used data structures containing subroutines to simulate objects. Now that we have objects built in to our programming languages, such exercises in programming virtuosity are no longer required. The main remaining application for storing subroutines in data structures is to facilitate a table-driven style of program. To illustrate this style, I will re-implement the toy command interpreter from chapter 4.

This time, I will construct a hash, whose keys are the commands that the interpreter understands. The value for each key will be a little subroutine that performs the necessary action in response to that command. As well as initializing globals as before, I could set up this hash before starting the main loop, as follows:

```
%commands = ( up    => sub { ++$n; },
              down  => sub { --$n; },
              zero  => sub { $n = 0; },
              '!'   => sub {
                              if ($last_cmd)
```

```
                            {  &{$commands{$last_cmd}}; }
                            else
                            {
                              print "No previous command to redo\n";
                            }
                          },
               quit => sub {
                              print "Be seeing you\n";
                              exit;
                            }

          );
```

I am treating the variable $n as a global, although I could easily have passed it to each subroutine as an argument, returning its updated value as the result. This seems unnecessary (and is inefficient) for such a tiny program. The body of each subroutine performs the required action more or less the same way as the in-line code from the original versions. Although it is possible to use the loop control transfer statements last, next and redo within the body of a function, and have them affect the flow of execution of a loop from which the function is called, the practice cannot be advised, so I have used the function exit within the code for the quit command; it terminates a program's execution. It is also necessary to add a little bit of logic to the main loop, to prevent infinite loops if a repeat command is repeated. Otherwise the loop is very simple. First, check whether there is an entry in the hash for the command you have just read, and if there is, call the corresponding subroutine.

```
while ()
{
  if (exists $commands{$ARG})
  {
    &{$commands{$ARG}};
  }
```

Otherwise, whatever you just read was not a command, so issue a message and try again.

```
  else
  {
    print "Unknown command <<$ARG>>\n";
    next;
  }
```

Remember the last command, unless it was a repeat:

```
  $last_cmd = $ARG unless $ARG eq '!';
}
```

The continue block remains the same as always.

```
continue
{  print "$n\ncommand?   "  ;  chomp($ARG = <STDIN>); }
```

Organizing the flow of control in this way separates the association of actions with commands from the interpretive logic, in rather a similar way to that in which the instructions of a program are separated from their fetching and execution in a stored program machine. The advantages are the same: it is possible to replace the hash %commands or alter it without touching the interpretive loop. Admittedly, for a toy like this example, the advantage is negligible, but for more realistic applications, this clean separation of concerns might be valuable. It also makes it easy to construct an interpreter dynamically, deciding what goes into the hash at run time.

Objects

8

If you have been paying any attention to developments in programming since the early 1980s, you will probably not have been very impressed by the way I manipulated the data structures in my implementation of topological sorting in the previous chapter. Although the hash %arrows was being used exclusively as a multi-map, I was manipulating its representation as a hash, using hash operations directly. In other words, I was treating an abstract datatype as a concrete data type. There was little harm done, but next time I need a multi-map, I will have to do the work again, or at least cut code out of this script and paste it into a new one. I would prefer to be able to re-use existing code, which I could do if I had been able to provide an abstract datatype for multi-maps, whose interface provided a set of operations suitable for such objects, and whose implementation was hidden, so that I did not need to consider multi-maps as anything but multi-maps.

Perl offers some support for a style of programming based on abstract datatypes, and its more illustrious relative, the object-oriented style. The emphasis is on making it easy to package code in a form that can be re-used; much less emphasis is placed on information hiding and representation-independence than in many other programming languages. Programming convention and documentation play as much of a part as do language features.

▶ Indeed, if you know C++ or Java, you may be tempted to conclude that Perl's 'object-oriented' features barely deserve that description, since so much of the mechanics of object-orientation found in those languages is missing from Perl. The omissions are partly a result of the difference of emphasis just mentioned, but partly a result of the fundamentally different nature of the languages. Since there are no declarations in Perl, there can be no static types, and hence the requirement for virtual functions cannot arise. Polymorphism is almost a meaningless concept in this context. Comparing Perl's approach to object-oriented programming with that of strongly typed languages is very difficult to do meaningfully, and criticizing Perl for not being C++ is neither fair nor useful. It is important to be aware of the differences, so that you can make the best use of Perl's features on their own terms.

◀

Packages, Objects and Methods

Up until now I have assumed that any Perl program is held in a single file and developed in one piece. However, Perl allows you to break your program into separate pieces, called packages, which may be in separate files. The same package may be re-used in several different programs. The existence of packages raises new questions about scope.

Packages

All the programs I have exhibited so far have consisted of a single package, one which is implicit in every program, called `main`. In general, a program has a `main` package, which may make use of some other, explicitly declared, packages.

A package declaration has the form

```
package ⟨name⟩ ;
```

Normally, a package declaration appears near the beginning of a file, which makes the rest of the file into the body of the package. Each package has its own symbol table (or 'namespace', if you prefer to be abstract about it), which means that the same name can be used in different packages to refer to different entities. Dividing a program into packages reduces the risk of confusion caused by using the same name for different purposes in different places; it also spares you from having to think up new names all the time. If you put a package into a file whose name consists of the package name with `.pm` (for Perl module) on the end, then you can incorporate the package into another part of your program, with a `use` directive, of the form

```
use ⟨name⟩;
```

In this way, Perl programs can be built up out of separate pieces.

Within a package, all undeclared variables (those I have so far considered to be global) are entered into and looked up in the symbol table belonging to the package. By default, they can only be accessed outwith the package by prefixing them with the package name and two colons. Thus, if I declared a package called `Wombles`, a subroutine `orinoco` declared within it could only be called in another package as `Wombles::orinoco`, although inside the package it could just be called as `orinoco`. Similarly, a scalar variable that was referred to inside the package as `$tomsk` would be referred to elsewhere as `$Wombles::tomsk`. (Notice that the prefix migrates all the way to the beginning of the compound name.)

You have, of course, seen the `use` directive before. As long ago as chapter 2 I advised you to put the incantation

```
use English;
```

near the top of your Perl scripts. As you can now see, this incorporates a package from the file `English.pm`, which defines long synonyms for built-in variables with cryptic names. (The English module is part of the standard library.) However, in apparent contradiction of what I just said, these long names are not usually referred to as `$English::ARG`, and so on. This is because a module may choose to *export* some of its names, making them accessible in unqualified form to the outside world. The mechanism for doing this will be described briefly in chapter 9. For now, you just need to know that the package name in a `use` directive can be followed by a list of strings, which are interpreted as names to be imported from the module. If no list is provided, a default set of the module's exports is imported. If you prefer to use fully qualified names for entities from other packages, you can add an empty list. Thus,

```
use English ();
```

would force you to refer to `$English::ARG`, and so on.

There is one other way in which packages interact with scope. It is possible to use `my` to declare variables at the package level (that is, outside any block in the package). Variables declared this way are local to the package, and their values cannot be accessed from outside it in any way.

▷ If you declare a variable local to a package, like this:

```
package private;
my $private_var;
```

and, in a separate package that uses `private`, you try to use a variable `$private::private_var`, it will be taken as a reference to an undeclared global ◁ `$private_var` in `private`.

Classes and Objects

A package can be more than a means of program decomposition. By following certain conventions, and using one extra piece of linguistical technology, a package can function as a class, and define an abstract datatype.

The essence of data abstraction is that an object belonging to a type can only be accessed by operations specific to that type. Clearly, this implies that an object *has* a type. In Perl, packages provide the types. Typed objects can only be created and manipulated through references. Associating a type with an object is achieved by a process known by the picturesquely meaningless name of *blessing* a reference to the object. The ceremony is simple:

```
bless ⟨reference⟩ , ⟨name⟩;
```

where ⟨*reference*⟩ is any expression producing a reference, and ⟨*name*⟩ is the name of a package, or some expression producing a string containing the name. Hence,

```
bless \$orinoco, 'Wombles';
```

enters the scalar contained in `orinoco` in the ranks of Wombles. Usually, a blessed reference is returned as the result of a subroutine, which functions as a creator (or *constructor*, in the jargon) of objects. The returned reference will point to a data structure that provides the concrete implementation of the abstract datatype.

It is important to understand that, although `bless` takes a reference as its first argument, it is the object referred to which receives the blessing. In terms of the model presented in chapter 7, r-values, not l-values, belong to a class. This implies that objects of any class may be stored in the same l-value at different times, and that subroutines are automatically polymorphic—they can take any kind of object as an argument.

Some subroutines, though, are designed only to take references to objects of one type as their first argument. These are the subroutines which provide the operations on the abstract datatype to which the object belongs. In deference to object-oriented usage, such subroutines are called *methods*. They are not declared in any special way, and they receive all their arguments through @ARG. They may be called using a special syntax, known as an 'object-oriented method call', though. If ⟨*method*⟩ is the name of a method declared within a package ⟨*package*⟩, and ⟨*object*⟩ is an expression (usually a variable) whose value is a reference to an object that has been blessed in ⟨*package*⟩, the call

   ⟨*object*⟩->⟨*method*⟩ (⟨*argument list*⟩)

(which looks vaguely like a call to a member function in C++) is equivalent to

   ⟨*package*⟩::⟨*method*⟩ (⟨*object*⟩, ⟨*argument list*⟩)

The method is looked up in the correct package on the basis of the type information in the blessed object.

Methods of the form just described are sometimes called 'instance methods', because they apply an operation to an object—an instance of a class. Another kind of method is also needed, which conceptually belongs to the class, but does not need a particular instance to operate on. An example might be a method to return a count of all the objects of a particular class presently in existence. Such methods are called 'class methods' in the object-oriented literature. In Perl, class methods are just subroutines that expect a package name as their first argument; they may be invoked using an object-oriented method call, but a string containing the package name replaces an object. Constructors are usually class methods; they cannot be instance methods, since they are there to create the instances. Since there is no syntactical distinction between instance methods and class methods, it is possible to write a subroutine that can function as either, examining its argument to determine how it is being called.

▶ Perl's methods correspond to C++'s member functions. Class methods are like static member functions. The terms 'instance method' and 'class method' are used in Java

with roughly the same meaning as in Perl. Unlike those in C++ or Java, constructors in Perl are just named methods like any other; no special name is reserved for them, and they are not invoked automatically. There is no method overloading in Perl; if
◀ you need more than one constructor, you just give them different names.

▷ An alternative form of method call, known as the 'indirect object' form, may also be used.

⟨*method*⟩ ⟨*class or object*⟩ ⟨*list*⟩

Here, ⟨*class or object*⟩ is either a string containing a package name, or it is any expression yielding an object. The ⟨*list*⟩ provides the arguments, and unlike an object-oriented method call, it only needs brackets round it where an ambiguity would result otherwise, just like an ordinary subroutine call. Sometimes, the indirect object syntax can be more natural, especially for class methods, but I will stick
◁ with object-oriented method calls for consistency.

Using Classes

Packages, blessed references and methods working together allow you to program with abstract datatypes in Perl. It is about time we did so.

As an example, I will consider wrapping up a hash of lists so that it looks like a multi-map. The wrapper will be a package called `MultiMap`. The first step is to decide how a multi-map should appear from the outside: what operations it needs, and what their behaviour should be. I chose the following specification (⟨*mmap*⟩ denotes a variable or expression having a `MultiMap` object as its value):

`MultiMap->new` returns a new, empty instance of the class MultiMap.

⟨*mmap*⟩`->insert(`⟨*key*⟩`,` ⟨*list*⟩`)` add the values in the ⟨*list*⟩ to the multi-map, under the ⟨*key*⟩.

⟨*mmap*⟩`->lookup(`⟨*key*⟩`)` returns the values stored in multi-map under the ⟨*key*⟩ as a reference to the stored list.

⟨*mmap*⟩`->present(`⟨*key*⟩`,` ⟨*list*⟩`)` If the list is empty or omitted, returns true or false depending on whether the ⟨*key*⟩ exists in the multi-map; if a non-empty ⟨*list*⟩ of values is provided, return a list consisting of the subset which are present in the multi-map under ⟨*key*⟩, or if a scalar is required, a count of them.

⟨*mmap*⟩`->remove(`⟨*key*⟩`,` ⟨*list*⟩`)` If the list is empty or omitted, delete the entry for ⟨*key*⟩ from the multi-map; if a non-empty ⟨*list*⟩ of values is provided, remove just those values from the entry for ⟨*key*⟩. If ⟨*key*⟩ is not present in the multi-map, do nothing.

⟨*mmap*⟩`->display()` print the multi-map in a suitable format.

A specification such as this should form part of the documentation of any class. Because of the absence of any type checking or formal mechanism for datatype specification, documentation has to be considered part of the interface to a class in Perl.

▷ Because convention plays such a large part in Perl's support for object-oriented programming, it is trivially easy to abuse it. The assumption is that you are interested in making your program work by using packages correctly. If you choose to subvert the conventions, it will be nobody's fault but your own if you end up in trouble. (In Perl's view, programming language abuse is a victimless crime. Whether this view holds up on large-scale projects is a debatable point. Perhaps there is some virtue ◁ in distinguishing between 'hard' and 'soft' programming abuse.)

Knowing the interface to MultiMap, we know enough to use it—that is largely what data abstraction is about. The way I have defined the constructor new means that multi-maps must be built up incrementally. For example, I could construct a multi-map called cities, keyed by countries, to record the names of cities in different countries:

```
$cities = MultiMap->new();

$cities->insert('Ireland', 'Dublin');
$cities->insert('Scotland', 'Edinburgh', 'Glasgow');
$cities->insert('Ireland', 'Cork');
$cities->insert('France', 'Paris', 'Lille', 'Calais', 'Moutiers');
```

As the Irish entry shows, there is no need to add all the cities for a country at once. The call

```
$cities->display();
```

produces

```
Scotland => {Edinburgh, Glasgow}
France => {Paris, Lille, Calais, Moutiers}
Ireland => {Dublin, Cork}
```

I can get just the Scottish cities using the method lookup:

```
$scots = $cities->lookup('Scotland');
```

which returns a reference to the list 'Edinburgh', 'Glasgow'. Or I can determine whether certain cities are in France:

```
@z = $cities->present('France', 'Moutiers', 'Edinburgh',
                                'Madrid', 'Paris');
```

sets @z to ('Paris', 'Moutiers'). I can remove Cork from Ireland, or remove France and all its cities entirely:

```
$cities->remove('Ireland', 'Cork');
$cities->remove('France');
```

All I need to do is implement the methods. They are all declared within the package MultiMap, which I put in a file called MultiMap.pm in a directory known to my Perl compiler, so that I can incorporate it with a use directive.

The constructor is simple, but crucial. It constructs a reference to an anonymous empty hash, blesses it, and returns it. I use the class name passed as an argument to determine which class to use in the blessing. This may seem odd: don't I know which class I'm in? Not always, as we will see.

```
sub new {
  my $class = shift;
  return bless {}, $class;
}
```

The insert method is just the code I used in my topological sort, made into the body of a subroutine taking the key and values as arguments. The hash I need to insert values into is accessible via the reference passed as the first argument to the method. It will be the object before the -> in the method call. Most methods begin by shifting the first argument into a local variable, often called $this, especially by C++ and Java programmers. There is nothing special about the name $this in Perl, though; many programmers prefer $self. You can call it $elvis if you prefer.

```
sub insert {
  my $this = shift;
  my $key = shift;
  my @values = @ARG;
  if (exists $this->{$key})
  {
    push @{$this->{$key}}, @values;
  }
  else
  {
    $this->{$key} = [ @values ];
  }
}
```

Because of the way I have specified it, lookup only needs to do an ordinary hash lookup.

```
sub lookup {
  my $this = shift;
  my $key = shift;
  return $this->{$key};
}
```

On the other hand, the specification of present makes me do quite a lot of work to accommodate it. First, I extract the arguments.

```
sub present {
  my $this = shift;
  my $key = shift;
  my @values = @ARG;
```

What happens next depends on whether any values have been provided. If they have, I construct a temporary hash to use in conjunction with the `grep` idiom I introduced on page 163 to determine the intersection of the values with those stored in the hash.

```
if (@values)
{
  my %values;
  map { ++$values {$ARG} } @values;
  return grep { $values{$ARG}} @{$this->{$key}};
}
```

If no values were provided, it is only necessary to see whether the key is present.

```
else
{
  return exists $this->{$key};
}
}
```

The logic for `remove` is very similar. If values to remove are specified, I use `grep` again to compute a new set of values to be stored under the key. Otherwise, `remove` is just a `delete` from the hash.

```
sub remove {
  my $this = shift;
  my $key = shift;
  my @values = @ARG;
  exists $this->{$key} or return;
  if (@values)
  {
    my %values;
    map { ++$values {$ARG} } @values;
    $this->{$key} = [ grep {!$values{$ARG}} @{$this->{$key}} ];
  }
  else
  {
    delete $this->{$key};
  }
}
```

Finally, `display` is just a double loop, that prints each key and its associated list of values, with appropriate formatting.

```
sub display {
  my $this = shift;
```

```
    my $k;
    foreach $k (keys %$this)
    {
      print "$k => {",
            join(',', @{$this->{$k}}),
            "}\n";
    }
  }
}
```

Last of all, I must provide an expression to be evaluated to indicate the successful completion of a use directive:

```
    1;
```

All modules end like this.

Beginnings and Endings

A package may contain one or more subroutines called BEGIN. These may be used to initialize the package: they are executed, in the order in which they appear, at the time the package is being compiled. Hence, they can be used to do processing that is necessary before the ordinary routines can be compiled. Such processing usually takes the form of somewhat esoteric symbol table manipulation; an example will be given in chapter 9.

In pleasing symmetry, you can also have subroutines called END, which are executed after the main part of your script has terminated, either naturally, or by dying. They can be used for cleaning up, but are rarely necessary, since perl does most of the cleaning up for you.

A class may also include a method called DESTROY, which is called when any object becomes inaccessible, either because control has left the scope region in which the only variable it is stored in is visible, or because all references to it have become inaccessible or undefined. For whatever reason, the object is no longer needed, and the DESTROY method (also known as a destructor) is called to clean it up. Because Perl is a language with garbage collection, most classes do not have a destructor—the storage de-allocation for which destructors are often used in C++ is unnecessary. There may be occasions when a destructor is required if an object is used to hold some resource, such as a database lock, which must be de-allocated.

Inheritance

Most experts on the subject consider inheritance to be the *sine qua non* of object-oriented programming, and the key to truly re-usable code. It is the ability to define new classes as extensions or refinements of old ones, by adding methods and data, or by re-defining methods. The old class thus extended is referred to as the *base class* of the new, which is said to be *derived* from it. All the classes derived from a particular base class will share some characteristics and behaviour, but each will add some of its own. A derived class may itself be a base for further derivation, so that hierarchies of related classes are built up by inheritance.

The slogan is: inheritance means 'is a'; although it would be more precise to say: inheritance models 'is a kind of'. For example, if you were writing a program to deal with town planning, you would be concerned with the class of buildings. You would observe that there were different kinds of buildings: some that people lived in, others that they worked in; and that the way you treated a building—for example, in computing its liability for local taxes or determining where it could be built—was different for different kinds of building, although all buildings had some things in common, including an address. You could use inheritance to capture the commonality while supporting the differences. Not only would this improve the structure of your program, it would enable you to re-use any code for common behaviour between the different classes of building, so that each derived class only need implement its own special behaviour.

Some modern programming languages provide extensive and elaborate linguistic support for inheritance. Perl provides a minimal framework, with which you can build your own inheritance.

This framework is built on an array called @ISA. When you call a method, either through an object or using a package name, it is first looked up in the corresponding package's symbol table. If the method is not found there, it is next looked up in the symbol tables of any packages whose names are stored in @ISA within the original package. This search algorithm is applied recursively, in a depth-first manner. The effect is that a package inherits all the methods belonging to the packages in its @ISA array; in other words, @ISA lists its base classes.

You will have noticed the plural in the previous sentence, arising from the fact that @ISA holds a list. When a class may have more than one base class, we say that a language supports *multiple inheritance.* Although multiple inheritance may appear to be a simple and natural generalization of *single inheritance*, where each derived class has only one base class, using it can lead you into some very unpleasant situations, and on the whole, it is best avoided unless you feel very confident about your understanding of inheritance. I shall restrict myself to single inheritance.

▷   In Perl, multiple inheritance is most often used by packages that do not implement classes, but simply provide a collection of subroutines. By 'deriving' the package from some library classes, it is possible to provide a standard interface for exporting names and only loading subroutines when they are needed. See the documentation
◁   on the modules AutoLoader and Exporter for more details.

In addition to @ISA, Perl provides a 'pseudo-package' called SUPER. When you use the name SUPER as if it was a package, it refers to the first package in the current package's @ISA array. In the case of single inheritance, SUPER is the current class's base class. By explicitly prefixing a method call with SUPER::, it is possible for a derived class to call a method from its base class, even if it has the same name as a method in the derived class. In this way, a derived class can add extra functionality to a method from its base, without duplicating code. A common use of this facility is to allow a derived class's constructor to call the constructor of its base class.

@ISA only provides inheritance of methods, but objects usually include some data, as we saw in the previous section. You must organize the inheritance of data yourself. The usual method is for the class at the base of an inheritance hierarchy to have a constructor, similar in form to that of the MultiMap class, which returns a blessed reference to a hash. Derived classes call their base class's constructor; these calls propagate to the base of the hierarchy. As the reference to the hash is returned down the chain of constructors, each class may add some entries to it, corresponding to the data belonging to that class. This mechanism offers no protection to the data; every derived class has access to the entire hash, and thus to the data belonging to its base class. Furthermore, a derived class has to know which hash keys have been added by its base class, and all its indirect base classes, right down the class hierarchy, otherwise, a hash element belonging to a base class may inadvertently get overwritten in a derived class. The mechanism is not, therefore, entirely satisfactory, but it works.

▷   Tom Christiansen[1] suggests a nice analogy: an object is a nice shiny box containing the complex behaviour that a class implements; users of the class can play with the box using the controls on the outside, but they should not open it up and mess around with its insides, or they void the manufacturer's warranty. This analogy can be pursued further: whereas C++ and other programming languages with a similar approach to object-oriented programming put a seal on the box, forcing you to break it open to gain access, Perl attaches a warning sticker, but lets you open it by releasing a simple catch. This doesn't really mean that Perl is irresponsible. After all, it is in the programmer's interest to use the module, not to break it, so why go
◁   to extreme lengths to protect it?

To illustrate how data inheritance works, the remainder of this chapter is devoted to an example. It is a simple simulation of local tax gathering from a collection of buildings in a town. The computation of taxes is based loosely on the incoherent legislation at present in force in this country: a dwelling's tax liability is computed as a function of the number of people living there and its putative market value, using a per capita rate and a domestic rate; a commercial building pays tax computed by multiplying its 'rateable value' (a somewhat arbitrary number) by a business rate; monasteries and government buildings pay nothing at all.

---

[1]One of the authors of the 'Camel book' (see page 249) and a leading light in the Perl world.

▶ I have used this example before. Interested readers might like to compare what follows with the version in my *Late Night Guide to C++* (John Wiley and Sons, 1996), pp120ff. In fairness to C++, it should be pointed out that the example occurs fairly early in that book, before some language features that would have permitted a ◀ simpler and more elegant formulation have been introduced.

As suggested at the beginning of this section, the different sorts of building will be derived from a common base class `Building`. This class will provide some methods common to all buildings, and will manage the data that all buildings possess; in this case, their address. In addition, the `Building` class will include an array containing references to all the buildings in existence. I will make this local to the package, using `my`. This means that the array cannot be accessed from outside the package, even by using the package name as a prefix, but it is accessible to the methods of `Building`. Each building will remember where it is in this array, and I will supply a method to return a reference to the array, so that methods that need to do so can find any building. As with any design, different arrangements are possible. Since the purpose of this example is to illustrate inheritance, validity checking and other distracting details have been kept to a minimum—this is not production quality code.

The package begins by declaring the array to hold all the buildings.

```
package Building;
my @buildings;
```

Next comes the constructor, which I called `build`, since that seemed appropriate. It first finds out what class of object it is building, by shifting its first argument. Here this is vital, since this constructor may be called from some derived class. It is going to do the blessing, and it cannot simply make the object into a building, it must know where it was called from, and hence what sort of building is being built.

```
sub build {
  my $class = shift;
```

The data common to all buildings is now entered into a hash: the address will be passed as an argument, the index is internal to the package.

```
my %this = ( address => shift,
             aindex  => scalar @buildings
           );
```

A reference to this newly constructed building is stored at the end of `@buildings`; the value just stored as the index will be correct, and the array will grow if necessary.

```
$buildings[$#buildings+1] = \%this;
```

A reference to the hash `%this` is blessed, using the constructor's argument as the object type, and returned.

```
    return bless \%this, $class;
}
```

The method to access the array of buildings is trivial.

```
sub buildings {
    return \@buildings;
}
```

In the way of things, buildings get demolished; here, demolition is achieved by setting the building's entry in @buildings to an undefined value. This action is the same, no matter what sort of building I demolish, so the method belongs here in the base class.

```
sub demolish {
    my $this = shift;
    undef $buildings[$this->{aindex}];
}
```

So does a method to return a building's address. Although this is just a hash lookup, it is better to provide a method, so that if the representation is ever changed (for example, by storing the number, street and district separately), scripts using the class do not need to be changed.

```
sub where {
    return shift->{address};
}
```

Finally, for debugging and monitoring, I will provide a method to print out information about every building. In the Building class, this can only print the information common to all types of building; derived classes will extend the method, to provide the extra information pertinent to each specific type of building.

```
sub describe {
    my $this = shift;
    my $index = $this->{aindex};
    my $address = $this->{address};
    print "building $index at $address\n";
}
```

Like all packages, this one finishes with

```
1;
```

For the remaining classes, this will be left out of the description.

I now need to derive some sub-classes from Building. The easiest is Monastery, which nevertheless shares its basic structure with the more elaborate derived classes. The simplicity derives from the fact that a monastery has no additional data beyond that of any building, and that monks do not pay tax in this simulation.

First, the package must incorporate Building and set @ISA to reflect the derivation.

```
package Monastery;
use Building;
use English;
@ISA = ('Building');
```

The constructor merely calls `Building`'s constructor, and returns the resulting reference. Because of the way the base class constructor is called, the result will be correctly blessed as a `Monastery`.

```
sub build {
  my $class = shift;
  return $class->SUPER::build(@ARG);
}
```

▶ C++ programmers will note that the call to the base class constructor must be made
◀ explicitly. Perl is more like Java in this respect.

Computing a monastery's tax is really quite easy:

```
sub compute_tax {
  return 0;
}
```

A `describe` method just has to call the base class's corresponding method, and then add the information that this is a monastery.

```
sub describe {
  my $this = shift;
  $this->SUPER::describe();
  print "a monastery -- Pax Vobiscum\n";
}
```

Each class derived from `Building` will supply these three methods. In every class they will perform the same conceptual task: building the building, computing its tax liability and describing it, but each class will implement them in its own way.

▶ Again, C++ programmers should note that there is no need for these methods to be declared virtual, although virtual functions would be required under the same circumstances in that language. The reason is that Perl variables do not have types, hence there is no question of distinguishing between a variable's declared (compile-time) and dynamic (run-time) type, and hence no need for virtual functions. All method lookups are inevitably done at run-time. Of course, it follows that any attempt to call a method through an object of the wrong type will only be diagnosed
◀ at run-time.

The class `Commerce` for modelling buildings that pay business rates is nearly as simple as `Monastery`. It needs one extra piece of data: the building's rateable value. This is set to zero by the constructor, and an extra method is supplied to change its value. Otherwise, the class presents the same interface as `Monastery`, and the common methods are very similar.

```
package Commerce;
use Building;
use English;
@ISA = ('Building');

sub build {
  my $class = shift;
  my $this = $class->SUPER::build(@ARG);
  $this->{rateable_value} = 0;
}
sub set_valuation {
  my $this = shift;
  $this->{rateable_value} = shift;
}

sub compute_tax {
  my $this = shift;
  my ($domestic, $per_capita, $business) = @ARG;
  return $this->{rateable_value} * $business;
}

sub describe {
  my $this = shift;
  $this->SUPER::describe();
  my $rv = $this->{rateable_value};
  print "a commercial building, with rateable value $rv\n";
}
```

The Dwelling class is much the same, although here there are two additional pieces of data: the number of inhabitants and the property's valuation for tax assessment. Also, when computing tax, a warning message is issued if an attempt to tax an empty house is made. (The function warn is built in to Perl for such a purpose.)

```
package Dwelling;
use Building;
use English;
@ISA = ('Building');

sub build {
  my $class = shift;
  my $this = $class->SUPER::build(@ARG);
  $this->{'no of inhabitants'} = 0;
  $this->{valuation} = 0;
  return $this;
}

sub inhabit {
  my $this = shift;
  $this->{'no of inhabitants'} = shift;
}
```

```
sub set_valuation {
  my $this = shift;
  $this->{valuation} = shift;
}

sub compute_tax {
  my $this = shift;
  if ($this->{'no of inhabitants'})
  {
    my ($domestic, $per_capita, $business) = @ARG;
    return $this->{valuation} * $domestic +
           $this->{'no of inhabitants'} * $per_capita;
  }
  else
  {
    warn "You can't collect tax--nobody lives here\n";
    return 0;
  }
}

sub describe {
  my $this = shift;
  $this->SUPER::describe();
  my $n = $this->{'no of inhabitants'};
  my $v = $this->{valuation};
  print "a dwelling with $n inhabitants, valued at $v\n";
}
```

Finally, we come to the most complex and interesting class derived from Building:

```
package TownHall;
use Building;
@ISA = ('Building');
```

Its three 'standard' methods are much the same as those of Monastery and will not be repeated here. However, a town hall administers the gathering of taxes, so it has some extra methods. First, one to set the rates for a year (the values are passed as arguments):

```
sub set_rates {
  my $this = shift;
  ($this->{domestic}, $this->{per_capita}, $this->{business})
                                                      = @ARG;
}
```

Next, a method to describe all the buildings in the town. This iterates through the @buildings array, calling the describe method of every building that has not been demolished. To get at the array, it calls the buildings method; the lookup algorithm ensures that this method is found in Building. Each building describes itself in its own way, since the `describe` method called is determined by its class.

```
sub report {
  my $this = shift;
  foreach $building (@{$this->buildings})
  {
    $building->describe() unless !defined $building;
  }
}
```

The method to collect the taxes works similarly, iterating through all buildings that are still standing, calling their `compute_tax` method. The specific computation is determined by the class of each building; the method lookup algorithm ensures that the right computation is performed. A test is added to make sure that the town hall does not tax itself.

```
sub collect_taxes {
  my $this = shift;
  my $revenue = 0;
  foreach $building (@{$this->buildings})
  {
    if (defined $building and $building != $this)
    {
      my $tax = $building->compute_tax($this->{domestic},
                                       $this->{per_capita},
                                       $this->{business});
      my $there = $building->where;
      print "$there paid $tax\n";
      $revenue += $tax;
    }
  }
  print "We collected $revenue in local tax this year\n";
}
```

If you are new to object-oriented programming, think about how you would have performed the tax gathering without it. Probably, you would have added a tag field to the data structure for each building, and used it to select the tax computation algorithm, and the form of description produced by `report`. Every time you needed to add a new sort of building, you would have had to change `collect_taxes` and `report`. With inheritance, you merely need to derive a new class from `Building` and provide it with the appropriate methods. Any old code that uses buildings is undisturbed by the change.

One way I might use my classes of buildings is within another class, Town. A town is not a kind of building, nor vice versa, so there is no question of using inheritance here. A town may include some buildings; in particular, I might assert that every town has a town hall. This is a rather convenient assertion, since a town hall knows how to collect tax from other buildings. The constructor used to found a town can create a town hall, and return a reference to it as the town object:

```
package Town;
use English;
use TownHall;

sub found {
  my $class = shift;
  my $town_hall = TownHall->build('1 Town Square');
  return bless \$town_hall, $class;
}
```

Even though the value returned by the town hall constructor is already a reference, I still need to generate a reference to the reference; merely blessing and returning $town_hall would lose its 'town hall nature', making it impossible to call any methods other than those of Town. As it is, within a method in the Town package, I can de-reference the object to get at a town hall. For example, if I really wanted to simulate economic activity within a town, I could define a method do_a_year, with the following outline:

```
sub do_a_year {
  my $this = shift;
  my $town_hall = $$this;

  obtain values for this year's rates

  $town_hall->set_rates($domestic, $per_capita, $business);

  simulate life, and rate valuations

  $town_hall->collect_taxes();
}
```

To set everything in motion, I just need to create a town:

```
$new_town = Town->found();
```

and then, within a suitable loop, keep simulating its activity for a year at a time:

```
$new_town->do_a_year();
```

Documenting Classes

Documenting your code is always important, but it is especially so if the code is intended to be re-used. Good documentation will allow another programmer to find out what your code does and how to use it. Since Perl provides no linguistical mechanism for protecting the internals of a package, or for asserting pre-conditions, the documentation of a module must also indicate any restrictions that a user must satisfy if the module is to perform according to specification. Comments are a clumsy method of providing the necessary degree of documentation, but if the documentation of a module is separate from its source, it is easy for the two to diverge as the module is developed, or to become separated when it is distributed. Perl provides a means of combining the source code with its documentation, which allows properly formatted versions of the latter to be generated for users, without separating the text from the code. The combined source and documentation is called a *pod*.

Pods

The acronym 'pod' stands for 'plain old documentation', and may be an allusion to *Invasion of the Body Snatchers*, or—even more sinister—to something in the C++ standard, or it may not. It is a characteristically Perl variation on the theme of 'literate programming', allowing you to mix the documentation and the source code for your program in the same file, which may either be executed by `perl`, or passed to a translation program which will generate a version of the documentation in some markup language, such as HTML or LaTeX, or even convert it into the `troff` source for a Unix manual page.

Figures 8.1 and 8.2 show the `Monastery` class as a pod. (I do not claim that it deserves this level of documentation.) Contrary to appearances, this is a legitimate Perl module, which can be used as it stands by a Perl script. It can also be passed to a pod-to LaTeX translator, which comes with the Perl distribution; Figure 8.3 shows the output produced by LaTeX from the result of doing so.[2]

The pod mechanism is simple. A pod consists of chunks of Perl code, interspersed with chunks of documentation (or vice versa, if you prefer to look at it like that). The chunks of documentation are introduced by a line that begins with an = sign, followed by a pod directive—one of the words listed below. Everything from that line up to and including a line beginning =`cut` is ignored by the Perl compiler. At a minimum, this mechanism allows you to include extensive comments, spanning several lines, without an excess of #s.

However, there is more to pods than that. Within the chunks of documentation, some elementary formatting commands can be included. The text is divided into paragraphs, separated by blank lines. The pod directives that can introduce a documentation chunk may appear at the beginning of a paragraph within one; in either place, they control some layout. At present, there are only seven directives, some of which take arguments, consisting of the remainder of the paragraph they begin. Paragraphs beginning =`head1` or =`head2` are level

---

[2]Since this book is typeset by LaTeX, the formatting of the section headings in the pod output is picked up from the book's style; if you just used LaTeX defaults, it would not look quite the same.

```
package Monastery;

=head1 NAME

Monastery -- a class to model monasteries in a town simulation

=head1 SYNOPSIS

    use Monastery;

    $st_chrisostoms = Monastery->build();
    $revenue += $st_chrisostoms->compute_tax();
    $st_chrisostoms->describe();

=head1 DESCRIPTION

Monastery is derived from the abstract base class Building.
It inherits the methods C<where> and C<demolish> and overrides
C<build> and C<describe>.  It adds its own method C<compute_tax>.

=cut

use Building;
use English;

@ISA = 'Building';

=head1 CONSTRUCTOR

C<build> makes a Monastery object by calling the constructor from the
base class C<Building>.

=cut

sub build {
my $class = shift;
return $class->SUPER::build(@ARG);
}

=head1 METHODS

=head2 compute_tax

A monastery pays no tax, so this method returns 0.

=cut

sub compute_tax {
return 0;
}

=head2 describe

To describe itself, a monastery calls the C<describe> method of its base
class, through the reference in $this, then adds specific information about
itself.
```

Figure 8.1   A pod

```
=cut

sub describe {
my $this = shift;
$this->SUPER::describe();
print "a monastery -- Pax Vobiscum\n";
}

1;

=head1 SEE ALSO

The base class for Monastery, described in L<Building>.

Related classes derived from the same base:

=over 4

=item *

Commerce: see L<Commerce>;

=item *

Dwelling: see L<Dwelling>;

=back

=head1 AUTHOR

Nigel Chapman, 1996.
```

Figure 8.2 A pod (continued)

one and two headings (section and subsection, if you like). The pair of directives =over and =back mark the start and end of an itemized list; =over is followed by a number, which may be used by a pod translator as the indentation for the list's items. Each item is introduced by =item, whose argument is the item's label. The following paragraph is suitably formatted according to the abilities of the system used to do the final typesetting. Some pod translators make use of the form of the first label to decide how to format the list; for example, if the first label is a number, it will produce an enumerated list, whereas if it is an asterisk, it will produce a list of bullet points, as in the example. Hence, it is a bad idea to mix styles of item.

The only remaining directives are =cut, which, as already explained, finishes off a block of documentation, indicating to the Perl compiler and to pod translators that what follows up until the next pod directive is Perl code, and =pod, which does nothing but can be used to introduce a block of documentation when you don't want a heading or a list. You can add an argument to

Monastery

NAME

Monastery — a class to model monasteries in a town simulation

SYNOPSIS

```
use Monastery;

$st_chrisostoms = Monastery->build();
$revenue += $st_chrisostoms->compute_tax();
$st_chrisostoms->describe();
```

DESCRIPTION

Monastery is derived from the abstract base class Building. It inherits the methods `where` and `demolish` and overrides `build` and `describe`. It adds its own method `compute_tax`.

CONSTRUCTOR

`build` makes a Monastery object by calling the constructor from the base class `Building`.

METHODS

compute_tax   A monastery pays no tax, so this method returns 0.

describe   To describe itself, a monastery calls the `describe` method of its base class, through the reference in $this, then adds specific information about itself.

SEE ALSO

The base class for Monastery, described in the *Building* manpage.
Related classes derived from the same base:

- Commerce: see the *Commerce* manpage;
- Dwelling: see the *Dwelling* manpage;

AUTHOR

Nigel Chapman, 1996.

Figure 8.3   Typeset documentation produced from a pod

these last two directives, to identify chunks and their corresponding cuts, or just to amuse yourself:

```
=cut to the chase
```

Within a documentation block, you can use some simple commands to change fonts and include cross references. Each of these commands is a single upper-case letter followed by some text in angle brackets. The commands I and B cause their arguments to be set in italic or boldface by a typesetting system that can do so. S prevents its argument from being broken across lines; C treats its argument as a code fragment and sets it literally; X creates index entries; F is used for filenames, which will be set in a distinctive style; and E is used to include HTML entity references (character escapes, such as `&eacute` for é). E escapes may be used inside the argument to C.

As the example pod demonstrates, it is possible to leave out C commands when their arguments are easily recognized Perl constructs, such as a scalar variable. The pod format is fairly loosely defined in this respect, and some translators may be more helpful than others. The format is also still evolving, and you should check the on-line reference for new developments.

Cross references, or links, to other pods can be included using the L command. What these do depends on the markup language that is ultimately generated from the pod. If it is HTML, then L commands are converted into hypertext anchors, so that when the document is viewed with a Web browser the links between documents can be followed by clicking with a mouse. For other forms of output, the link will be converted to a suitable textual cross reference. (Notice how the pod to LaTeX translator converts `L<Dwelling>` to 'the *Dwelling* manpage', which you may or may not consider suitable.) Provided you set everything up in a coordinated manner, you can easily construct a collection of interlinked documents for a set of scripts. You will need to consult the documentation for individual pod translators to find out how you have to organize your documents if links are to operate correctly. It is usually sufficient to have them all in one directory or folder.

If none of the facilities for formatting pods serves your purpose, you need only begin a paragraph with a space or tab, and it will be reproduced exactly as you type it, with all its characters and spacing intact. Such verbatim paragraphs are useful for showing example pieces of code; you can also use them for simple tables, and even for diagrams constructed out of ASCII characters.

I have described pods as a means of documenting modules, which is arguably their most important use, but *any* Perl script can be combined with its documentation into a pod. It is not even necessary for a pod to include any code, you can just use it as a form of manual that is independent of any specific markup language. The on-line Perl reference is produced in this way.

Using Modules

9

Some programmers who are used to object-oriented programming will want to make use of the facilities described in the previous chapter to write their Perl scripts in that style; for many more, the interest of modules and packages lies in using them, rather than writing them. A large and growing collection of modules is available over the Internet, in addition to the library modules provided in the standard Perl distributions. A great deal of repetitive or specialized programming can be avoided by using these modules instead of doing everything yourself.

It would be futile to try and describe all the available modules—any such description would be out of date as soon as it was written. Instead, in this chapter I will illustrate different ways of using modules. The way you can use a module depends on the interface it presents, so before looking at any specific modules, I will consider the possibilities offered by Perl's module interface mechanism.

Module Interfaces

Module writers have used the package mechanism in different ways to provide a variety of interfaces to their code. A little more detail about what goes on when you use a module will help you understand how these different interfaces come about.

The use directive is not an indivisible primitive operation. When you write, for example,

```
use SomeModule (⟨list⟩);
```

it is expanded into

```
sub BEGIN {
  require SomeModule;
```

```
    SomeModule->import(⟨list⟩);
}
```

▷ The equivalence is not quite exact. If ⟨*list*⟩ is the empty list, the call to the import
method is not made. If the ⟨*list*⟩ and brackets are missing, import is called with
an empty list, which has the effect of importing the default set of symbols, rather
◁ than nothing. This is another case of Perl being more convenient than consistent.

   Being the body of a BEGIN subroutine, this code is executed at compile-
time. The require function *is* primitive, and it incorporates, compiles and
executes the contents of SomeModule.pm; since the contents will typically be
declarations only, this has the effect of compiling any subroutines declared
in SomeModule.pm and building its symbol table. In most modules, the only
thing that is actually executed is the expression 1 at the end, which indicates
the success of the require operation. The implementation of require ensures
that a module is not incorporated more than once; it also knows where to look
for modules in standard places. (The array @INC holds a list of directories that
are searched for modules.)
   Once SomeModule has been incorporated by require, its names are available, provided you qualify them with the package name and two colons, or call
them as methods, using the package name or an object. The latter is what immediately happens: a method called import is called. Module writers can, if
they like, define import themselves, to do anything that seems good to them,
but, most often, packages make use of a definition of import inherited from a
package called Exporter, which is part of the standard distribution. Depending on which side of the module you look from, Exporter's import exports
or imports selected symbols. It does this by planting entries for the selected
symbols in the importing package's symbol table. (Some sleight of hand ensures that, if a module neither inherits nor defines an import method, no error
message is produced by the attempt to call it.)
   On the exporting side, a module wishing to export some names begins like
this:

```
package SomeModule;
use Exporter;
@ISA = ('Exporter');
@EXPORT = ⟨list of names⟩;
@EXPORT_OK = ⟨list of names⟩;
```

The array @EXPORT holds a list of names which will be exported when
SomeModule is used without any argument list; @EXPORT_OK holds a list of
names that *may* be exported, if they are specified in the argument list to use.
Software engineers like to tell us that we should exert the finest control over
exports and imports, so module writers are advised to use @EXPORT_OK in pref-
erence to @EXPORT, forcing module users to select the names they want to import.

Exporting names in Perl is just a matter of scope: exported names can be used in the importing package, just like that package's own variables. Names that are not exported can still be used, but only if they are qualified by their package's name; there is no question of protecting variables from interference, just of protecting the importer's namespace from unwanted names.

The consequence of all this is that module writers can do several different things to control the way their modules interact with other parts of a program. They can do nothing, so that any names declared in their module must be fully qualified. Or, they can inherit the standard import method from Exporter, and export some names. Most modules providing this type of interface export subroutine names, so that they behave much like traditional function libraries. Some exceptional modules export only the names of variables.

Module writers of an object-oriented bent do not need to bother about exports. Instead, they must design their modules to implement a class. If methods that expect either a package name or a blessed reference as their first argument are provided, they can be called using the object-oriented method calling syntax, and the method lookup algorithm will find the method in the correct package. As a somewhat orthogonal issue, programmers who choose to implement classes may also choose to design them to be used as base classes for inheritance.

It is common to find modules that provide both a procedural interface, consisting only of exported subroutines, and an object-oriented interface. Usually, the subroutines encapsulate common tasks, while the objects and methods of the object-oriented interface provide knowledgeable users with fine control over the details.

Interfaces based on exports and classes do not exhaust the possibilities. A rather specialized, but very convenient, interface is provided by a built-in function called tie. In effect, tie overloads some of the notation for operations on hashes, scalars and arrays, causing expressions that look like, for example, an assignment to an array element, to be interpreted as calls to specially named methods in some class. A class designed for tying *must* provide a specific set of methods with standard names.

You tie a variable to a class as follows:

```
tie ⟨variable⟩, ⟨class⟩, ⟨arguments⟩;
```

The type of the variable, as indicated by its prefix, determines what operation the class must provide. For example, you can only tie an array to a class that has the following methods: TIEARRAY, DESTROY, FETCH and STORE. The first is a constructor, the second a destructor, called automatically at the end of each object's lifetime. FETCH takes a numerical subscript as its second argument (since it is a method, its first is a blessed reference); it is called when an expression like $tied_a[$i] is used in an r-context. STORE takes a subscript and a value, and is called when a value is assigned to a subscripted expression. Array variables can thus be tied to a class which adds extra (or different) functionality to the array type. Hashes can be tied to classes that implement methods corresponding to lookup in l- and r-context, and to the `exists`, `delete` and `each` functions. One use of tied variables is to provide arrays and hashes with persistence. That is, a class implementing an indexed or sequential file on disk can be manipulated like an array or hash. Looking at it another way, values stored into a hash that is tied to a database can persist between invocations of a program, and be accessed by different programs at different times.

Packages, and hence modules, can be nested—or, at least, can appear to be. A module name may have the form

$\langle name_1 \rangle :: \langle name_2 \rangle$

as if it was a module that was local to another, as a variable may be local to a module. The nesting is only apparent, though. If a module is called `Outer::Inner`, then there is no special relationship between the names in `Outer` and `Inner`. Anywhere you use a name from the inner package, you must prefix it with `Outer::Inner::` (unless it has been exported). The inner package itself must be declared as

```
package Outer::Inner;
```

Nesting is a way of grouping together related modules. The files containing nested packages will be held in nested directories. Usually, the outer module has no methods of its own; at most it will have `use` directives for all its sub-modules, so that they can all be incorporated at once. For example, in recent releases of Perl, a collection of modules relating to input and output is available; each is a sub-module of IO, such as `IO::File` and `IO::Handle`. These sub-modules all reside in the IO sub-directory of the Perl library; at the top level of the library is the module IO, which contains `use` directives for all the others, so to access the entire collection of IO modules, it is sufficient to write

```
use IO;
```

There is one extra dimension to Perl's modules. They do not necessarily have to be written in Perl. Some modules are written in C or C++. They are usually called 'extension modules', because they extend the power of Perl beyond what is built into it. Extension modules may provide access to additional operating system or network functions, or they may be used for efficiency reasons. From the interface, it should not be possible to tell the difference between an extension module and one written in Perl. The procedure for installing extension modules may be more complex, especially on systems that do not support dynamic loading. Several modules in the standard distribution are provided to assist with the production and distribution of extension modules, but since they are inevitably system-dependent, their workings will not be described here.

In the following sections, some examples of modules providing a variety of different forms of interface will be given. The modules used are all either part of the standard distribution or readily available from the CPAN archives (see page 251). I have tried to credit the authors of all these modules; where no credit is given, the module is part of the standard distribution, and presumably written by Larry Wall. All have their own on-line documentation in pod form, which should be consulted if you want a full description. In general, when using modules, you can expect a specification of the interface to be available to you in a pod.

The intent of this chapter is to convince you that it is worthwhile using modules to avoid extra work. However, a warning is in order. No quality control is applied to the modules that are made available; there is no validation process. Some modules are pretty flaky. It is possible that, instead of saving the time you would have spent writing your own code, you will spend it debugging somebody else's. In time, no doubt, the best modules will achieve a reputation for reliability and usefulness, while the poor ones fade away. Sticking to modules from the standard distribution where possible, or ones by programmers with some standing in the Perl community, is generally advisable, unless you enjoy tinkering.

Programming Aids

An important group of modules does not add any extra functionality to Perl, but provides assistance in the task of Perl programming. These modules tend to have slightly unusual interfaces. Among them, we are familiar with `English`, which exports only variable names, no subroutines.

Pragmas

A small number of so-called pragmatic modules, or pragmas,[1] do not export anything at all. Instead, their `import` methods set the bits of a mask variable used by `perl` to control various aspects of the compilation and interpretation of your script. These modules behave like the compiler directives, also sometimes known as pragmas, in other languages. The arguments supplied to the `use` directive for pragmas control which bits are set.

By convention, pragmatic modules have names beginning with a lower case letter, whereas other modules' names usually begin with a capital letter.

I mentioned the pragma `integer` in chapter 3. Putting

```
use integer;
```

at the head of your program causes all arithmetic to be performed in integer mode.

The remaining pragmas cause extra levels of checking to be applied to your script.

```
use diagnostics;
```

---

[1]I know it should be 'pragmata', but I didn't have much of a classical education, so I don't really care.

turns on those compiler warnings I have mentioned several times, and replaces the terse error messages normally issued by longer explanations—the very ones you can find under `perldiag` (Perl diagnostics) in the online documentation.

```
use strict;
```

enforces three extra restrictions on your script. First, it prevents you using soft references, causing any attempt to de-reference a string to generate a run time error. Second, it prevents you using bare words as strings. As explained in chapter 3, any sequence of characters matching `[A-Za-z_]\w*` is treated as a single-quoted string if it could not be anything else. The danger here is that a mis-spelled subroutine name will be parsed as a string, with unpredictable consequences. If the `strict` pragma is in force, a bare word can only be used as a string if it is a hash key, that is, within curly brackets as a hash subscript or on the left hand side of a =>. Finally, under `strict`, you cannot access a global variable unless you qualify it with its package name. This forces you to make all variables local to a package using `my`, or to prefix them with the package name, or to pre-declare them, as described next. This restriction is even applied to the package `main`.

You can choose to enforce only some of these restrictions. The directives

```
use strict 'refs';
use strict 'subs';
use strict 'vars';
```

turn on each of the three separately.

For small Perl scripts, you may find that using `strict` is *too* strict, and reminiscent of what caused you to take up Perl instead of C++ in the first place. For larger scripts, or for modules that you are expecting other programmers to use, it provides an extra level of security and confidence that is well worth having.

To avoid error messages when using `strict` or when the compiler's warnings are turned on, you can pre-declare global variables by using the `vars` module:

```
use vars ⟨list of names⟩;
```

declares the variables in the ⟨*list of names*⟩ (which is usually specified using the `qw` operator). In a similar spirit,

```
use subs ⟨list of subroutines⟩;
```

pre-declares a list of subroutines. Here, the main benefit is that you can use them without bracketing the arguments or prefixing them with &, even before they are defined.

▷ You can turn off pragmas within a block by using the `no` directive, which has the form:

> no ⟨*pragma*⟩;

or

> no ⟨*pragma*⟩ ⟨*list*⟩;

For example, to relax the restrictions caused by the `strict` pragma I could put

> no strict;

If I only wanted to relax the restriction on using soft references, I could put

> no strict 'refs';

◁ In both cases, the effect would extend to the end of the enclosing block.

Configuration Information

If you are interested in writing Perl scripts that are portable, you should investigate the `Config` module, which provides a host of information about the version of `perl` that is running your program. You can obtain a summary of the major features of any Perl implementation using the following script:

```
use Config ('myconfig');
print myconfig;
```

The output provides a summary of the operating system you are running under, the compiler and linker options used to create `perl`, and the support for dynamic loading.

Each Perl implementation's `Config` module is created (possibly automatically) when the `perl` system is built. It holds its information as a large collection of variables. You can access their values via a hash exported by `Config`, called `%Config`. For example, the operating system name is `$Config{osname}`. A typical use of this element is to set the separator character for path names on different operating systems:

```
use Config;
$pathsep = $Config{osname} eq 'MacOS'? ':' :
          ($Config{osname} =~ 'DOS' ||
           $Config{osname} =~ 'Windows')? '\\' :
           $Config{osname} =~ 'Unix'? '/' :
   die "This script does not understand your OS's paths\n";
```

Most of the elements of `%Config` have a much more technical flavour, and their documentation is thin on the ground, so you may have to do some investigation to find out what they all mean, and whether you should care. To see everything that `Config` knows, use the following:

```
use Config ('config_sh');
print config_sh;
```

Note that the only thing `Config` exports by default is `%Config`; its subroutines must be explicitly imported, as in these examples. In fact, `%Config` is not just a simple hash; although it looks like one, it is actually an example of a tied variable. It is tied inside the package in such a way that it becomes read-only; the values of the configuration parameters can only be interrogated, not changed.

Timing

The module `Benchmark`, by Jarkko Hietaniemi and Tim Bunce, provides facilities for finding out how fast your code is running. It has a hybrid interface, with some rudimentary object-oriented features, as well as some subroutines to handle the most common tasks.

`Benchmark` uses a method of timing that can only be guaranteed accurate to within a second, so to get useful measurements out of it for anything except long-running programs, it is necessary to run code several times. The most straightforward way of doing so is by calling the subroutine `timethis`, which takes two arguments. The first is a number, which is the number of times the code to be tested will be run; the second is a string, which may contain the code itself, if you are interested in the performance of short sequences; or it may be a reference to a subroutine. For example, suppose you had coded up an algorithm in a really smart way as a subroutine `really_smart`. You could time 500 executions of it like this:

```
timethis(500, "\&really_smart");
```

assuming your script included

```
use Benchmark;
```

to get output of the form:

```
timethis 500: 61 secs (61.18 usr  0.00 sys = 61.18 cpu)
```

A different way of using `Benchmark` is to compare different algorithms. This is done using `timethese`, which takes a count and a reference to a hash, with keys providing names for a set of code strings which you want to time. For example, is it really faster to double a variable by adding it to itself instead of multiplying it by two, like they told you when you learned Fortran? Or should you do as the compiler writers do (and hope the signs stay sane)?

```
use Benchmark;
timethese(200000, { addition       => '$x += $x',
                    multiplication => '$x *= 2',
                    arithmeticshift => '$x <<= 1'});
```

You have to use pretty big numbers of repetitions for such small pieces of code; otherwise, the way the timing is done, you can end up with negative running times. The output is clear and informative:

```
Benchmark: timing 200000 iterations of addition, arithmeticshift...
addition: 19 secs (19.45 usr  0.00 sys = 19.45 cpu)
arithmeticshift:  4 secs ( 3.90 usr  0.00 sys =  3.90 cpu)
multiplication: 25 secs (26.28 usr  0.00 sys = 26.28 cpu)
```

A lower level of interface, which works with Benchmark objects, is provided for timing sections of a program. The constructor new produces an object whose value is the current time. By creating such objects before and after the execution of a piece of code you want to time, and then finding their difference, you can obtain the information you need. The difference between two Benchmark objects is computed by a method timediff, which returns a Benchmark object, and a readable version of the time is produced from an object by timestr. Code timed in this way looks like:

```
use Benchmark;
$t0 = Benchmark->new;

Code being timed

$t1 = Benchmark->new;
$dt = $t1->timediff($t0);
print "the code took:",$dt->timestr(),"\n";
```

(You can write the call to timediff as an ordinary subroutine call if you feel more comfortable with it.)

Finally, the function timeit does the same as timethis, taking the same arguments, but returns a Benchmark object with the result instead of printing it.

Dates

Because of the quirky nature of our calendar, and the multiplicity of formats used for writing down the date, manipulating calendrical data can be tricky. Because of the way most of our lives are organized, dates play an important part in them, and so computer programmers are often required to do such tricky manipulations. One approach, exemplified by my speculations on Friday the 13th in chapter 5, is to develop special-purpose algorithms based on the arithmetical properties of a particular problem. An alternative is to use a general-purpose module that encapsulates all the quirks of the calendar.

Such a module is Date::Manip, written by Sullivan Beck. Its interface is purely procedural, making no use of object-oriented features.

The first facility this module provides is a parser for dates in a multitude of formats: day of the month, month and year may be given as numbers, separated by slashes, dots or space; the year may be four or two digits; month names may be fully spelled out, or abbreviated to the conventional three letter abbreviations. A day of the week may be included, and a check is made whether it corresponds correctly to the rest of the date. A time may be appended to the date, in either the twenty-four hour or twelve hour format (with am or pm added in the latter case); a time zone may also be added. Options set through a function `Date_Init` can specify a global time zone, whether the components of dates are to be written in the European or American order, and a language (from a small set) to be used for the names of months and days. Finally, a collection of special forms, such as 'second Friday in September 1996', 'now', '3 weeks ago' or 'tomorrow' is recognized.

The parser is a subroutine `ParseDate`, which takes a string (or a reference to one) and returns a string holding the argument in a canonical form (YYYYMMDDHH:MM:SS), which collates correctly using Perl's string comparison operators. Hence, values returned from `ParseDate` can be compared or sorted easily.

The second sort of data this module implements represents the difference between two dates. The documentation refers to this as a date 'delta'. Deltas can be written in several different ways, too, but they are all variations on two basic formats. In both, a delta may have up to six fields (years, months, days, hours, minutes and seconds). Each field is a number, optionally preceded by a sign. In the more austere format, the fields are separated by colons, and leading fields may be omitted, although minutes and seconds must always be specified. For example, a difference of two days less than a month would be +1:-2:0:0:0. In the second format, each field is identified by the name of the unit, or an abbreviation, which means that any missing values can be omitted, as in 1 year 1 day. You can add the word ago to a delta, to negate it. Deltas are parsed by `ParseDateDelta`, which returns a canonical string for its argument.

The canonical forms chosen for dates allow you to compare them, but to compute with them you must use the function `DateCalc`. This takes up to four arguments. The first two are compulsory and can be either dates or deltas, or strings which can be parsed into dates or deltas. If they are both dates, the function returns a delta for their difference; if both are deltas, it adds them together; if there is one of each, it computes the date separated from its date argument by the delta. The third argument is a reference to a scalar, which is set to an error code if something goes wrong with the calculation. The final argument stipulates the mode in which the computation is carried out. The default mode performs exact computations. The most interesting alternative possibility occurs when the mode is set to 2. Then, the computation is carried out in 'business mode', in which deltas represent only working days, so weekends and holidays are ignored. This is the mode to use to find out when your parcel ought to be delivered. You can customize the behaviour of business mode by setting up a configuration file listing holidays in your country. (See the pod for details of this, as well as other features of this extensive package.)

To undo the parsing of dates, `Date::Manip` provides a function called `UnixDate` (because it duplicates the facilities of a Unix function), which is rather like `sprintf`, in that it takes a string and a date, and formats the date according to control sequences found in the string. The control sequences are simpler than those of `sprintf`, consisting simply of a % sign followed by a letter. There are nearly fifty sequences, allowing you considerable freedom in how you represent a date. For example, %A is replaced by the name of the day, %a its three letter abbreviation and %v its shorter abbreviation. Consult the documentation for the full set.

This module could have been used to perform the Friday the 13th investigation, in a way requiring far less explanation than the version in chapter 5. First, the start date is used to initialize a 'current date' variable.

```
use Date::Manip;
$date = ParseDate('13th September 1996');
```

As before, we loop backwards through the century. I have combined the extraction of the year and day from the current date with the loop test for convenience. The extraction is done by `UnixDate`, using the control sequences %y, to get the year as a two digit number, and %A, to get the day's full name.

```
while (do {
    ($year, $day) = UnixDate($date, '%y', '%A');
    $year > 0;})
```

Since the day is in the form of a string, I can use a hash indexed by names to hold the counts.

```
{
    ++$counts{$day};
```

The computation of the previous month's date is particularly easy. I omit the fourth argument to `DateCalc` to get the default exact mode of computation:

```
    $date = DateCalc('1 month ago', $date, \$error);
    $date or die "Problem with date calculation: $error\n";
}
```

All that remains is to print out the results. I want the days of the week in the right order, so I cannot just use the keys of %counts. I still need a list of the names, but this time I will use a temporary.

```
foreach $d (qw(Sunday Monday Tuesday Wednesday Thursday
                                    Friday Saturday))
{
    print "$d: $counts{$d}\n";
}
```

This script is undeniably more readable and readily comprehensible than the version based on modular arithmetic, but it illustrates one of the hazards of using modules. The run time of this script is over 350 times that of the earlier version. A great deal of work is going on inside the subroutines in order to provide the module with its generality. A hand-crafted script will often be more efficient than one using a general-purpose module. On the other hand, some modules have been written (often in lower-level programming languages) specifically to provide Perl programmers with access to efficient implementations of the algorithms they implement. It is important for you to understand the efficiency implications of using any particular module. Ideally, the module's documentation will provide the necessary information.

Filehandles Revisited

Filehandles are great for the simple tasks, such as those you can do within the file processing idioms introduced in the early chapters of this book. When you try to use them in more ambitious ways, you discover that filehandles have some undesirable properties. You cannot treat them like other values; there are only some things you can do with them. In particular, if you try to pass a filehandle to a subroutine, or create a reference to a filehandle, you will find that the obvious way does not work, and you need to resort to the technique of 'typeglobbing', which is as nasty as its name.

The module IO::File, part of a collection of IO modules developed by Graham Barr, provides an object-oriented wrapper for filehandles, allowing them to be treated like objects of any other class.[2] The constructor for IO::File returns a reference to an object that includes an anonymous filehandle. It doesn't need a name, because you can use the methods of the class to perform all the filehandle operations through the reference. In many cases, the methods present a more convenient interface than do the primitive filehandle operations.

The method open is used to open a file and associate it with an IO::File object. It may take a single argument, which is a string that could have been passed to Perl's ordinary open function; alternatively, it may take one or two extra arguments. In that case, the first argument is a file name, and may contain spaces and other unconventional characters; the second argument is then the mode in which the file is to be opened. It may take the form of the prefixes used on file names with the open function (<, >>, and so on), or it may take the form of mnemonic letters (r for read, w for write, and so on); finally, if you are familiar with POSIX, you can use constants such as O_RDWR or O_CREAT, together with a third argument in the form of a permissions mask, to exert fine control over the way the file is opened. The version with a single argument is usually perfectly adequate.

As an additional convenience, you can create and open a filehandle all in one, by giving extra arguments to IO::File's constructor, new; these arguments are passed on to the open method.

IO::File has methods print and printf, which do what the functions of the same name do. You can also use an IO::File object with the <> operator

---

[2]If you have not got a recent release of Perl, you may find the module IO::File is missing from your library. You should have FileHandle instead, which provides similar functionality.

to read lines from the filehandle, but there are two methods, `getline` and `getlines`, which provide a safer means of doing so. The `getline` method reads exactly one line, whether it is called upon to return a scalar or a list, unlike <>, whose effect depends on the context; `getlines` always reads all the remaining lines in a file, returning a list; it produces an error if it is called when a scalar is needed. Although they are not as slick-looking as <>, these two methods can prevent some errors that might otherwise be hard to track down.

▷ Other methods in `IO::File` allow you to change the formats associated with a filehandle. Recall that normally, the format used by `write` has the same name as the filehandle. You *can* change this, but only awkwardly, by selecting the filehandle as the 'current filehandle', then changing the format by assigning to a special variable. This is a recipe for confusion, since you might fail (accidentally or deliberately) to select the previously current filehandle, with the risk of subsequent output going to the wrong place. With `IO::File` objects, the format is clearly associated with the filehandle. You associate a new format with an `IO::File` object by calling the method `format_name` through the object, passing it the format as an argument; the method `format_top_name` sets the format for page headers in a similar way.
◁ See the documentation for full details.

Inheritance Revisited

Wrapping filehandles in a class hides their inconsistent nature, making them more convenient to use. It provides another advantage that should not be overlooked. Any well-designed object-oriented module can serve as a base class from which you can derive new classes that add extra functionality to it.

Suppose, for example, that you like `IO::File`, but feel that it lacks a couple of features you would like to see. You certainly don't want to throw it away and start afresh on your own filehandle abstraction. Only a few years ago, I would have taken a copy of the `IO::File` source and hacked it, but where would I have been when the new version of `IO::File` was released? Using inheritance to add just a little bit more to the available class is a much better option.

To illustrate the advantages of object-oriented file handling, and object-oriented module interfaces in general, I will begin by extending `IO::File` with some additional methods, to produce a class I call `DeluxeFile`.

```
package DeluxeFile;
use English;
use IO::File;
@ISA = ('IO::File');
```

The main extra facility I want is the ability to look at the next line of input without reading it. That is, I want a method `first` that returns the next line of input, and will continue to return the same line if it is called repeatedly without any intervening call to a method `next`, which returns the next line and then moves on, like `getline`. While I am extending the base class, I will add a different version of `getlines`, which takes a numerical argument, and reads that many lines, returning them in a list. I will also add a `rewind` method, which seeks to the beginning of the file, and a `destroy` method, which deletes the file. The methods `look` and `next` require me to buffer a line of input as data inside the `DeluxeFile` object; `destroy` requires me to remember the file's name when I open it, so I can subsequently use `unlink` to delete it.

Thus, I need somewhere to keep these pieces of data. On investigation, it turns out that the blessed reference of an `IO::File` object refers to a typeglob—something I mentioned briefly on page 148. A typeglob is a composite of all the different types of entity a name may belong to: a scalar, an array, a hash, a filehandle, a directory handle, and a subroutine. You can think of it as being a symbol table entry, as partially illustrated in Figure 7.3 on page 149. When you use a typeglob, context determines which of its components is used. Thus, after de-referencing the typeglob returned by `IO::File`'s constructor, I can treat it as a hash, ignoring the other components.

My constructor (`new`) will open a file as well as constructing the object, so that it can immediately read the first line to prepare for the `first` method. (Don't try anything like this with a handle connected to a terminal.) It opens the file by passing its arguments to the `IO::File` constructor (which will check them for validity).

```
sub new {
  my $class = shift;
  my $this = $class->SUPER::new(@ARG);
  $this || die "Failed to open DeluxeFile(@ARG):$OS_ERROR\n";
```

Next, the first line is read from the file, and stored in the object's hash under the key `DeLuxeFile_peep`. Using names beginning with the class name and an underline for hash keys is a convention suggested by the author of `IO::File`, so I have followed it.

```
  $$this->{DeLuxeFile_peep} = $this->getline;
```

Before returning the reference (which will have been correctly blessed by the base class's constructor) I also store the file's name, which has been passed as an argument, having first stripped off any >, < and + characters.

```
  my $filename = $ARG[0];
  $filename =~ s/^[<>+]*//;
  $$this->{DeLuxeFile_filename} = $filename;
  return $this;
}
```

Using the **peep** element, `first` and `next` are easy to implement.

```
sub first {
  my $this = shift;
  return $$this->{DeLuxeFile_peep};
}
```

```
sub next {
  my $this = shift;
  return $$this->{DeLuxeFile_peep} = $this->getline;
}
```

The only difficulty with `getlines` is ensuring that `peep` is dealt with correctly. The method lookup algorithm ensures that it is this version of `getlines` which is called if a `DeLuxeFile` object is being used.

```
sub getlines {
  my $this = shift;
  my $n = shift;
  $n > 0 || return ();
  my ($line, $i);
  my @lines;
  $lines[0] = $$this->{DeLuxeFile_peep};
  undef $$this->{DeLuxeFile_peep};
  for ($i = 1; $i < $n; ++$i)
  {
    $line = $this->getline;
    defined $line || return @lines;
    push @lines, $line;
  }
  $$this->{DeLuxeFile_peep} = $this->getline;
  return @lines;
}
```

The `rewind` method just conceals a special case of `seek`, which is available as a method in `IO::File`.

```
sub rewind {
  my $this = shift;
  $this->seek(0, 0);
  $$this->{DeLuxeFile_peep} = $this->getline;
}
```

Finally, `destroy` closes the file and then uses the name that was stored by the constructor to delete it, using the `unlink` function in an entirely normal way.

```
sub destroy {
  my $this = shift;
  $this->close;
  my $filename = $$this->{DeLuxeFile_filename};
  unlink $filename;
}
```

I will use `DeLuxeFile` objects to implement another classic algorithm: merge sort. In chapter 5, I told you that you need never write a sort routine in

Perl, unless you wanted to. This was not entirely true: if you are working with large quantities of data, you may find one day that you need to sort a collection of records so large that it will not all fit into your computer's memory at once.

If you work for a company that produces expensive shrink-wrapped software, you will probably just tell your customers that they need 128 megabytes of memory to run your program—and probably get away with it. If you aspire to a higher level of craftsmanship in your programming, you will sort the records in a more intelligent fashion. It is actually very easy.

If you have never met sorting algorithms that use external merging before, it is probably easiest to understand what is going on by considering a method you might use to sort a large collection of record cards, each bearing a serial number, by hand. You could pick up a bunch of cards small enough to sort while holding them, and arrange them in order, the one with the lowest serial number at the front. Putting that pile to one side, you could then pick up a second bunch, and sort those. You would proceed in this fashion until you had divided the whole set of cards into piles, each pile being sorted. Now all you would need to do is put all these piles face up and merge them into one big pile by choosing the card with the smallest number from those you could see, taking it off its pile and putting it face down on the final pile of cards. You carry on picking the smallest card until every card has been transferred to this final pile. Since all the small piles were in order, the algorithm will sort the entire collection of cards. (Try it if you don't believe me.)

With the aid of `DeLuxeFile` objects, it is easy to translate this algorithm into a Perl script. I will write a subroutine `merge_sort` taking three arguments: the name of a file to be sorted, a name to be given to the file of sorted records, and the number of records in each of the sorted bunches. Choosing this last value requires some judgement: it must be small enough to ensure that each bunch of records can be held in memory at once, but not so small that the number of intermediate files required is prohibitive. This subroutine calls two others, `first_pass` and `second_pass`, to do the actual work. A `DeLuxeFile` object, opened on the input file is passed, together with the buffer size, as an argument to `first_pass`, which returns as its result a list of `DeLuxeFiles`, each of which is attached to a temporary file, corresponding to one of my intermediate sorted card piles. This list is passed to `second_pass`, together with a `DeLuxeFile` object opened on the output file. Hence, `merge_sort` just looks like this:

```
sub merge_sort {
  my ($infile, $outfile, $buffer_size) = @ARG;
  my $infile_handle = DeLuxeFile->new($infile);
  $infile_handle or die "could not open $infile: $OS_ERROR\n";
  my $outfile_handle = DeLuxeFile->new(">$outfile");
  $outfile_handle or die "could not open $outfile: $OS_ERROR\n";
  second_pass($outfile_handle,
              first_pass($infile_handle, $buffer_size));
}
```

The first pass is a simple loop that reads an appropriate number of records, sorts them and writes them to a temporary file. A little preparation is required; the arguments are extracted, an array is declared, which will hold the list of DeLuxeFiles for the temporary files, and a string is initialized to generate names for these temporary files—something more imaginative would be called for on a shared system.

```
sub first_pass {
    my ($infh, $buffer_size) = @ARG;
    my @outfhs;
    my $temp_file_name = 'TEMP00';
```

With DeLuxeFiles, the value returned by the first method will be undefined at the end of the file; this is used to control the main loop.

```
while (defined $infh->first)
{
```

First, a temporary file is opened for writing and reading; the special behaviour of ++ is used to generate a sequence of names for these files. Since some operating systems impose a limit on the number of files you can have open at once, this operation may fail, so the value returned must be tested. If you were doing this job seriously, you would need some expedient for coping with the possibility of running out of files. I am sure you can devise at least two for yourself.

```
my $temp_file = DeLuxeFile->new('+>' . $temp_file_name++);
$temp_file or
    die "Failed to open a temporary file: $OS_ERROR\n";
```

Since this file will have to be read from later, it must be opened for reading and writing. The temporary files should not exist, but if they do, we certainly do not want their old contents, hence, for once, +> is the right way to open the file.

The correct number of records is read using the convenient getlines method provided by DeLuxeFile, then the buffer is sorted and printed to the temporary file, which is rewound in preparation for the second pass, before being added to the array of objects to be returned.

```
my @buffer = $infh->getlines($buffer_size);
@buffer = sort @buffer;
$temp_file->print(@buffer);
$temp_file->rewind;
push @outfhs, $temp_file;
}
```

On exit from the loop, all of the input file has been processed, so a reference to the list of temporary DeLuxeFiles is returned as the result.

```
    return \@outfhs;
}
```

At this point, the result just returned corresponds to my collection of sorted bunches of cards, face up (rewound), waiting to be merged, which the function `second_pass` does. To simplify matters, I am going to sort the list of `DeLuxeFiles` so that I always know that the next record to be added to the sorted output file comes from the object at the beginning of the list. The sort should be done by comparing the first records of each file.

```
sub second_pass {
  my $out_fh = shift;
  my $temp_fhs = shift;
  my @handles = sort { $a->first gt $b->first } @$temp_fhs;
```

Whenever a temporary file becomes empty, I will remove it from the array `@handles`, so I know I must continue processing until the length of that array becomes zero.

```
  while (@handles)
  {
```

I begin by taking the first object from the list of handles and writing its first record to the output:

```
    my $first_fh = shift @handles;
    $out_fh->print($first_fh->first);
```

I must use `next` to read the following record; provided there is such a record (I am not at the end of this file), I must put the handle back into `@handles` in its proper place. I just use a linear search to do this—there should not be a huge number of temporary files.

```
    if (defined $first_fh->next)
    {
      my $i = 0;
      my $line = $first_fh->first;
      while ($i < @handles)
      {
        if ($line lt $handles[$i]->first)
        {
          splice @handles, $i, 0, $first_fh;
          last;
        }
        else
        { ++$i; }
      }
```

When I reach this point, either the handle has been put in place, or I reached the end of `@handles`—it belongs on the end:

```
      $i < @handles || push @handles, $first_fh;
    }
```

If the file whose record I just wrote is now empty, I need to close and delete it. Nothing remains to be done; the loop will finally lead to this action being taken for all the temporary files, after which all the records will have been sorted.

```
    else
    {
      $first_fh->destroy;
    }
  }
}
```

The simplicity of this implementation is due to the abstraction provided by DeLuxeFile, which, in turn, was easily implemented because it could be derived from IO::File (itself derived from IO::Handle, a more abstract class, suitable as a base for other handle-like classes). Passing around bare filehandles as typeglobs and using only the available built-in functions and operators would have led to a much more obscure formulation. There really is more to object-oriented programming than hype.

Persistent Hashes

In the section on 'Module Interfaces', at the beginning of this chapter, I described how the function tie can be used to associate a variable with a class having a special set of methods. Several suitable classes are available in library modules. The most widely used are a collection of modules that provide persistent hashes by tying a hash variable to a *DBM file* on disk. The name DBM is used loosely to refer to a family of C libraries which provide access to indexed disk files. By tying a hash to a DBM module, you can access indexed files using the normal Perl hash indexing notation. Looking at this another way, you can make a hash persistent—values stored in it will survive the execution of any particular Perl script.

The most highly developed and flexible version of DBM is Berkeley DB; the Perl module DB_File, written by Paul Marquess, is used to provide Perl scripts with access to its facilities. Of course, before you can take advantage of DB_File, you must have Berkeley DB linked in to your perl system (either statically or dynamically). If this cannot be arranged, you have a choice of other versions; at the very least, you can use SDBM and the corresponding module SDBM_File, since this is built in to the Perl distribution. Some older versions of DBM are said to be somewhat slow and to place limits on the size of databases, though.

Assuming you can use DB_File[3] you tie a hash to a file in the following way:

⟨*scalar variable*⟩ = tie ⟨*hash variable*⟩, 'DB_File', ⟨*file name*⟩,
⟨*flags*⟩, ⟨*permissions*⟩, ⟨*organization*⟩

[3]If you cannot, consult your local documentation for the fine detail of the other versions.

The first three arguments to `tie` should be self-explanatory. The ⟨*flags*⟩ specify the operations you wish to allow on the DBM file; they are usually written as a combination of symbolic constants, following POSIX conventions;[4] for example, an argument `O_RDWR|O_CREAT` specifies that the file should be opened for reading and writing, and created if it is not found. The ⟨*permissions*⟩ argument is a Unix-style mode specification: if you are not familiar with these, 0644 is quite a good choice. (If you want to know what is going on, look in a good Unix book). The final argument may be `$DB_HASH`, which stipulates that the indexing of the disk file is to be performed using a hashing algorithm, or `$DB_BTREE`, which causes a B-tree structure to be used instead.

▷   You can also tie an array to an indexed file with the `DB_File` module. In that case, you use `$DB_RECNO` as the final argument, causing the file to be indexed by record (i.e., line) number. You can then perform random access reads and writes to the file by indexing the array. The random access uses record numbers to identify positions in the file, which may be more convenient than using byte offsets, as you
◁   do with the `seek` function or method.

The value returned from `tie` is a `DB_FILE` object. You can call the methods of this class directly through this reference, and you sometimes need to do so, although most of the operations you naturally need to perform on a DBM file can be done using the ordinary hash operators on the variable you have tied.

To break the association between a hash variable and a DBM file, you pass the variable to the function `untie`. A standard way of closing the file associated with a `DB_FILE` object is to undefine the value of the object.

Tied hashes differ from ordinary hashes in one important respect: you cannot successfully use a reference as the value—if you try, the string returned by the `ref` function is stored in the file, which is unlikely to be of any use to you. Complex data structures like hashes of arrays cannot, therefore, be directly stored in a file.

As a simple, but representative, illustration of how tied hashes are used, consider a script to assist the financially incompetent with their book-keeping. At the end of the tax year, accountants like to be presented with neat records, showing all the transactions on your business account, broken down by category, in chronological order. Which is fine, if you employ a book-keeper, or are naturally well organized. Some of us reach the end of the year with a large envelope stuffed with barely legible receipts and scruffy bits of paper with enigmatic notes on. This program is intended to help impose some order on such records. The intended pattern of use is that, whenever the harassed small businessperson (or writer) can face doing so, they will run this script and enter whatever transaction details they can lay their hands on at the time. This information will be held in a DBM file; during subsequent sessions, more information will be added. At the end of the accounting year, all the data in the file can be printed out to be handed over to the accountant.

---

[4]Look at `POSIX.pm` or `Fcntl.pm`, in the standard Perl library, to find which values are available. You will need to `use` one of these modules to make the names available.

The script begins by opening or creating a file for the book-keeping records, tying it to a hash variable.

```
my $books = tie %books, 'DB_File', 'books.db',
                O_RDWR|O_CREAT, 0640, $DB_HASH;
defined $books or
        die "Unable to open or create books file: $OS_ERROR\n";
```

Next, it calls a subroutine to process the user's commands. I will not show the details of this; in chapter 4 you saw several ways of organizing a simple 'call and response' command interpreter; more sophisticated interactions will use system-dependent facilities. When the user wants to add a new record to the books, the following subroutine is called:

```
sub add {
  my ($code, @rest) = get_record;
  $books{$code} = join '|', @rest;
}
```

The function `get_record` (again, the details are of no interest) returns a list, whose first element is a unique transaction code identifying this particular record. The remaining elements are combined by the `join` function to produce a single string, which is then entered into the database by assigning to an element of the tied hash `%books`. All that distinguishes this operation from storing the record in an ordinary hash is that I have had to join the elements of `@rest`, instead of storing a reference to the list itself.

Retrieving data from the database is also easy; for example, the following subroutine prints all the currently available records, ordered by their codes. The output format for the `STDOUT` filehandle causes the values in the global variables beginning with capital letters—`$Date` and so on—which hold the values of the individual fields, to be printed with a suitable layout.

```
sub report {
  my $k;
  foreach $k (sort keys %books)
  {
    $Code = $k;
    ($Date, $Amount, $Direction, $Payee, $Remarks) =
                                 split '\|', $books{$k};
    write STDOUT;
  }
}
```

Although the use of tied hashes is intended to make the existence of DBM files transparent, it is important not to forget that you are dealing with potentially large files of data when you use a tied hash, and that it is only the hash itself that is stored in disk. Here, for example, the expression `keys %books` causes an array holding all the separate code values from the database to be constructed. This is just an ordinary array, held in memory, so if your database is huge, this will be a huge array. Where possible, you should try to process the records from your database one at a time, unless you know that the database is relatively small, and you are only using the DBM files for persistence.

If you need to use a program like this, it is extremely unlikely that you will be entering records in correct chronological order, so it must somehow sort them for you by date. Doing this in the obvious way, by sorting `keys %books` using a comparison function that extracts the associated dates from the database and compares them would be inefficient. An alternative, which also avoids the construction of a potentially large array, is to construct a temporary DBM file, keyed by date. By using the B-tree organization for this file, sorting can be avoided entirely, since B-trees are sorted, and the function `each` will return the records in the desired order.

The only problem is that it is extremely unlikely that the dates of all the records would be unique—it would be an extremely strange business that never performed more than one transaction on any day. However, unique keys can be generated from dates: assuming that the dates are stored in the canonical form using by `Date::Manip` (see page 205), whenever I find a date that is already in my temporary database, I can add one second to it. This will not affect the part of the data I am interested in.

I begin by declaring some local variables, and then opening the B-tree file, tying it to a local hash.

```
sub show {
  my ($d, $code, $date, $amount, $direction, $payee,
                                  $remarks, $data);
  my %by_date;
  my $by_date = tie %by_date, 'DB_File', 'TEMP.db',
              O_RDWR|O_CREAT|O_TRUNC, 0640, $DB_BTREE ;
  defined $by_date ||
        die "Unable to create temporary file: $OS_ERROR\n";
```

Next, I loop through all the records in my permanent database, extracting all the individual fields, generating a unique date key, joining the other fields back together, and storing them in the B-tree.

```
  while (($code, $data) = each %books)
  {
    ($date, $amount, $direction, $payee, $remarks) =
                                  split '\|', $data;
    while (defined $by_date{$date})
    {
      $date =~ s/(\d\d)$/sprintf("%02d", $1+1)/e;
    }
    $by_date{$date} = join '|',
          ($amount, $direction, $code, $payee, $remarks);
  }
```

(The test `defined $by_date{$date}` ought to be `exists $by_date{$date}`, but in the version of DB_FILE presently available, the method EXISTS is not implemented. The logic of this code is such that defined works correctly.)

Now I only have to loop through the records in the B-tree and write them out.

```
while (($Date, $data) = each %by_date)
{
  ($Amount, $Direction, $Code, $Payee, $Remarks) =
                                    split '\|', $data;
  write STDOUT;
}
```

Finally, I must clean up. First, I break the association between the hash and the file; next, I set the DB_FILE object to an undefined value, which has the effect of closing the file, which I then delete.

```
untie %by_date;
undef $by_date;
unlink 'TEMP.db' || warn "Could not delete TEMP.db: $OS_ERROR\n";
}
```

As this example shows, DBM files are useful for simple record-keeping tasks, but although DBM stands for 'Data Base Management', on their own, they do not really deserve to be dignified by the title 'database'. For serious database work you need a serious database management system. However, you do not need to abandon Perl to do so. Several extension modules are available for interfacing Perl to commercial DBMSs. A framework providing a uniform interface to many such systems is Tim Bunce's DBI module (not included in the standard distribution), which you use in conjunction with a 'driver' for a specific DBMS. Drivers are available for Oracle, Informix and Ingres, among others.

Other Modules

The examples in the preceding sections have shown you the range of interface styles used by Perl modules. They have by no means exhausted the application areas for which modules are available.

The Standard Library

The standard Perl distribution includes a library of nearly 100 modules. Many of these provide facilities for programmers wanting to develop other modules and extensions. If you are not intending to do so, they will be of no interest to you, but if you are, you should make use of them, not only to save yourself effort, but also to help ensure that your module presents a standard appearance.

Most of these modules can be found within `ExtUtils::*`.[5]

Earlier in this chapter, I described some of the programming aids available in the form of modules. There are several others, including `GetOpt::*`, which provides sub-packages for processing command line options; `Carp` provides alternatives to the `warn` and `die` functions, called `carp` and—somewhat tastelessly—`croak`, respectively. These are used by module writers to produce error messages that refer to the user's code where a subroutine in the package was called, instead of some statement deep inside the module where the user's error eventually caused the program to stop.

There are also modules in the standard library for parsing path names, traversing a directory hierarchy, performing tests or other actions on the files satisfying some condition, copying files, and creating or deleting directories. These modules are in `File::*`. In distributions later than release 5.003, `IO::*` is a collection of modules providing an object-oriented handle interface to several different sorts of devices.

There are also a few modules in the standard library for inter-process communication (`IPC::*`) and some elementary network operations; there are, however, much more elaborate modules for these available separately from the standard distribution. Similarly, there are a few mathematical modules in the standard library, and some for performing text processing, but many more are available separately.

Finally, as well as modules for interfacing to the different versions of DBM, including `AnyDBM_File`, which will interface to whichever of the versions it can find, there are several `Tie::*` modules, which provide base classes from which you can derive your own modules to use with the `tie` function, with a minimum of effort.

All of the standard modules are documented as pods, which you can find in the `lib` sub-directory of your Perl installation. As time goes on, the composition of the standard library will no doubt evolve.

Separately Available Modules

The Internet is central to the Perl way of life, and if you have not got access to it, I am afraid that you will miss out on some of the advantages of Perl modules. You will find it hard to get hold of anything beyond those in the standard distribution.[6] If you do have Internet access, though, you will find a wealth of useful modules at your nearest CPAN host (see page 251).

The Perl module list, maintained by Tim Bunce and Andreas König, can be found in the modules directory at CPAN; it lists the modules available there

---

[5]The notation ⟨*module*⟩`::*` means all the sub-modules within ⟨*module*⟩, so `ExtUtils::*` means `Extutils::Install`, `Extutils::MakeMaker`, and several other related modules.

[6]Perl CD-ROMs, including modules and other material, do exist, but may be hard to track down. I found out about them…on the World-Wide Web.

under 22 headings, which provide a good indication of the extent of the fields covered:

- Perl core modules, Perl language extensions and documentation tools;
- Development support;
- Operating system interfaces;
- Networking, device control (modems) and inter-process communication;
- Data types and data type utilities;
- Database interfaces;
- User interfaces;
- Interfaces to or emulations of other programming languages;
- File names, file systems and file locking;
- String processing, language text processing, parsing and searching;
- Option, argument, parameter and configuration file processing;
- Internationalization and locale;
- Authentication, security and encryption;
- World Wide Web, HTML, HTTP, CGI, MIME;
- Server and daemon utilities;
- Archiving, compression and conversion;
- Images, pixmap and bitmap manipulation, drawing and graphing;
- Mail and Usenet news;
- Control flow utilities (callbacks and exceptions etc.);
- File handle, directory handle and input/output stream utilities;
- Microsoft Windows modules;
- Miscellaneous modules.

The modules vary in complexity, from simple packages that encapsulate a single task, to large libraries providing a collection of services for an entire application area, such as mail handling or graphics. The collection is constantly growing and evolving, and it is likely that there is a module among it that would help with most programming tasks you might undertake with Perl. You should be warned, though, that portability is not a universal goal among module implementors, so if you do not run `perl` under Unix, you may find that you have to do quite a lot of work to install a module and get it working correctly under your system.

Perl and the World-Wide Web 10

In both of my big local book shops, all the books about Perl are shelved under 'Internet/WWW'. The preceding chapters should have demonstrated that Perl can be used for a vast range of programming tasks that have nothing at all to do with the Internet, and the shops' shelving policy has more to do with fashion than anything else. Nevertheless, the requirements of programming for the 'net and the Web are well met by Perl, and these areas provide some interesting examples of how Perl can be used.

I will largely confine myself to the World-Wide Web, since that is where most of the fun is. Perl scripts can use other Internet protocols, too, to provide useful services, and some of the relevant modules will be mentioned at the end of the chapter.

Even if you never intend to write Perl scripts for the World-Wide Web, you may find it interesting to learn how they work. As an added incentive, a few new features of Perl, which we have not needed until now, will be introduced along the way.

Preliminaries

You know all the Perl that is required to write scripts for the World-Wide Web, but there are a few additional things that you need to understand before you can get started.

HTTP, CGI and All That

This is not the place for a detailed account of Internet protocols, but some knowledge of what is going on when you access a Web page is necessary before you can understand how Perl can be used on the Internet.

The provision of information on the World-Wide Web is based on the client/server model of distributed computation. In this model, programs called *servers* spend their time listening on a communication channel for requests from programs called *clients*, which are usually running on some other machine, connected to the server's machine by a network; whenever a server receives a request, it sends a response, which provides some service or data to the client. The requests and responses conform to a communication protocol (a set of rules governing how data is exchanged), so that servers and clients can understand each other.

World-Wide Web servers and clients communicate with each other using the HyperText Transfer Protocol, usually abbreviated to HTTP. HTTP is a very simple protocol, designed for the fast transmission of hypertext information, which is usually in the form of documents marked up using the HyperText Markup Language, HTML. However, the information in the World-Wide Web is more properly described as hypermedia, and may include graphics, sound, video, MIDI and other sorts of data, and even programs.

Interaction between a Web client and server proceeds in four stages. First, the connection is opened: using lower level protocols, the client contacts the server; the identity of the server to be contacted is usually extracted from a URL. The client then sends a request. Typically, this will ask the server for a Web page, whose pathname is also extracted from a URL. The request must contain some additional information. In particular, it must specify one of the methods supported by HTTP; the most common method is GET, which is used to obtain some data. The request may also provide the server with information about the client: what software it is running, what types of data it is prepared to accept, and so on. The server sends a response, which contains the requested data, if it was found. The response too must include some extra information, in particular, the type of the data (HTML text, GIF graphics, sound, etc.) it is sending. Finally, the connection is closed.

HTTP requests and responses consist of a string of eight bit characters, so they can be treated as text by programs that read them. Requests and responses both consist of one or more *headers*, which may be followed by some data. Headers are separated from the data by a blank line. We will see examples of the information that can be transmitted in headers in both directions, later.

World-Wide Web clients are usually browsers, such as Netscape Navigator, Mosaic, or Internet Explorer, which allow us to access Web pages interactively. This is not the only possible form a client can take though. We will see towards the end of this chapter that Perl scripts can be used as special-purpose clients, to automate repetitive retrieval tasks.

The story so far does not leave much scope for Perl programming on the server side. One could write a server in Perl (several have been), but writing servers is a somewhat specialized pastime. However, the story is not over. Some HTTP requests do not identify a file containing data, they identify an executable program to be run on the same machine as the server and generate some data for the client dynamically. Such programs are called CGI programs (or CGI scripts), because the mechanism by which they communicate with the server is called the Common Gateway Interface, or CGI. This name draws attention to the fact that CGI scripts are often 'gateways' between the server and some other resource, such as a database. The CGI standard specifies how data is passed from the server to a CGI script and back.

As we will see, CGI scripts must process textual data, and this is one reason why Perl has become popular as a CGI scripting language. Other reasons are its portability, the availability of excellent library modules for carrying out the repetitive sub-tasks of processing input from the server and preparing output to send to it, and finally, security features built in to Perl, which help prevent malicious or incompetent Web surfers from causing damage on the server machine.

Much CGI programming in Perl is no different from any other sort of programming in Perl, although you need some more details about the CGI definition before you can start writing scripts. Before you plunge on ahead into those details, though, you need to ask yourself a few questions.

'Am I allowed to do this?' CGI scripts only work in conjunction with an HTTP server. If you are running your own server, or are employed as a Webmaster, there is no problem. Otherwise, you may find that whoever is in charge of the machine where you keep your Web pages is reluctant to let you install CGI scripts. Internet service providers often only allow customers to install scripts if they pay extra for the privilege, and system administrators are often unwilling to let ordinary users in their organization install scripts. This may seem unreasonable, but CGI scripts are a security risk for the machine running the server.

▷ Interestingly, at least one leading UK Internet service provider will only allow customers to install their own CGI scripts (even after they have paid rent on their Web space) if they are written in Perl. Scripts written in any other language must be submitted for scrutiny and compilation by their system programmers, a 'service'
◁ for which the customer must pay again.

Even if you only wish to use a Web browser to interact with a collection of hypertext documents on your own machine, you must be running a server in order for the CGI scripts to work. If you try accessing a CGI script using an 'open file' command, or a `file://` URL, it will not work.

If you want to write CGI scripts purely for your own entertainment or education, a positive answer to the previous question is all you need. If you are developing a serious Web site, you should also consider the following two questions.

'Is this the best way to get the job done?' When the Common Gateway Interface was the only mechanism available for executing a program over the World-Wide Web, CGI scripts were used for tasks for which they were not really the best mechanism. Making Web pages more lively with interactive elements is something that can be done with CGI scripts, but because the script runs on the server machine, interaction requires traffic over the network, and puts a load on the server machine. Unless the interaction requires data or some special facility that is on the server machine, it is better to do the computation locally, on the same machine as the client—but this poses security problems. The programming languages Java and JavaScript can be used to write programs to be downloaded and executed in a secure way[1] by the client. Interactivity can also be provided by other mechanisms, using 'plug-ins', such as ShockWave, in the browser. Interpretation of mouse clicks on 'image maps'—once a mainstay of CGI programming—can now be done on the client's side, by the browser. Finally, even computation that must be done on the server machine does not necessarily have to use the CGI mechanism. Increasingly, servers are providing their own proprietary interfaces, which are often more efficient than CGI. For specific classes of interaction, such as querying databases, special-purpose interfaces, which do not require conventional programming, are available.

▷ An exciting development for Perl programmers is Penguin, a Perl extension written by Felix Gallo, who describes it—only partly in jest—as 'Java done right'. It allows you to send Perl scripts to and and receive them from other computers, and have them executed in an arbitrarily restricted environment, which guarantees that a script you receive from somewhere else will only be allowed to perform operations that you trust the sender with. PGP encrypted signatures are used to verify that the sender really is someone you trust. Among their potential applications, Penguin scripts could be used to add interactive features to Web pages, in the same way as
◁ Java applets are.

'Has it been done already?' If you want to add a guest book or a visitor counter to your home page, or use a Web site as an on-line product catalogue with secure ordering facilities, you will find that sophisticated scripts are already available (although you may have to search your favourite archives to find them). Generally, Perl scripts are freely distributed, subject only to the restrictions of the GNU Public Licence or the Perl Artistic Licence. Even simple CGI applications can hold unexpected surprises (what happens if someone types HTML into your guest book?), so you may save yourself some grief, as well as time and effort, by using a tried and tested script written by some other programmer.

Practical Considerations

Different servers have different conventions about CGI scripts, and system administrators at different sites may impose their own additional restrictions. Consult local documentation and people for the specific rules at your site. Some broad restrictions will apply almost everywhere. CGI scripts usually have to be

---

[1]There is some dispute about *how* secure.

placed in a special directory before the server can execute them. This directory is often called CGI-bin or cgi-bin, although where many users have Web space on the same machine, a more complex path name may be used. CGI scripts must be executable. On machines running Unix, this means that the userid under which the server runs CGI scripts must have execute permission for your script (which usually means you must give execute permission to the world), and the script must begin with a line like

```
#!/bin/perl -wT
```

The precise command following the #! may differ—it is the full path name required to invoke the Perl interpreter. (The T will be explained shortly.) On other systems, you may have to save your script in a special format, or give it a distinguishing extension, such as .acgi.

One thing any competent system administrator will certainly do is ensure that, when CGI scripts are run, they have restricted privileges. On a Unix machine, they will usually be run as if they belonged to a user called nobody, or www or some such, with minimal privileges. On any system, restrictions may be placed on the files which a CGI script can access; for example, they may only be allowed to read or write files in a special World-Wide Web sub-tree of the directory hierarchy, and may not be able to resolve symbolic links or aliases. All of these restrictions are for your own good, and those of your fellows, but may be inconvenient. For example, if you want a CGI script to read files in your own private directory, you may find that you cannot, or you may have to make sure that you have set the permissions correctly, to enable user nobody to read them.

If you have never done any network programming before, you may find the concern with security that surrounds the subject offensively paranoid. It isn't. A CGI script may, in effect, be executed by anybody anywhere on the Internet, who can feed it whatever data they like, and there are some strange and mean people out there. Some of them are also very clever at subverting scripts, and using them to open up holes through which they can do very unpleasant things. You have to protect yourself from potential malicious behaviour, such as attempts to crash your machine, or overwhelm your server with requests, or deliberately delete files or corrupt disks; from invasions of your privacy, or that of other people sharing a machine with you; and, if you are working in industry, from industrial espionage. On a shared machine, a system administrator will impose restrictions on what you can do, aimed at protecting the community of that machine's users from such attacks.

There are some things that you can do to help. The first is read about security issues affecting CGI scripts. You can find some good tutorial information on the World-Wide Web itself, by following links from some of the pages listed on page 251. If you are actually running your own server, you should read a good book on security, too. You should use the -T switch to perl. This catches a lot of potential security problems by restricting the way in which you can use data that has come from a remote user. In particular, it stops you passing that data out to system commands. If you are using Perl on a Unix system, it is tempting to use the features specific to that system which allow you to call a system program and have it send its results back to your script. It is easy for someone with malicious intent to manufacture input that causes mayhem when you do this. Note that it is not safe to assume that input generated from a form using radio buttons and pop-up menus is safe, just because the form restricts the user's choices. As we will see, you can invoke the CGI script associated with a form without using the form, and pass whatever data you want to it.

In general, you should check that any data typed by a remote user appears to be what it claims to be. If you are using the –T switch, you are effectively forced to do so before you can use the data in a potentially dangerous way. Data sent by a remote user is described as 'tainted'; `perl` does dataflow analysis to ensure that copies of tainted data are tainted too, and cannot be used in a dangerous way. The only way that you can 'untaint' a value is by extracting strings from it using a pattern matching operation. For example, if you have asked for an e-mail address, it should match a pattern such as /^[-\w.]+@[-\w.]+$/. Hence, any string with the form of an e-mail address can be untainted in the following way:

```
if ($suspect_address =~ /^([-\w.]+@[-\w.]+)$/)
{
    $clean_address = $1;
}
```

The protection offered by –T is not infallible. Although you are assured that `$clean_address` has the form of an e-mail address, you still do not know who's address it is, if anyone's. Furthermore, it is up to you to ensure that the pattern you use to extract untainted strings does do some checking.

HTML and CGI

Most CGI scripts are inseparable from HTML. HTML is a simple, but rather verbose and rigid mark-up language. Special formatting commands, called tags, are interspersed with the text of a document. Most tags describe the desired appearance of the formatted text in terms of the document's structure, but some cause the incorporation of graphics and other non-textual elements, while others are responsible for the hypertext links between Web pages. Tags and their arguments or *attributes* are enclosed in angle brackets, to distinguish them from ordinary text. Fortunately, nowadays, you do not need to write HTML by hand, unless you really want to. There are many dedicated Web page editors available, as well as HTML modes for the super-charged text editors like Gnu-Emacs and Alpha, which will insert the appropriate tags for you, allowing you to compose your page in terms of the abstract structures, such as headings and tables, which the tags implement. As we will see, you can generate HTML from within a Perl script, in a way that also hides the syntactical details of

HTML tags. If you need to know much about HTML, consult the books listed in chapter 11; here, only the relevant structures will be described.

Since most HTML commands are concerned with document layout and structure, if you have any experience with a markup language such as LaTeX you will find no conceptual difficulty with these aspects, or with using Perl function calls to generate them. If your experience is restricted to word-processing or page layout, you may have to make some adjustments to get used to separating the logical structure of a document from its appearance. Using one of the current generation of HTML editors is a good way for anyone to get used to HTML's capabilities.

The most distinctive aspect of HTML is its support for hypertext links. These are what make the World-Wide Web possible. A link appears as some highlighted text. In the HTML source, the tag used to create the link specifies a URL; when the user clicks on the link, the browser sends an HTTP request constructed from the URL. If the URL points to another HTML document, that document is loaded into the browser and displayed; if the URL points to a CGI script, that script will be run. You can also cause a CGI script to be run by giving its URL to the browser and asking it to open that location.

The URLs of CGI scripts are also associated with fill-in forms that can be incorporated in HTML documents. Forms contain elements such as text fields to be filled in by the user, check boxes, radio buttons and pop-up menus from which choices can be made, and a submit button. Clicking on this last element causes a request to be sent, which causes the server to execute the CGI script associated with the form. Any data from the form is sent with the request, either as a query string appended to the URL sent to the server, or as the body of the request. The mechanism used depends on the method of the HTTP request sent by the browser; this is stipulated by an attribute of the HTML <FORM> tag, which introduces forms. The URL of the associated CGI script is also an attribute of this tag. Additionally, this URL may have extra path information appended; this is recognized by the server (which understands where the pathname of the CGI script ends), and passed to the script for its use.

Some HTML documents include a special <ISINDEX> tag, identifying them as interfaces to a searchable database or document collection of some sort. When these documents are displayed, the browser will add to them a text field and a prompt for keywords. (You will probably have come across such pages on Web index sites, or providing a front end to publishers' catalogues, and the like.) When the user has filled in some keywords, a script is invoked to carry out the search. Usually, such HTML documents are themselves created on the fly by CGI scripts, which are re-invoked when the keywords are submitted.

If your browser displays the URL it is currently accessing, you will be able to see when it is calling a CGI script, and see any query strings appended to URLs. Another helpful way of finding out what is happening is to download Web pages that do interesting things, and examine the HTML, either by hand, or by loading them into an HTML editor and letting it display the relevant information to you.

Simple CGI Scripting

Entire books are devoted to CGI programming. In the space available here, I cannot provide a complete account of all aspects of it, but I hope to convey the flavour and some of the techniques, while further illustrating the power of Perl modules.

Accessing the Data

When a CGI script is invoked, the data from the request must be passed to it. The server may pass this data on to the CGI script in more than one way. Information from the HTTP header is mostly passed in environment variables, which are accessible inside a Perl script as elements of the built-in hash %ENV (even on systems that do not actually have any concept of an environment); any data from the message body is sent to the standard input of the CGI program; keywords for an index search are passed as command line arguments. To complicate matters further, the format of the query string appended to a URL is different for search keywords from a document containing an <ISINDEX> tag, and data derived from a form. As a final complication, there are restrictions on the characters that may be used in URL query strings, and any other characters must be specially encoded, although this encoding is not necessary if data is passed in the body of an HTTP request.

Thus, when the data arrives in your CGI scripts, you must determine how it is being passed to you, decode it if necessary, and then store it in a data structure where it will be useful to the rest of your script. This is tedious and demanding work, so it is as well that there are Perl modules that do it for you.

The CGI module[2] by Lincoln Stein takes care of the task of finding data and parsing it for you. It also provides facilities allowing you to construct HTML dynamically, without having to spell out all the tags in detail. This module makes simple CGI scripting very easy.

The module's interface is object-oriented, although, for simple use, the objects themselves can be implicit, so that the interface appears to be procedural, for programmers who find that more natural or familiar. Only one class is provided: CGI. When you create a CGI object, by calling its constructor, new, it does all the tedious work of examining the environment and parsing query strings, and stores the data so you can access it using the methods of the CGI class. The values of environment variables that hold data from the request header can be obtained using methods provided for the purpose. For example, if $the_cgi is a CGI object, $the_cgi->remote_addr() returns the IP address of the remote host from which the request was sent. If extra path information has been sent in the URL, $the_cgi->path_info() returns it as a string.

---

[2]Slightly confusingly, the same author has also created a collection of CGI sub-modules, CGI::*, for more advanced use. Here I am only describing the single module, which is kept in the file CGI.pm, not the directory CGI.

The data from a search query consists solely of keywords. You can obtain a list of their values by calling `$the_cgi->keywords()`.

The data from a form that has been filled in takes the form of a set of keyword and value pairs; the keywords are the names given to the form elements by its designer, the values are the user's input to the corresponding elements. You can find all the names of these keywords (or *parameters*, as they are usually called) by calling `$the_cgi->param()`. You can find the value corresponding to a particular parameter by passing the parameter to the `param` method, as a string. Sometimes, a parameter may have more than one value associated with it; in that case, if you call the `param` method in a context where a list is required, you will get a list of all the values.

Constructing the Response

With the few methods just described, a CGI script can obtain any data that is available to it from the HTTP request that invoked it. Normally, the script will do some computation with these values, and return a response. This must begin with a header. The CGI method `header` builds a suitable string. The response from a CGI script is sent to its standard output, so the header string merely has to be printed. Usually, the script only fills in part of the required information in the header, leaving the server to put in the rest before forwarding the response to the client. The most important information that the CGI script must supply is the type of data contained in the body of its response. By default, if you don't provide any arguments to `header`, this is set to `'text/html'`, which indicates that the body is an HTML document. The argument string is what is technically called a MIME type; you can specify a different one by providing it as an argument to `header`. For example, a GIF image would need the header generated by `$the_cgi->header('image/gif')`.

A useful class of CGI scripts does nothing more than select a file and wrap it up in an HTTP response. Being a program, it can select the file dynamically, according to some criteria it computes. As a trivial example, you could point a link labelled Surprise Me from a Web page to a CGI script that replied with a randomly chosen image, like this:

```
#!/bin/perl -wT
use English;
use CGI;
use IO::File;
```

Assume that the script begins by initializing a variable `$the_dir` to hold the name of a directory, readable by CGI scripts, containing some images in GIF format, and that `$pathsep` is set up as usual to hold the separator character for pathnames on the machine running the server. We begin by opening the directory and reading its contents.

```
opendir DIR, $the_dir or die "I can't open $the_dir: $OS_ERROR\n";
```

```
@files = readdir DIR;
```

Next a file is chosen at random, by constructing an index into `@files` from the current time. While this is not random enough to please a statistician, it is good enough for this purpose.

```
$file = $files[time % ($#files+1)];
```

Next, an `IO::File` object is constructed and associated with the file. If this operation fails, the program calls `die` in the usual way. A helpful server might pass on the error message to the browser, but more likely it will just get logged on the server machine, and a general-purpose failure message will be sent to the browser. Shortly we will see a more robust way of handling errors detected by CGI scripts.

```
$image = IO::File->new("$the_dir$pathsep$file") or
         die "I can't open the file $file: $OS_ERROR\n";
```

Next, construct a CGI object, and send the header—the type of the data is `image/gif`.

```
$the_cgi = CGI->new;
print $the_cgi->header('image/gif');
```

Finally, just copy the image file as the body of the HTTP response.

```
print $image->getlines;
```

The chosen image will be displayed as a nice surprise in the browser's window (assuming it is capable of displaying images).

▷ You can take this idea further, by returning random pages from anywhere on the World-Wide Web. The method `redirect` takes a URL as its argument, and generates a special redirection request, which is sent back to the remote client, which immediately requests the indicated page. For example,

```
print $the_cgi->redirect('http://www.perl.com/');
```

would whisk the remote user off to the Perl language home page (see page 251.)

◁ Redirection can be used less playfully to install 'forwarding addresses' for Web pages whose URL has been changed, or to connect you to a less busy mirror site.

Virtual HTML Documents

A more common pattern of behaviour for CGI scripts is the construction of a 'virtual document' to be transmitted as the body of the response. A virtual HTML document consists of text marked up with HTML tags, so that, when it is displayed by a browser, it looks like any Web page. There is, however, no physical file containing the document. Since its contents are constructed dynamically by a CGI script, a virtual document can contain information that is computed when it is built. As a trivial example, the following script constructs and transmits a virtual document that includes the current time, and some information derived from the HTTP request that called it. Like all the CGI scripts in this chapter, it uses the CGI module; henceforth, use CGI will be omitted.

Computation of the date and time is something we have seen before; it is done no differently just because this is a CGI script.

```
($sec, $min, $hour, $month_day, $month,
    $year, $week_day, $year_day, $summer_time) = gmtime();
++$month;
$year += 1900;
$the_day = (qw(Sun Mon Tue Wed Thur Fri Sat))[$week_day];
```

A CGI object is created so that the response can be built. This begins with a header; since we are making a virtual HTML document, the MIME type is the default text/html so no arguments need be passed to the header method.

```
$the_cgi = CGI->new;
print $the_cgi->header;
```

To construct the HTML itself, there are methods in the CGI module that correspond to HTML tags, or more accurately, to the logical markup operations those tags represent, such as headers, emphasis or lists. These methods return strings, which can be printed immediately or manipulated in more complicated ways if necessary. For example, to combine different effects (say an emphasized list element) you can pass the result from one method as an argument to another. For now, though, we only need simple things.

Any virtual HTML document is begun by calling start_html; this may take several arguments, but usually a single argument giving the title (which is displayed by most browsers as the window title) is sufficient. I will call this document 'Arrival'.

```
print $the_cgi->start_html('Arrival');
```

Once this string has been sent, the actual content of the document can follow. I will provide a welcoming heading (not to be confused with an HTTP *header*). HTML supports six levels of heading, corresponding to sections, subsections, subsubsections, and so on. The methods h1 to h6 are used to generate these. Here I will choose a level 1 heading.

```
print $the_cgi->h1('Welcome');
```

The date information does not need any special markup, so it is just printed, as it would be if I wanted to display it to a terminal. However, after it, I want to start a new paragraph; the method to do this is simply called p.

```
print "You arrived at ", sprintf("%02d:%02d", $hour, $min),
    " on $the_day, $month_day/$month/$year", $the_cgi->p;
```

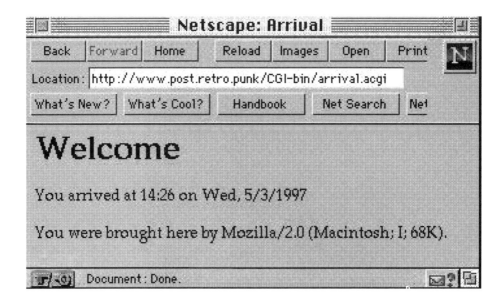

Figure 10.1   A Virtual Document Displayed

Web browsers usually do automatic text justification and line breaking. Spaces, tabs and newlines are all treated as a single space, so it is necessary to include tags to force line breaks and new paragraphs.

As a bonus, I will tell the user what sort of browser they are using. I get this information from the `user_agent` method.

```
print "You were brought here by ", $the_cgi->user_agent, ".";
```

Finally, every document must be finished off by the `end_html` method.

```
print $the_cgi->end_html;
```

Figure 10.1 shows the output of this script as displayed in a (somewhat squashed) browser window.

HTML Forms and Search Queries

The most characteristic use of CGI scripts is in conjunction with HTML forms, to provide an interface to some form of database or information server. Examples abound on the World-Wide Web. The most straightforward approach is for the Web page designer to construct a form, using the HTML tags for forms and form elements, as part of an HTML document stored on disk, and to write a CGI script, designed in parallel with the form, to deal with data sent by a user

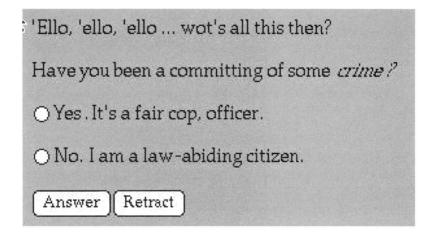

Figure 10.2   A New Weapon in the Fight Against Internet Crime

who accesses that page. The CGI script may store that data in a database—perhaps of visitors who have registered their interest in the site or answered a marketing questionnaire—or it may use the data to construct a database query and return some results to the user. Whichever end of the transaction gains the most benefit, the technique is the same.

To begin with, I will concentrate on the CGI script's interaction with the remote user, using a simple—not to say facetious—example, where the response is computed from the data, without recourse to any database on the server machine. It is my contribution to a solution to the problem of Internet crime which has been exercising the minds of politicians recently.

Figure 10.2 shows the display of a form, designed to be a substitute for a police officer on the beat, which will interview any Web surfer who passes this page. Disarmed by the cheerful demeanour of a cartoon constable, the user may select one or other of the options, and then, by pressing the button labelled Answer, transmit the proof of their innocence or guilt to a CGI script associated with the form, which will take appropriate action. (The Retract button causes the form to be cleared without sending any data. This is handled by the browser.)

When I created the form, I specified that the two radio buttons should be considered as a group called confess, and that the value produced when the first is selected is yes, and that for the second is no. When the CGI script is invoked, I can create a CGI object, which will collect the data for me so that I can call the param method with the string 'confess' as its argument, and get back the value 'yes' or 'no' to show which button the user selected. The browser ensures that no more than one of the two buttons can be selected. It is possible that neither will be, and I have to be prepared for that possibility, too.

The actual script is trivial, because the CGI module is doing all the hard work. All I need to do, once I have fetched the parameter from the CGI object, is print a suitable message, wrapped up in an HTTP response, with the starting and ending HTML rubric.

```perl
my $interview = CGI->new;
my $confession = $interview->param('confess');
print $interview->header;
print $interview->start_html;
if ($confession eq 'yes')
{
  print "I shall have to ask you to report to a police station";
}
elsif ($confession eq 'no')
{
  print "That's all right, then.  Mind how you go.";
}
else
{
  print "You have a right to silence, if you insist";
}
print $interview-> end_html;
```

Apart from its obvious deliberate silliness, this script is technically suspect, in that it is an example of using CGI for purposes that do not require it. No attempt is made to discover the identity of the remote user and record it in a database on the server's machine—that would be unethical. Therefore, all the processing could be done on the client machine, perhaps using JavaScript or Penguin. For a more sensible use of CGI scripting, we should look at how a script can provide an interface to data stored on the server machine.

The simplest such interface uses the HTML <ISINDEX> tag. When this tag appears in a document, the browser will display a prompt for keywords. After the user has typed these, they are sent to a CGI script. Although it is possible (according to the HTML3 specification, anyway) to provide the URL of such a script as an attribute of the tag, most browsers will ignore this, and re-invoke the URL which was used to access the document itself. Thus, if anything desirable is to happen, the document must be generated by a CGI script, which will be called again when the keywords have been entered. A script used in this way must see whether it has been passed any keywords; if not, it displays the document, if so, it searches through its data and displays the results.

This style of interface is designed to provide a gateway to databases that are searchable by keywords. These are often full text databases. For large databases, the searching is generally passed on to a purpose-built search engine. As we know, Perl is good at searching text, so for smaller databases, a Perl script will suffice.

As a simple example, assume that I have a collection of files, consisting of paragraphs separated by blank lines. Each paragraph may be a quotation, or perhaps the abstract of a research paper, or a newspaper clipping. The following script makes it possible to search in one of these files for paragraphs matching a set of keywords, over the World-Wide Web. Since the task is fairly simply achieved, a few extra flourishes have been added.

First, we need a subroutine to search a collection of paragraphs for keywords. I will assume that there is no requirement that the keyword appears only as a complete word (although it would be easy to implement such a restriction). I am also going to make life simple by assuming that the entire database can be read into memory at once. Assuming otherwise adds some slight complexity without contributing any extra understanding. With these assumptions, I can write a subroutine that takes a reference to an array of strings (the paragraphs) to be searched, and a reference to an array of keywords, and returns the strings in which all the keywords are found. It uses a nested call to grep. (The final expression in the first argument to the outer call of grep compares the number of keywords matched in the target with the total number supplied, so it is only true for target paragraphs that contain all the keywords.)

```
sub find_matches {
  my ($targets, $keywords) = @ARG;
  return
    grep
    {
      my $target = $ARG;
      my $hits = grep { $target =~ /$ARG/} @$keywords;
      $hits == @$keywords
    } @$targets;
}
```

This time, I want to do something better than dying in the case of anything going wrong. I will return a small HTML document, giving some details about the error. This is sent as the body of a response whose header includes a status code indicating that something has gone wrong. HTTP designates certain numerical status codes for specific errors in a transaction. Anything that I can catch in my CGI script will count as a server logic error, which has code 500. I can add a message to the code, but I have no guarantee that every browser will do something with it. The following subroutine constructs an error response. It takes as arguments a CGI object, so it can call CGI methods, an informative message, and the name of a file, since all errors that can be detected by this script involve a file.

```
sub error {
  my ($query, $mess, $file) = @ARG;
  print $query->header(-status => "500 Server Error $mess");
  print $query->start_html(-title => 'Unexpected Error');
  print $mess;
  print $query->hr;
  print $query->end_html;
  die "$mess: $file\n";
}
```

The calls to header and start_html illustrate a style of argument passing that is supported by most of the methods in the CGI module. Instead of a simple list of argument values, you can provide a list of pairs, usually written, as I have here, using the => symbol normally used for hashes. This style is easier to use when there are long lists of arguments, many of which you want to omit. Since this module supports either style of argument passing, the keywords for named parameters begin with a minus sign, so that the method can determine which style you are using. The method hr causes a horizontal rule (printers' jargon for a straight line) to be drawn across the page.

▷   Named arguments are not a new language feature. They are still passed in @ARG (re-
    member, => is just a fancy comma). It is the called method that extracts name/value
◁   pairs.

With these supporting subroutines in place, the real work can begin. First, a CGI object is created, and then any keywords are fetched from it using the keywords method provided for the purpose.

```
my $search = CGI->new;
my @keywords = $search->keywords;
```

If there are no keywords, we must display a page inviting the user to enter some.

```
unless (@keywords)
{
  print $search->header;
  print $search->start_html(-title => 'Remote Search',
                            -BGCOLOR => 'blue');
```

Again, I have used named arguments to start_html. The second one causes the page to be displayed on a rather lurid blue background. Next, I send the <ISINDEX> tag, using a method of the same name.

```
  print $search->isindex;
}
```

And that is all I need to do, for now. Figure 10.3 shows how this virtual document is displayed. Everything you can see is inserted by the browser, which also handles the interaction with the user to obtain the keywords.

▷   HTML experts will tell me that the <ISINDEX> tag is supposed to be in the document
    head, not its body. The CGI module does not presently let you put it there; the tag
◁   is still *allowed* in the body, even if putting it there is disapproved of.

If there were keywords, I need to search for them. Where? I will assume that a key such as quotations or abstracts, identifying one of several databases is appended to the URL as extra path information; this information will be planted

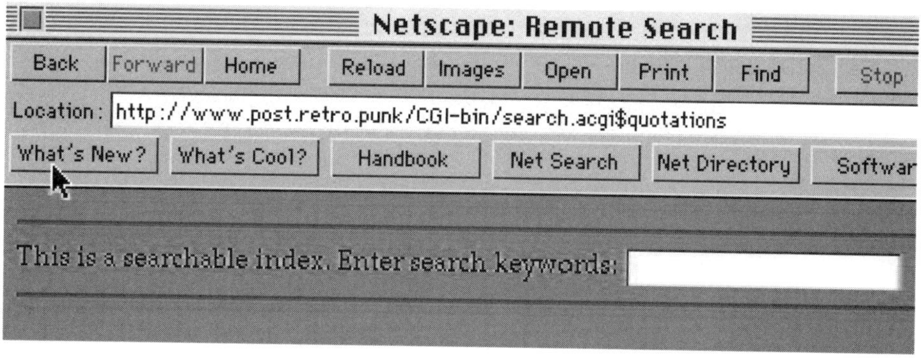

Figure 10.3 Prompting for keywords

in the link that originally referenced my CGI script, or it could be specified explicitly by a knowing user. I can find out what it is using the path_info method, and then call a subroutine which_file to map it to a file name, so I can create an IO::File object, or call my error subroutine if that fails.

```
else
{
  my $database = which_file($search->path_info);
  my $data = IO::File->new($database) or
              error $search,
                "CGI script was unable to open the database",
                $database;
```

▷ The form of the extra path information suggests that the file name itself should be passed, and the information is sometimes used in this way. However, remote users have no business knowing path names on a server machine, and malicious ones could substitute booby traps for path names. Somewhat alarmingly, the value ◁ returned by path_info is not tainted. Hence, the indirect route is preferred.

By setting the input record separator to a null string, I can read each paragraph as a single record. I read all the paragraphs at once and pass a reference to them to find_matches with the keywords. Only the matching paragraphs will be returned.

```
$data->input_record_separator('');
my @relevant = find_matches [ $data->getlines ], \@keywords;
```

Now I prepare to write the virtual document containing the search results. I will want to include a record of the keywords used, so I set $LIST_SEPARATOR to a comma—I will print the list the lazy way, later. Next, I print the HTML header, and a heading; this time I will make the background green. (I don't recommend this practice as good page design; I am only illustrating the use of the argument.)

```
$LIST_SEPARATOR = ', ';
print $search->start_html(-title => 'Results of Remote Search',
                          -BGCOLOR => 'green');
print $search->h1('Relevant Paragraphs');
```

If there were any matching paragraphs, I print a little introductory text, throw a paragraph, then print each one separated by horizontal rules. It is possible that the text in the database is formatted specially; a database of quotations might include poetry, for example, whose line breaks must be respected. I therefore pass them to the method pre, which outputs HTML to tell the browser to treat them as 'pre-formatted' text, and not change the layout.

```
if (@relevant)
{
  print "These paragraphs include @keywords";
  print $search->p;
  print $search->hr;
  my $paragraph;
  foreach $paragraph (@relevant)
  {
    print $search->pre($paragraph);
    print $search->hr;
  }
}
```

It is always conceivable that no matches were found. In that case, print an apologetic message.

```
else
{
  print "Sorry, but none of our paragraphs uses @keywords";
}
}
```

In all cases, it is necessary to finish off the virtual HTML document properly.

```
print $search->end_html;
```

A More Complex Example

Imagine a dealer in second-hand computer equipment—let's call him Honest Mac—who finds he is having difficulty in getting hold of second-hand computer equipment to deal. He suspects that part of the problem is that people don't like to ring him up for a price, because they are embarrassed, and fearful that they might be browbeaten into accepting an offer they are not happy with. Mac reckons that people might be happier using the World-Wide Web to find out what he would offer them, so he decides to set up a Web site, which includes a form that prospective sellers can fill in with the details of their old equipment, and get back a price.

Honest Mac doesn't accept any old rubbish. He knows what he wants, so he decides to use pop-up menus as the elements of the form. Of course, as new models are introduced, the contents of those pop-up menus will change; so will the prices. Therefore, he decides that the form will be generated dynamically, and be built from the database of equipment and prices that he needs anyway. So, like the previous example, his CGI script works by finding out whether it has been sent any parameters; if not, it sends the form, if so, it works out a price.

Naturally, the script will use the CGI module; it will use DBM files to hold the equipment data—one file for each kind of component (processor, monitor, keyboard, accessory, printer and portable). Also, since this is a relatively complex script, it will be compiled using the `strict` pragma, so some global variables need to be declared. Thus, the script begins like this:

```perl
#!/bin/perl -wT
use DB_File;
use Fcntl qw(O_RDONLY);
use CGI qw(:all);
use English;
use vars qw(@components $component %hashes @names);
use strict;
```

Furthermore, I will assume that all subroutines are declared before being used, although the script will be described in a top-down way starting with the main program.

The `use CGI` line requires some explanation. As you would expect, it is importing some names from the CGI module, but the argument has a special form, beginning with a colon. A name of this form is called an export tag, and it identifies a set of names. (The correspondence between tags and sets of names is set up by an exporting module that is derived from `Exporter` as a hash called `%EXPORT_TAGS`.) Here, the tag `:all` causes all the methods of the CGI class to be imported as subroutine names, so that they can be called without using a CGI object. In fact, an object *is* created, but it is invisible to the user. As we will see, this alternative interface is more convenient and readable when only one object is involved (as it usually is).

The main part of the program initializes an array with the names of all the different kinds of equipment, and calls a subroutine to open all the databases—whatever happens, these are going to be needed. Next, it looks for parameters and takes appropriate action, depending on whether it finds any.

```perl
@components = qw(processor monitor keyboard accessory printer
                                                    portable);
open_databases;
```

```
@names = param;
unless (@names)
{
  send_the_form;
}
else
{
  send_the_price;
}
```

An error routine is required. Compare this version, using an implicit CGI object and the subroutine interface to the module, with the version in the previous section.

```
sub error {
  my ($mess, $file) = @ARG;
  print header(-status => "500 Server Error $mess"),
        start_html(-title => 'Unexpected Error'),
        $mess, hr, end_html;
  die "$mess: $file\n";
}
```

The subroutine open_databases ties a hash to a DBM file for each sort of component. The file's names are constructed from the strings in the @components array; a reference to the tied hash is stored in the hash %hashes. I have used default values for the last two arguments to tie, which gives me the hashed file I require.

```
sub open_databases
{
  foreach $component (@components)
  {
    my %temp;
    my $tie = tie %temp, 'DB_File', "$component.db", O_RDONLY;
    defined $tie ||
      error "Unable to open database file: $OS_ERROR\n",
            "$component.db";
    $hashes{$component} = \%temp;
  }
}
```

▷ I have opened the DBM files in read-only mode (O_RDONLY), assuming that this script will be disabled while they are updated. This frees me of any obligation to obtain a lock on the files to prevent any attempt to simultaneously read them and write them. Many CGI scripts that use DBM files would have to worry about locking. Locking a file through a tied variable is not entirely trivial, but there is a recipe in the DB_FILE pod, which, if followed carefully, gives perfect results every time. ◁

Now for the real CGI part. The form that is sent initially begins, as always, with an HTTP header, and the start of the HTML body. Next is a suitable heading, and some welcoming text (dictated by Mac himself). The br method causes a line break.

```
sub send_the_form
{
  print header,
    start_html(-title => q[Honest Mac's Bargains]),
    h1(q[Honest Mac's Price Calculator]),
    "Use the pop-up menus to tell us what sort of ",
    "kit you have for sale",
    br, "If it ain't there, we don't touch it";
```

Next comes the form itself. The methods startform and endform surround the body of the form, which, in general, consists of a mixture of ordinary text and formatting tags, and special form elements, such as the radio buttons you saw previously, text fields, check boxes, and—the one to be used here—pop-up menus. A pop-up menu has a name, a set of values and a default. When it is first displayed, it appears as a box containing the default; when a user clicks on it, the values pop up so that one can be selected. The method popup_menu takes the name, values (as a reference to a list) and default as arguments, and produces the appropriate HTML tags.

The form for Honest Mac has a pop-up menu for each class of equipment, whose values consist of the keys from the corresponding tied hash, together with the default value 'None'. The menus are set as separate paragraphs, labelled with the name in boldface. A reset button and a suitably labelled submit button complete the form (and the document), which is generated by the following code:

```
print startform;
foreach $component (@components)
{
  my @models = keys %{$hashes{$component}};
  push @models, 'None';
  print p, b($component), ' ';
  print popup_menu(-name    => $component,
                   -default => 'None',
                   -values  => [ @models ] );
}
print p, reset, ' ', submit(-label => 'Give me a price');
print endform;
print end_html;
}
```

Figure 10.4 shows the resulting form half filled in, having been displayed after the CGI script was invoked with no parameters.

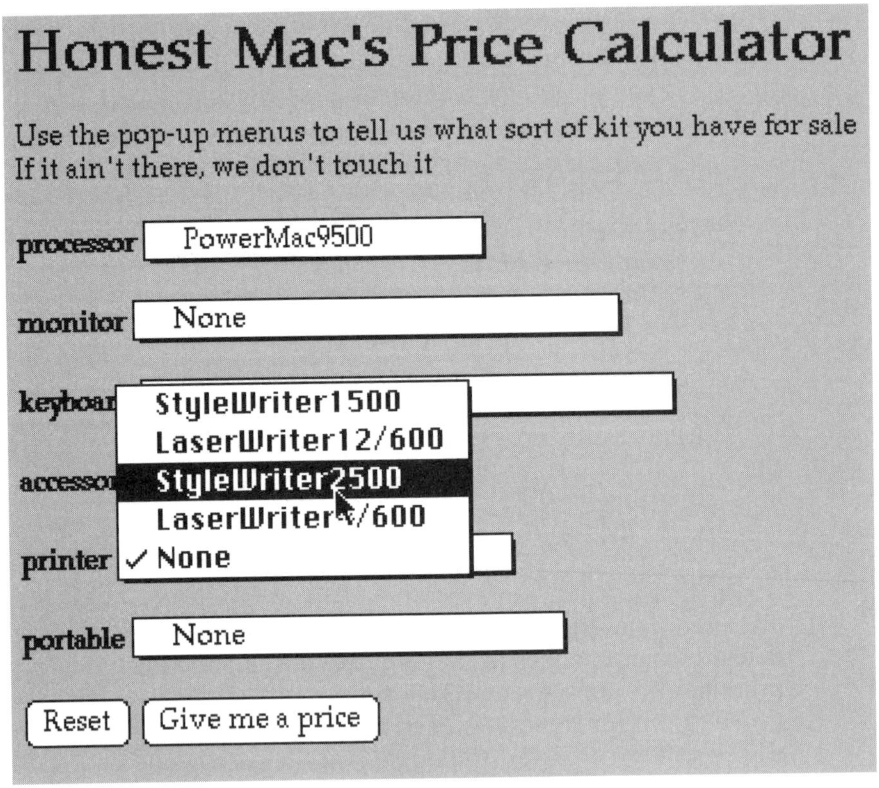

Honest Mac's Price Calculator

Use the pop-up menus to tell us what sort of kit you have for sale
If it ain't there, we don't touch it

processor   PowerMac9500

monitor   None

keyboar   StyleWriter1500
accesso   LaserWriter12/600
              StyleWriter2500
printer   LaserWriter4/600
              ✓ None

portable   None

[Reset]   [Give me a price]

Figure 10.4   Filling in the form

The logic required to deal with the submitted data and produce a price is obvious: for each sort of equipment, find out what, if anything, the user has to offer, and look up the price in the corresponding hash. The problem is making the displayed prices look nice. The table features of HTML will be used for this purpose. (Not every browser can handle tables; I will indicate a possible response to this situation later.) A table is constructed by the method `table`, whose argument is the body of the table, which consists of several table rows, constructed by the TR method,[3] which takes as *its* argument the values for each column of the row; these are constructed by the `td` (table data) method. The table body is constructed incrementally by concatenating the rows as they are built. In parallel with the construction of the table, the total price will be calculated.

The first thing is to build the response header and start the HTML, in a way

---

[3]The anomalous use of capital letters is due to the conflict with the `tr` operator.

that should have become familiar.

```
sub send_the_price
{
  print header, start_html(-title => q[Honest Mac's Bargains]);
```

Next, initialize the total price and the table; its first row consists of the column headings.

```
  my $total_price = 0;
  my $table_body = TR(td('Item') . td(q[Mac's Price]));
```

Now, for every sort of component the user is offering, build a row of the table, comprising its name and the price offered. This price is added to the running total. It is possible that the user will have sent data directly, instead of using the form, so some checks have to be added in case of invalid data.

```
  foreach $component (@components)
  {
    my $model = param($component);
    unless (!defined($model) || $model eq 'None')
    {
      my $price = $hashes{$component}->{$model};
      next unless defined $price;
      $table_body .= TR(td($model) . td($price));
      $total_price += $price;
    }
  }
```

It is quite possible that somebody will have filled in the form by selecting None from every menu. In that case, the total price will be zero, and we send a suitable response.

```
  if ($total_price == 0)
  {
    print "If you have nothing to sell, we can't help you.";
  }
```

If there is something to sell, send a suitable heading, and some explanation for the international market.

```
  else
  {
    print h1(q[Honest Mac's Best Offer]);
    print em("All our prices are in Euros"), p;
```

Next, finish off the table, and send it.

```
    $table_body .= TR(td('TOTAL') . td($total_price));
    print table($table_body);
```

Honest Mac never forgets his origins as a humble market trader:

Honest Mac's Best Offer

All our prices are in Euros

Item	Mac's Price
PowerMac9500	1850
LaserWriter4/600	295
TOTAL	2145

Because I like your face, I'll give you 2037 for the lot

Don't forget to tell your friends about Honest Mac

Figure 10.5 Honest Mac's response

```
if ($total_price > 1000)
{
  $total_price -= $total_price/20;
  print p, "Because I like your face, I'll give you ",
        int($total_price), " for the lot";
}
}
```

(If you think that -= should be a +=, you don't know Honest Mac.) Whether a price has been sent or not, there's no harm in appending a little advert. The blink method makes its argument blink in a suitably tacky way on browsers that recognize it.

```
print p, "Don't forget to tell your friends about ",
        blink('Honest Mac');
print end_html;
}
```

Figure 10.5 shows an example of the response sent by this script.

This script is a basic first attempt at providing the necessary service; its scope can easily be extended by adding more and bigger databases. Two of its more fundamental defects can be fairly easily remedied, although the details will not be spelled out here.

First, what about browsers that cannot cope with HTML tables? A CGI script can ascertain, using the `user_agent` method, which browser software is sending it a request. It can test the value, and generate different HTML code to fit the capabilities of the browser. Here, for example, the table could have been sent as pre-formatted data, or simply as a list of bullet points, to browsers incapable of displaying tables. Some research is required, both to discover what each browser is capable of, and also what name it uses to identify itself. As Figure 10.1 shows, this is not always obvious.

Another failing of the second-hand dealer's script is that, having made an offer to the seller, it gives them no opportunity to accept it. At the very least, it should let them send an e-mail message to Honest Mac. The easiest way to do this is to generate a link containing a URL such as `mailto:mac@honest.co.uk`; clicking on the link would then cause a mailing window to be opened. Unfortunately, not all browsers understand `mailto` URLs, so if all comers are to be accommodated, some other expedient is required.

Most Web servers run on Unix machines. On such a machine, the canonical way to send such a message is to display a form allowing the user to enter their e-mail address and the body of the message. On receiving the data from this form, the GCI script opens a pipe to the `sendmail` program, to send the message. On systems other than Unix, you may be able to use the `mailtools` modules, mentioned later, to send the message yourself.

Among its other virtues, the `CGI` module is equipped with excellent documentation, armed with which you should be able to accomplish many CGI scripting tasks with ease. It also allows you to perform some testing of your script without going through a server. If you run the script in the normal way, you can enter keyword and value pairs from your keyboard, to simulate the data passed in an HTTP request from an HTML form.

`CGI`'s only drawback is that it is a large and monolithic module, which can be sluggish to start up. For simple tasks, you may prefer to use the module `CGI_Lite`, by Shishir Gundavaram. For more complicated tasks, on the other hand, you may find the separate `CGI::*` modules better. These enable you to implement advanced CGI scripts that interact with the same user over a sequence of related transactions. Again, they are well documented, but you would probably find it helpful to learn more about HTTP before trying anything too ambitious.

Other Tasks

CGI programming is where Perl has attracted most attention in the Internet world, but it by no means exhausts the language's possibilities. Perl modules are very good at hiding the grubby details of all sorts of network programming, and make it possible for just about anybody to write scripts that manipulate resources over networks.

Web Clients

Web browsers have become so ubiquitous that it is easy to think that accessing a Web page is synonymous with opening it in a browser window. However, browsers do not have a monopoly on the World-Wide Web, and they are not always the most suitable interface to it. Some tasks can be much better achieved by a Perl script.

Needless to say, the key to writing Web clients in Perl is a set of modules. They are collectively known as libwww-perl, and were written by Martijn Koster and Gisle Aas.[4] Like other powerful modules, libwww-perl offers both a procedural and an object-oriented interface. The module LWP::Simple provides subroutines for carrying out common everyday tasks, such as fetching a document from a remote server. The other LWP::* modules allow you to exert fine control over sending of HTTP requests and dealing with the responses.

If all you need to do is fetch a document whose URL you know, you call the get subroutine from LWP::Simple, and it will return it (or an undefined value if the request fails). The subroutine getprint will get the document and print it for you, while getstore will get it and store it in a file, whose name you provide as a second argument. Both these two subroutines return the response code as their result; you can use the subroutines is_success and is_failure to see whether the response code indicates success or failure.

With these simple routines, you can automate many repetitive tasks that would otherwise require you to stare at a browser window, clicking on links. As an example, consider Figure 10.6, which shows the structure of the part of the British Broadcasting Corporation's Web site concerned with its schedules. The progbyday page contains nine links, each pointing to a page for one day's programme schedules. Each of these nine pages has nine links, three to TV channels, one to the World Service, and five to radio stations. Following one of these links brings you to a page that actually contains the programme schedule for one channel or station on one day out of the nine displayed at any time. These pages are leaves in the page structure: they only contain one link, all the way back up to the BBC home page. If you want to download, say, an entire set of Radio 3 schedules so you can peruse them at your leisure without using Internet bandwidth or running up phone bills, you must start at the progbyday page, follow a link to the first day, then another to Radio 3, download that page, go back up two levels, then down to the next day, and from there to the next Radio 3 page, and so on.

Fortunately, the URLs of these pages follow a pattern. Each page of Radio 3 schedules has a URL of the form

```
http://www.bbc.co.uk/schedules/auntr30n.wir.html
```

(something of a BBC in-joke, one suspects), where n is a number between 1 and

---

[4]With, as the documentation puts it, 'lots of help from Graham Barr, Tim Bunce, Andreas König, Jared Rhine, and Jack Shirazi'.

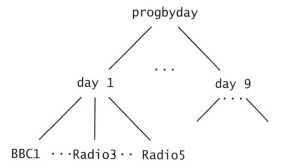

Figure 10.6 Part of a Web site

9. It is easy to write a Perl script that constructs these URLs and then fetches each page and stores it in a file.

```
use English;
use LWP::Simple;

$url_start = 'http://www.bbc.co.uk/schedules/auntr30';
$suffixes = '.wir.html';

$file_start = 'radio3_schedule';
for $i (1..9)
{
  $url = $url_start . $i . $suffixes;
  $file = $file_start . $i . '.html';
  print "getting $url\n";
  $response_code = getstore $url, $file;
  is_success($response_code) or
    print "Couldn't get it: response code was $response_code\n";
}

print "finished for this week\n";
```

All the Radio 3 fan has to do is run this script once a week, and they will never need to buy a listings magazine again.[5]

If you did not know when the BBC updated their Web page, and wanted to keep your own mirror of it at all times, you could use the subroutine `mirror` instead of `getstore`. It takes the same arguments, but assumes that the file name belongs to an existing file that contains a local copy of the document identified by the URL. The remote document will only be fetched if it appears to have been updated more recently than the local one.

---

[5]No URL is set in stone, so don't necessarily expect the script to work by the time you read this. A little investigation with a browser will be needed to verify the URLs.

The final subroutine exported by `LWP::Simple` is `head`, which sends a request with method `HEAD`, causing the server to send only the header of the response, not the body. If the request succeeds, `head` returns a list comprising the content type, the document length, the time it was last modified, the time it expires (i.e. when a client that caches documents must fetch a new copy), and the name of the server. This method is handy for quickly finding out whether a document exists on a remote server; if it doesn't, the request will fail and `head` will return an empty list.

To use the object-oriented interface to `libwww-perl` effectively, you need to know more about HTTP than it is appropriate to describe in this book. Fortunately, `libwww-perl` is well endowed with good documentation, which should take you a long way with this sort of programming. Also included in the distribution are several Perl scripts for doing common tasks.

Using Other Protocols

The Internet does not end with the World-Wide Web, and for those who know an RFC from a CCITT, there are Perl modules for almost any network programming task you can imagine. Thanks to these, even with a small amount of knowledge it is possible to automate FTP accesses, news reading and the handling of mail.

The relevant modules are largely the work of the prolific Graham Barr. His `Net::*` collection includes modules that let you use FTP, SMTP, POP3, Telnet, NNTP and SNPP. (The `libwww-perl` modules call on some of the `Net::*` modules for lower-level network services.) If you know what those letters stand for, you will find the modules' interfaces easy to use.

The `Mail::*` modules (sometimes known as `mailtools`), also by Graham Barr, provide facilities for composing messages in the correct format for different mail systems, and automating tasks like sending and replying to messages, or examining headers. It is quite simple to put together scripts using these modules for filtering mail, or automatically forwarding messages on certain subjects to a chosen destination, and so on. Graham Barr has written a series of tutorials in the *Perl Journal* (see page 250), explaining the use of several of his modules.

Inevitably, some features of these network modules are not portable. If you are not using a Unix system, you may have to do some experimenting to discover what works; in some cases, there are extra modules available that provide equivalent services for other platforms.

The Final Chapter

11

I have not told you everything about Perl—I never said I would. By following the suggestions in the next section, you can truly find out all there is to know.

As well as sending you off towards new discoveries, the final chapter is a good place to reflect on what has been learned, and try to assess Perl's place in the programming world.

Further Information

The definitive reference material is the Perl on-line documentation, which will fill in all the details that have been glossed over in this book, and tell you about additional features. In particular, you will find out just how much I have been concealing about Perl's intimate relations with Unix. For the most part, this consists of many built-in functions, which provide Perl with direct access to operating system services or the contents of system files. The documentation also covers advanced topics, which are not presently described anywhere else, particularly writing extension modules in languages other than Perl.

Reading documentation on line is never very comfortable. You can always print it, of course, but if you prefer to read real books, several useful ones are available.

Literature

For reference purposes, there is only one choice.

Larry Wall, Tom Christiansen, and Randal L. Schwartz. *Programming Perl.* O'Reilly and Associates, Inc., 2nd edition, 1996.

Larry Wall is the designer, chief implementor and guiding spirit of Perl; his co-authors are prominent members of the Perl inner circle. Most of their book—

usually referred to as the 'Camel Book', in honour of the animal on its cover—reproduces the on-line documentation. As well as being nicer to handle than the electronic version, the material has been edited and cleaned up somewhat, to provide an essential reference manual. There is also some material of a tutorial nature. There are even some funny jokes.

▷   If somebody offers you a copy of the first edition of the Camel Book, don't refuse it. Although it is out of date, describing only Perl4 and thus omitting many important innovations in the current version of the language, it includes many examples of Perl idioms which can still be used in Perl5, and complete Perl programs. True, rather too many of these are Unix system management tasks to be of general interest, but they provide a helpful insight into how Perl is used in practice.

     It may just be nostalgia, but there seem to be more funny jokes in the first
◁   edition.

If you are happy to read the full documentation on-line, but do not always want to dive into it to check what order the arguments to some function must be in, you might benefit from:

Johan Vromans. *Perl 5 Desktop Reference.* O'Reilly and Associates, Inc., 1996.

As well as the published version, the reference guide exists in several different electronic formats, for those who prefer doing their own printing and stapling to contributing to the funds of O'Reilly and his associates. Links from the Web sites mentioned later in this section will lead you to it.

     If chapter 10 whetted your appetite for CGI scripting, you will need to know about concepts that the CGI module conveniently hides from you, and the specialized techniques used to achieve more advanced effects. There are a number of books on this topic available.

     A fine book on HTML, which also deals with CGI programming and the HTTP protocol, is:

Ian S. Graham. *The HTML Sourcebook.* John Wiley & Sons, 2nd edition, 1996.

A good book that describes how to write CGI scripts without using the modules, if you prefer to do so, is:

Shishir Gundavaram. *CGI Programming on the World Wide Web.* O'Reilly and Associates, Inc., 1996.

     If you have become interested in Perl and want to keep up with developments, consider subscribing to *The Perl Journal*, which describes itself as 'A quarterly newsletter devoted to the Perl programming language'. Recent issues have featured tutorials on CGI programming, building graphical interfaces with Perl and Tk, and using mail, news and FTP modules, as well as articles describing applications of Perl, an obfuscated Perl contest (for those who like that sort of thing), and many other useful things. Consult *The Perl Journal*'s home page, `http://orwant.www.media.mit.edu/the_perl_journal` for more details, and subscription information.

The Comprehensive Perl Archive Network (CPAN)

CPAN is a set of FTP servers, each of which has a copy of the Comprehensive Perl Archive, a collection of material related to Perl, including the Perl distribution, versions of Perl for a large number of platforms, Perl modules, Perl documentation and Perl scripts. The easiest way to connect yourself to a CPAN host is by pointing a Web browser at the URL `http://www.perl.com/CPAN/` (with the trailing slash); this will cause you to be magically transported to the host nearest to you.

For those who prefer to access CPAN with a dedicated FTP client—or a Perl script—instead of a Web browser, Figures 11.1 and 11.2 list all the sites available at the time of writing. These lists demonstrate the extent of the Archive Network. As you can see, the root directories are not the same on every host, but beneath them the archive always has the same structure. If you already have a Perl system, the most interesting sub-directories will be `doc`— which has the reference manual in several different formats—and `modules`. Within `modules` you will find the module list, again in several different formats, and sub-directories `by-author`, `by-category` and `by-module`, allowing you to search for a module in different ways, depending on what you know about it already. The `scripts` directory contains a collection of Perl scripts which you may find useful.

If you need to obtain Perl and you are running any version of Unix, or one of its close relatives, you should look in the `src` directory. The file `latest.tar.gz` is the distribution kit for the most recent production version (in the form of a `tar` archive, compressed by GNU-zip). Version 5.004 is reported to build 'out of the box' on all varieties of Unix, Plan9, VMS, OS/2, QNX and AmigOS. If you are not using any of these systems, look in the `ports` directory, where there are versions for Acorn RiscOS, MacOS, MVS, and other systems including MS-DOS and more varieties of Windows than it is comfortable to contemplate.

World-Wide Web Sites

There are many sites scattered over the World-Wide Web which contain some material that is of interest or of use to Perl programmers. The following four are good starting points. All of them include much good material of their own, and provide links to other sites.
`http://www.perl.com/perl`
The *Perl Language Home Page* is maintained by Tom Christiansen, and is presently the best single Web site specializing in Perl. As well as providing automated access to CPAN, it includes links to FAQ lists and other documentation, details of mailing lists and newsgroups and book reviews. One of its best features is a page entitled 'What's New in PerlLand', with up-to-date news on recent developments.

Africa	South Africa	ftp://ftp.is.co.za/programming/perl/CPAN/
Asia	Hong Kong	ftp://ftp.hkstar.com/pub/CPAN/
	Japan	ftp://ftp.jaist.ac.jp/pub/lang/perl/CPAN/
		ftp://ftp.lab.kdd.co.jp/lang/perl/CPAN/
	South Korea	ftp://ftp.nuri.net/pub/CPAN/
	Taiwan	ftp://dongpo.math.ncu.edu.tw/perl/CPAN/
		ftp://ftp.wownet.net/pub2/PERL/
Australasia		
	Australia	ftp://coombs.anu.edu.au/pub/perl/CPAN/
		ftp://ftp.mame.mu.oz.au/pub/perl/CPAN/
	New Zealand	ftp://ftp.tekotago.ac.nz/pub/perl/CPAN/
Europe	Austria	ftp://ftp.tuwien.ac.at/pub/languages/perl/CPAN/
	Belgium	ftp://ftp.kulnet.kuleuven.ac.be/pub/mirror/CPAN/
	Czech Rep.	ftp://sunsite.mff.cuni.cz/Languages/Perl/CPAN/
	Denmark	ftp://sunsite.auc.dk/pub/languages/perl/CPAN/
	Finland	ftp://ftp.funet.fi/pub/languages/perl/CPAN/
	France	ftp://ftp.pasteur.fr/pub/computing/unix/perl/CPAN/
	Germany	ftp://ftp.leo.org/pub/comp/programming/languages/perl/CPAN/
		ftp://ftp.rz.ruhr-uni-bochum.de/pub/CPAN/
		ftp://ftp.uni-hamburg.de/pub/soft/lang/perl/CPAN/
	Greece	ftp://ftp.ntua.gr/pub/lang/perl/
	Hungary	ftp://ftp.kfki.hu/pub/packages/perl/CPAN/
	Italy	ftp://cis.utovrm.it/CPAN/
	Netherlands	ftp://ftp.cs.ruu.nl/pub/PERL/CPAN/
		ftp://ftp.EU.net/packages/cpan/
	Norway	ftp://ftp.uit.no/pub/languages/perl/cpan/
	Poland	ftp://ftp.pk.edu.pl/pub/lang/perl/CPAN/
		ftp://sunsite.icm.edu.pl/pub/CPAN/
	Portugal	ftp://ftp.ci.uminho.pt/pub/lang/perl/
		ftp://ftp.telepac.pt/pub/CPAN/
	Russia	ftp://ftp.sai.msu.su/pub/lang/perl/CPAN/
	Slovenia	ftp://ftp.arnes.si/software/perl/CPAN/
	Spain	ftp://ftp.etse.urv.es/pub/mirror/perl/
		ftp://ftp.rediris.es/mirror/CPAN/
	Sweden	ftp://ftp.sunet.se/pub/lang/perl/CPAN/
	Switzerland	ftp://sunsite.cnlab-switch.ch/mirror/CPAN/
	UK	ftp://ftp.demon.co.uk/pub/mirrors/perl/CPAN/
		ftp://sunsite.doc.ic.ac.uk/packages/CPAN/
		ftp://unix.hensa.ac.uk/mirrors/perl-CPAN/

Figure 11.1   Registered CPAN Sites, Eastern Hemisphere

North America

	http://www.perl.org/CPAN/
Ontario	ftp://ftp.utilis.com/public/CPAN/
	ftp://enterprise.ic.gc.ca/pub/perl/CPAN/
Manitoba	ftp://theory.uwinnipeg.ca/pub/CPAN/
California	ftp://ftp.digital.com/pub/plan/perl/CPAN/
	ftp://ftp.cdrom.com/pub/perl/
Colorado	ftp://ftp.cs.colorado.edu/pub/perl/CPAN/
Florida	ftp://ftp.cis.ufl.edu/pub/perl/CPAN/
Illinois	ftp://uiarchive.cso.uiuc.edu/pub/lang/perl/CPAN/
Massachusetts	ftp://ftp.iguide.com/pub/mirrors/packages/perl/CPAN/
New York	ftp://ftp.rge.com/pub/languages/perl/
North Carolina	ftp://ftp.duke.edu/pub/perl/
Oklahoma	ftp://ftp.ou.edu/mirrors/CPAN/
Oregon	ftp://ftp.orst.edu/pub/packages/CPAN/
Pennsylvania	ftp://ftp.epix.net/pub/languages/perl/
Texas	ftp://ftp.sedl.org/pub/mirrors/CPAN/
	ftp://ftp.metronet.com/pub/perl/

South America

Chile	ftp://sunsite.dcc.uchile.cl/pub/Lang/perl/CPAN/

Figure 11.2   Registered CPAN Sites, Western Hemisphere

`http://www.panix.com/~clay/perl`
The *Perl Reference* provides an extensive collection of links to specialized information about Perl on the Internet.

`http://www.virtualschool.edu/mon/Perl`
With the wonderfully apposite title *Perl: The Swiss Army Chainsaw*, this page—part of Brad Cox's *Middle of Nowhere Web*—is a rich source of links which are useful to Perl programmers. It is particularly helpful if you are looking for material about the MacOS and Windows ports of Perl.

`http://www.perl.org`
The home page of the *Perl Institute* is an alternative source of information and links. It is also the place to go if you like joining organizations. The Perl Institute is a non-profit-making organization, 'run by and for the Perl community'. It describes its goals as being to help keep Perl useful, available and free. It intends to act as a coordination centre for Perl users, information and resources. At the time of writing, it is a new organization, and it is too early to know how it will develop. For now, it runs a CPAN server and a useful Web site, which includes information about the Institute's activities, and details on becoming a member, on top of the usual links.

If you just want to find as many Perl Web sites as possible, start at `http://www.yahoo.com/Computers_and_Internet/Programming_Languages/Perl` (or your local equivalent; for example, substitute `.co.uk` for `.com` in the domain name if you are in or near the UK).

Frequently Asked Questions, Newsgroups and Mailing Lists

An extensive set of Frequently Asked Questions (FAQs) about Perl is available—with answers—in the `doc` directory of CPAN. There are also specialized lists covering CGI programming and CGI security, and the MacOS and Windows ports of Perl. The easiest way to find these is by following the links from one of the Web sites listed above. The quality of the Perl-related FAQ lists is generally high, although they are not always entirely up to date.

Perl is well served by newsgroups: `comp.lang.perl.misc` is the high-volume, low signal-to-noise ratio group for seriously addicted newsgroup readers; `comp.lang.perl.announce` is a moderated group, which keeps you up-to-date on new modules and new releases of Perl;[1] `comp.lang.perl.modules` is for discussion of modules. There are also some specialized mailing lists, including two dedicated to MacPerl, and another to the '32-bit' Windows version of Perl. Details of these, and other lists, can be found on the Perl Language Home Page.

Precursors and Influences

Perl is extraordinary, but it is not unique. There have always been programming languages that are not quite like the others, and some of them clearly pre-figure Perl. You may find it interesting to learn something about where Perl has come from, and about some other contemporary programming languages that are similar to it.

Nothing springs from nothing, and every antecedent has its antecedents, so any attempt to trace Perl's roots is doomed to recede into the earliest programming languages and beyond to natural languages and mathematical notations pre-dating computers. Nevertheless, it is possible to identify certain older languages as important precursors. The following pages convey the flavour of several of these.

Snobol

Snobol[2] is one of Perl's most obvious precursors; pattern matching and replacement, and associative arrays are two key features of Perl that made an early appearance on the programming language scene in Snobol. Although different, Snobol's facilities in these areas are of comparable power to Perl's. Snobol is often described as a 'string manipulation language', and it was used most extensively in areas such as text processing, natural language analysis and symbolic algebraic manipulation. Unlike Perl, Snobol lacks most of the

---

[1] An archive of postings to `comp.lang.perl.announce` can be found in the `clpa` directory of CPAN.

[2] In the following description, Snobol refers to Snobol 4, the last and most widely used version of the language, which was released in 1969 and flourished until about 1980.

conventional control structures found in other languages, and it offers nothing comparable to Perl's modules. It does, however, have some features that will seem familiar, including dynamically typed variables, which do not have to be explicitly declared.

Patterns in Snobol are roughly equivalent to regular expressions, although some of the notation used is different. Concatenation is implicit and alternation is a vertical bar, as in Perl, but the other familiar operators are replaced by a collection of built-in functions. These include LEN(n), which matches any string of a certain length n, (like .{n}); SPAN(s), which matches any sequence of characters in a string s (like [s]+); BREAK(s), which matches any sequence of characters not in a string s (like [^s]*); and REM which matches everything that hasn't been matched by a sub-pattern to its left, up to the end of the string (like .*$). Typical examples are: LEN(7), which matches any seven characters; SPAN('0123456789') REM, which matches any run of digits and anything which follows it; and BREAK(",.;:!?"), which matches everything up to a punctuation mark.

Patterns are used in the characteristic Snobol statement, which has the form

⟨*subject*⟩ ⟨*pattern*⟩ = ⟨*replacement*⟩

which is roughly equivalent to the Perl statement

⟨*subject*⟩ =~ s/⟨*pattern*⟩/⟨*replacement*⟩/;

None of the qualifiers available in Perl is available. There is no automatic setting of variables like $1 to the substrings matched by sub-patterns, but you can use a dot operator to attach a variable name to a sub-pattern, and the variable will be set to the substring which matched it. For example, if I had performed the assignment

```
ARTIST = 'Blind Lemon Jefferson'
```

the effect of

```
ARTIST "Lemon " REM . SURNAME = "Melon"
```

would be to transform an early blues singer—perhaps unkindly—into a contemporary pop group, while remembering his surname in the variable SURNAME.[3] (Variables do not have prefixes.)

Extremely sophisticated effects can be achieved using the full range of patterns, of which I have only sketched a few, available to the Snobol programmer.

Flow of control in Snobol is based on the success or failure of pattern matching.[4] Any statement may be labelled with a name, which is separated from the statement proper by a colon. Any statement may also be followed by an annotation of the form :F(⟨*label*⟩), :S(⟨*label*⟩) or both, or just :(⟨*label*⟩).

---

[3] Since Snobol dates from a time of teletypes and limited character sets, variable names must be entirely upper-case.

[4] Actually, it is based on a more general concept of success or failure; other types of statement, which we won't consider, can succeed or fail in their own ways.

If a match succeeds and a :S annotation is present, the correspondingly labelled statement is executed next. If it fails, the statement whose label goes with the :F annotation, if one is present, is jumped to. Annotations without F or S cause an unconditional jump. If no destination is specified for the outcome of the pattern match, control drops through to the following statement in the program. Thus

```
LAB:  ASTRING 'IBM' | 'MicroSoft' =  :S(LAB)
```

will repeatedly strip out occurrences of the names IBM and MicroSoft from ASTRING (since the replacement is the null string) until none is left, after which the following statement will be executed.

This control flow mechanism can be tricky to manage and, even though Snobol allows you to define and call functions, it is a major obstacle in the way of using the language for large programs.

Input in Snobol is somewhat reminiscent of filehandles: the variable INPUT, whenever it is used, has as its value the next line from the standard input. An attempt to read beyond the end of file causes a statement using INPUT to fail. Output is symmetrical: to write a string to the standard output, you assign it to the variable OUTPUT, so

```
RD:   OUTPUT = INPUT                   :S(RD)
```

copies the standard input to the standard output.

While Snobol is best known for its pattern-matching facilities, in some ways its tables were as important an innovation. They provide associative storage structures that look like arrays indexed by strings—just like hashes. Also like hashes, their entries do not need to be initialized, and they expand as necessary to accommodate new entries. As an innovation in programming language design, Snobol's tables are very important. They are not, however, perfect: for example, the only convenient way to get at all the elements of a table is to convert it into an array with two columns (using a built-in function) and access each key and value via a numeric index. Combined with the primitive flow control structure, such operations are inevitably clumsy. Perl demonstrates what can be achieved with associative data structures in a more powerful setting.

Awk

Before Awk, programming languages with built-in support for pattern-matching, string manipulation and high-level data structures, such as Snobol and even Lisp, were generally perceived as 'special-purpose' languages, fit only for a restricted range of computations within a specialist field such as text processing or artificial intelligence. With Awk, this perception began to change. The language *was* devised with a restricted range of applications in mind— converting between data formats, extracting selected information from structured files, data validation, and simple counting computations—but, as it became adopted by users beyond its designers' immediate circle, it began to be applied to more diverse tasks, including the writing of small database systems and compilers. People extended the range of applications Awk was used for because they liked it. By doing so, they provided a demonstration that such languages were not just for specialists. They could be used for a wide range of jobs, even some hard-core computer science ones.

Almost everything in Awk is present in some form in Perl; in fact, the very first version of Perl was developed as a substitute for Awk, to get round some of its limitations. Nevertheless, programming in Awk is quite a lot different from programming in Perl, because, like Snobol, Awk has an unusual control structure, which is driven by its input data. In Awk's world, data consists of records divided into fields, like my video clips database from chapter 5. The main part of an Awk script consists of a set of *actions*, consisting of imperative code written in a language syntactically resembling C. Each action is enclosed between curly brackets; it may be preceded by a *pattern*—which, in Awk terms is any expression that may evaluate to true or false, its value usually depending in some way on current record. If the pattern is true of a record, we say that it *matches* that record. Each action is applied to the current record if its associated pattern matches. If there is no pattern, the action is applied unconditionally to every record. The patterns do not have to be mutually exclusive, so it may well happen that several actions are performed on a particular record.

When Awk is used for simple data processing, the patterns are usually patterns in Perl's sense of regular expressions; the action associated with each regular expression pattern is applied to every input record (usually a line) that matches the pattern, so the execution of an Awk script closely resembles the execution of a Perl script written in the file processing idiom I started my description with. The loop is implicit. Also implicit is an operation equivalent to a call of Perl's `split` operator, which breaks the current input record into its component fields. These are made available in pseudo-variables $1, $2, and so on.

▷ By using suitable compiler switches, you can make `perl` behave almost like Awk, by wrapping an implicit loop around your code and splitting each input line. Consult ◁ the manual for details, if you want to do so.

Two special patterns, just written as `BEGIN` and `END`, match an empty record before and after the real data, respectively. They are intended to allow you to write initialization and clean-up code. For example, you might set the value of the field separator in the action that went with `BEGIN`. Ironically, although the implicit record-splitting loop is handy for simple off-line editing jobs, it makes tasks that are slightly more complex awkward, and you find that many reasonably complicated Awk scripts do all their work in the action for `BEGIN`, perhaps calling some functions defined by the programmer, and never use the implicit loop. Although Perl may make you write a few more characters in your script, its more conventional control structure is usually easier to work with.

Something of the flavour of Awk is conveyed by the following example, which performs some analysis on the video clips data. This script shows how records satisfying some condition can be picked out: it only adds up the size and duration of clips compressed by Cinepak. The job is particularly suitable for Awk, since it relies on record-splitting and a loop that reads every record and selects some to perform an action on.

```
BEGIN  {
  FS = "|"
}

$3 ~ /Cinepak/  {
  total_size += $4
  split($2, duration, ":")
  total_duration += (60*duration[1] + duration[2]) * 25 + duration[3]
  print
}

END  {
  print "Total size is ", total_size,
        " and total duration is ", total_duration, " frames\n"
}
```

Notice the absence of semi-colons. In Awk, they can be omitted just before the end of a line. The assignment to FS in the BEGIN action sets the field separator. The fields of a record are numbered from 1, not 0, so the comparison $3 ~ /Cinepak/ picks out records whose compressor field is Cinepak. Within the action corresponding to this pattern, the explicit call to Awk's split function splits the duration sub-record on the colon separator, with the resulting components being stored in the array duration. As with Perl, variables do not have to be declared; they do not bear any prefix to identify their type, which is deduced from the way you use them.

Apart from the implicit loop, Awk would hold few surprises for a Perl programmer. It might prove irritating, because it is missing some of Perl's features; it would certainly seem limiting, because it does not have the range of Perl's functions, nor any module facilities. Although Awk saved many programmers a lot of time and effort in writing little text and data manipulation programs, from the present perspective, its real importance appears to be that it was the immediate ancestor of Perl.

Unix

It seems strange—almost syntactically incorrect—to be describing an operating system as an influence on a programming language, but 'Unix' is more than just the Unix operating system. It is also a set of tools and utilities, a view of human-computer interaction, and a general philosophy of offering convenience and power to users (as well as enough rope to shoot yourself in the foot, as the saying is). All of these make themselves felt in Perl.

Most immediately noticeable is the wealth of Perl functions providing access to system calls and system files. The tight interaction between the language and operating system these provide makes Perl a powerful tool for system administration, one of its main application areas. It does, as I have insinuated before, interfere with portability.

Unix has had more subtle influences on Perl, too. One of the things that made Unix seem so wonderful against the background of operating systems like OS/360 was its shell, or command language. The shell—or, to be more precise, shells, since several now exist—is more than a command language, it is a programming language, too, although a limited one. As well as providing you with a simple collection of commands that invoke system functions, it provides you with control structures that allow you to arrange the execution of a sequence of system functions using conditionals and loops, to achieve some larger-scale operation.

Among the linguistic features of shell languages that have found their way into Perl are the use of special variables, automatically set by the system, and interpolation of variables into double-quoted strings. The 'back-tick' quoting operation, also known as command interpolation, which allows you to use the output of a command as the value of a string, as in `ls -l`, whose value is a string consisting of the output of the `ls` command, is a shell feature, too. So are the file test operators described in chapter 6. The syntax for file open modes, and pipes, can also be found in the shells.

Among the Unix tools with a perceptible influence on Perl are the off-line editor `sed` and the `grep` family of file searching programs. Awk, which has already been described, was originally conceived more as another Unix 'power tool' than a programming language. The C programming language, whose influence on Perl extends beyond syntactical forms to library functions such as `sprintf`, was developed in parallel with, and has long been intimately bound up with, Unix.

All of these combined influences mean that Perl will always have a flavour of Unix about it, no matter which system it is ported to.[5]

Perl's Cousins

Perl is one issue of the mixing of text processing and command languages, at present the most widely used, but it is not the only one. If you have read this far and you *still* aren't convinced that Perl is Just The Thing, perhaps nothing is going to satisfy you, but before you go back to Java, consider investigating Tcl or Python.

Tcl—which you are supposed to pronounce 'tickle', if you can do so with a straight face—stands for 'tool command language', which tells you straight

---

[5]But then, recent announcements suggest that almost every operating system will soon have a flavour of Unix about it.

away what it is intended for. It is often described as a 'glue language', because you can use it to stick together facilities provided by several different packages to make a complex application. Tcl caused a lot of excitement when it first appeared, largely because of a package called Tk, which could be used in conjunction with it to allow you to build graphical interfaces for the X Window system, formerly a daunting task when you had to use a C library to do it. Tcl is sufficiently hospitable to be used to control many other tools, though; it is, for example, used as the language for writing extensions to the Alpha editor. Tcl and Tk have been ported to systems other than Unix, and now provide a means of implementing platform-independent graphical interfaces.

There is a noticeable whiff of Lisp about Tcl's syntax, with most expressions taking the form of a function applied to some arguments. Even the evaluation of an arithmetic expression requires a call to the function `expr`. Tcl also incorporates a few of the features of the Unix shells, and has elaborate rules for interpolation in strings. It supports regular expressions (although not quite as fully as Perl does), lists, and some string operations.

Although you will sometimes see people trying to debate the relative virtues of Perl and Tcl, the two are not really rivals; the jobs they are primarily designed for are different, although there is some overlap in what they can do. It is worth noting that there are Perl extension modules that allow you to call Tcl code from Perl, or to use the Tk library directly from Perl.

Python, on the other hand, *could* be seen as a direct rival to Perl. It does many of the same things, and does them in similar ways. Like Perl, it is easily extended by modules, and there is an extensive library available, which includes modules for interfacing to databases and networks. To a large extent, which of the two you prefer will depend on factors independent of the languages themselves, particularly the programming languages you have previously used.

There is a big difference between the two languages' syntax: Python has taken very little from C, being descended from a language called ABC, with some influence from Modula-3; it is thus closer to the Algol and Pascal tradition. The most striking thing about Python's syntax at first glance is that it uses program indentation, instead of { and }, or `begin` and `end` to delimit blocks and compound statements. Although it may be more a matter of culture than of language facilities, Python is more object-oriented than Perl. Whereas Perl programmers tend only to use classes for re-usability, Python programmers use them as a fundamental program structuring technique, almost as casually as they use functions. Interestingly, Python's facilities for building graphical interfaces are implemented using Tk.

All programming languages have their virtues, and in an ideal world we would all learn all of them. Unfortunately we must choose, and also unfortunately, there are no rules that always apply for determining the best language. This is not the place to compare Perl, Tcl and Python, and choose a 'best buy', but this book would not be complete without some attempt at a retrospective assessment of Perl's virtues and vices.

Hats Off to Larry?

Sometimes, it may seem as if Perl deliberately trails its coat in front of the mainstream programming languages, trying to start a fight. But, really, many of the things about Perl that seem to be provocative do not really deserve anybody's attacks: the use of prefix characters to identify the types of variables, scalar and list contexts, the absence of instance variables in objects. These things are different, but not necessarily wrong. Programming languages do not all have to be the same, and the examples throughout this book ought to have convinced you that many of Perl's unique features are positive assets—variable prefixes make interpolation simple, for example. You could be forgiven for thinking that if Perl can break so many of the conventional rules and come out so good, it may be the conventional rules that are at fault.

Perl is vulnerable to some attacks, though. To be without strong type checking or data hiding is not necessarily a sin. On the contrary, badly designed but strongly enforced type systems can make programming an ordeal, and encourage the use of dangerous tricks to circumvent the type checks that were supposed to protect the programmer in the first place. A language like Perl, with its more relaxed attitude to types, may feel more natural to programmers, and by allowing them to express their computation in a way they find easy to think about, make them less likely to make mistakes. But type checking has one great virtue: it can happen at compile-time. Now, of course, a Perl programmer can write code to check the validity of arguments passed to a subroutine, but those checks can only be made when the program runs, and if they fail, the program will most likely have to stop running, which might be, quite literally, a disaster, if the program was responsible for air traffic control, for example. A flexible type system that allows programmers to define their own types and constraints on the way those types are used, coupled with compile-time type checking, can enable a compiler to catch errors in program logic before anybody attempts to run the program. But strong type checking is not the cure-all it sometimes seems to be presented as.

Taking advantage of a sophisticated type system requires considerable programming skill and discipline. It does not suit everybody all the time, and often—probably more often than most software engineers would believe—the rewards may not be worth the effort. Sometimes, though, there is no room for mistakes; we *must* take the most pessimistic view possible, and assume that anything that can go wrong, will go wrong, and then try to ensure that nothing can go wrong. Perl offers very little assurance; it offers the promise that its power and expressiveness will make it easy for you to write a correct program, but it is up to you to make sure that you don't write an incorrect one.

Another area in which Perl is weaker than the mainstream programming languages is its support for decomposition of large-scale programs. You can use Perl in an object-oriented fashion; you can use inheritance to re-use existing code, but only up to a point. In Perl, the implementation and interface of a class are not cleanly separated; part of the interface has to be in the documentation, part of it relies on convention. Confronted with a module, you need to examine the code to determine whether constructors will function correctly if they are called from a derived class's constructor; or to find out which hash keys are used to store data local to the base class, so you can avoid clashes. There is no access protection to prevent accidental interference with the internal state of an object by other parts of a program. As with type checking, arbitrary amounts of protection can be added by the programmer, but not in a way that can be checked before the program runs. For small projects, or single programmers, these omissions are not important. For large projects, worked on by teams, they may restrict the potential benefits of object-oriented programming in Perl.

The conclusion would appear to be that the use of Perl should be restricted to applications that are not life-threatening, or overly complex. The trouble is that there is no hard, fixed line dividing large, complex and potentially dangerous programs from small, simple, harmless ones. I don't suppose that anybody would write an air traffic control system in Perl, but people seem happy to entrust their credit card details to Perl scripts. We don't really know enough about how people write programs to be able to lay down rigid guidelines. And the ease of programming in Perl tends to lead you on into ever more ambitious projects; there are no warning signs saying 'Turn back! You are entering a zone of excessive program complexity.' You will only find out if everything starts falling apart.

Another area in which Perl seems vulnerable is its apparent lack of support for modern graphical interface programming. The impression of such a lack comes from the documentation, which is firmly based in a world of command line interfaces. In fact, though, you can overcome this limitation by using extension modules: for the X window system, there is Perl/Tk, which provides access to the Tk library, originally developed in conjunction with Tcl; for MacOS and Windows, there are system-dependent modules providing access to those systems' facilities.

There is one other tangible limitation to Perl programming: efficiency. This is usually put down to the fact that the standard Perl implementation is an interpreter, and everyone knows that interpreters are slow. Things are not quite that simple. For a start, interpretation and compilation are not two distinct language implementation strategies: any interpreter does some compilation. At the least, its input will be converted to a stream of tokens; more likely, as with Perl, the entire program will be parsed and converted to an internal data structure, before being interpreted. However, the compilation phase is not generally decoupled from the interpretation, so your script has to be compiled every time you run it. If you use a lot of large modules, the overhead of doing so will produce a noticeable delay when you start up.

In Perl, the internal data structure produced by the compiler resembles a tree. The interpreter examines each node of this tree, and then executes an appropriate routine. Interpretation like this is usually contrasted with code generation, where each node of the tree is examined, and appropriate machine code is generated, to be executed later. The trade-off is supposed to be between fast execution of that machine code, with no interpretive overhead due to the examination of the tree and the calling of the runtime support routine, and the size of the generated machine code output. For languages with powerful high level data structures and operations built into them, the generated code sequences for single operations in the source language can be very large (think of a substitution operation in Perl). Consequently, their compilers tend not to generate in-line code for every operation; they generate calls to library routines. Thus, the distinction between interpreted and compiled code is not clear-cut; neither is the trade-off between speed and compactness of code.

The fact is, if a language provides powerful primitive operations, it will not be possible to execute programs written in that language extremely fast. It is the price you pay for generality and easier programming. Clever interpretive strategies are one way of ameliorating the situation; compilers are another, but they cannot magically offer the Perl programmer execution speeds comparable to C. Malcolm Beattie's Perl Compiler does not claim to do so. It does de-couple the compilation and interpretation phases, and takes advantage of the consequent fact that compilation time is no longer seen by the user as part of the program's run time to spend some extra time on optimization (although it should be noted that the standard `perl` system implements many of the standard compiler optimizations already). It can generate three different forms of output. Two of these are, by most standards, actually self-contained interpreters; the third is C code, with extensive use of calls to functions. The compiler kit takes the form of several extension modules, and is available from CPAN. However, even with its help, Perl is unlikely ever to be the language of choice for digital video capture or 3D scene rendering.

If this assessment of Perl appears to have concentrated on negative points, it is because I hope that the examples and descriptions in the preceding chapters have demonstrated Perl's positive advantages. Throughout the writing of the book, I have continually had to resist the temptation to follow example scripts with some such comment as, 'Ha! Try doing that in C++'. I have come to respect and admire C++ for its power and flexibility, but C++ programming is a hard discipline. It is difficult to feel any affection for C++, whereas Perl's cheerful anarchism is hard to resist. Programming in Perl is not just easy, it's fun. It is possible that nothing I can say will convince you, but try using Perl, and you will soon wonder how you managed without it.

Epilogue

Three prominent experts on programming languages—let's call them Ed, Bernie and Harry—met, late one night, in a small café. After the customary pleasantries, their conversation turned to their common interest.

ED   I despair sometimes, I really do. It seems as though Hell has reserved a special torment for anyone who ever tries to think rationally about programming languages.

HARRY   (*Sympathetically*) What is it that's upset you?

ED   This Perl ... *thing*. What I mean is, we've spent all this time—since the early 1960s—before the Beatles—developing semantic theories, so that we can design simple and elegant programming notations that are easy to reason about...

HARRY   Well, I...

ED   ... *and* we know how to develop a program and its proof hand in hand, so that we can *know* the program is correct—provided we write it in a programming language with clean semantics and no side-effects, aliases or abrupt transfers of control—so we don't have to rely on mere testing, and, after all that, people go on using programming languages with nothing but side-effects and aliases and abrupt transfers of control.

HARRY   Well, you...

ED   And this Perl is the worst of the lot. Trying to produce a formal semantics of something like that, or develop a program from a proof, is just a bad joke.

HARRY   But we...

ED   (*Self-pityingly*) But, do you know what makes me really despair? People *like* Perl, they prefer it, and...

264

HARRY   (*While he has the chance*) It gets their jobs done.

BERNIE   I do think you're being unrealistic, Ed. You can't really expect people to develop the sort of large-scale systems we're seeing nowadays from a formal proof. Even *you* can't claim to have a formalism that can deal with the specification of a complete windowing system, or an image-editing program, let alone a proof.

ED   Then you shouldn't attempt to write those programs.

BERNIE   Now that *is* unrealistic—society has come to depend on complex computer systems.

ED   So much the worse for society. Haven't you noticed? These systems *don't work.* They're full of what everyone insists on calling 'bugs'— programmers' mistakes. So now you've got a whole culture of software so-called maintenance—which just means trying to correct those mistakes. And new releases, where you charge customers for those corrections, and give them some new mistakes in the guise of extra features.

BERNIE   But it doesn't have to be that way.

ED   That's right. You can develop your programs formally, or have the courage to admit that there are some programs that are too difficult.

BERNIE   Those aren't the only choices. If you use a programming language that helps you re-use existing code, and uses strong type checking on a rich and extensible system of types, you can assemble systems out of reliable components, and the type checker will make sure, at compile time, you only assemble them in ways that make sense.

ED   But you can't really prove that those components are reliable, and you know what they say about testing.

BERNIE   Yes, I know they say testing can only show the presence of bugs...

ED   Mistakes.

BERNIE   ...not their absence. But if you combine testing with the sort of *informal* reasoning about program behaviour...

ED   (*Disgusted*) Behaviour!

BERNIE   ...that experienced programmers are actually very good at, then you *can* produce reliable software components, and all you need is a framework for putting them together. It can be more like production engineering than mathematics. You don't expect to prove a central heating system.

ED   And you don't expect it to work right, either.

BERNIE   Maybe not straight away, but fixing it is usually just a matter of tightening a few things up, or putting them on the other way round. It's good enough.

HARRY   And...

ED   Good enough when people's lives might depend on it? Their livelihood? Twelve months of their work?

BERNIE   It *could* be good enough, if programmers were prepared to work within the discipline. But perhaps you're right. As you say, this Perl ...*thing*. It just makes a mockery of all any of us are trying to do. No type checking, no access protection—just some conventions and tricks.

ED   We can agree on that, anyway. It's really hardly worth considering such a poorly defined and sloppy notation, especially when it does nothing to enforce a rigorous programming discipline.

HARRY   But what about the people?

ED   What?

BERNIE   Who?

HARRY   The people. The people who write the programs. Programming is a human activity. Your programming languages have to be fit for people. That's why Perl is popular—it fits people, it does what they expect, it's like a natural language: flexible, comfortable...human.

ED   Well, mathematicians are people too, you know.

HARRY   Yes, and look at how they behave. They don't really write down a set of axioms and rules of inference in a specified alphabet, and then prove theorems by writing down the premise as a string over the same alphabet, and using the rules of inference to derive the conclusion by a series of logically valid steps...

ED   Not in fact, but in principle.

HARRY   But *in fact* they produce quite different sorts of argument, to convince other mathematicians that the proof would be possible. And to do that, they make up notations, however they like—gloriously informal notations that work for the job they need to do. Like Perl.

BERNIE   But programming languages are not like mathematical notations—they have to cope with real computers in all their variety, and work within performance constraints, and...

ED   (*Down but not out*) In the end, everything is symbol manipulation.

HARRY   Yes, yes, fine...but *who* is manipulating these symbols?

BERNIE   Programmers are, and, as you insist, programmers are people. And people make mistakes.

ED   Bugs?

BERNIE   Now, a well designed programming language can help protect programmers from their mistakes. Strong typing means it is possible to catch many errors at compile time, when they can't do any harm. Contrary to what a lot of people seem to think, languages like C++ don't do type checking to stop people doing things they want to, they do it to prevent accidents.

HARRY I'm just not convinced those are the sorts of mistakes people make. I think it's better to let programmers express their intentions in the most natural way, so they don't end up making mistakes because you have forced them into thinking in ways they aren't good at. I know it's hard to believe, but a lot of programmers—even a lot of computer scientists—aren't actually very good at maths. Most people aren't.

BERNIE Which may be why they need help from their programming language.

HARRY The question is: What sort of help? For over a decade, the orthodox view has been that programming languages should enforce paranoia—I think it dates back to when Ada was being designed and the US DoD made everybody think about programming languages in a military way. And who uses Ada now? Programming is a human activity, it's a social activity, and it should—no, it can't help but reflect people and society. You can theorize or dictate all you want, but, as the wise man said to the frog, 'peoples is peoples'. And they like Perl more than they like C++ or maths.

A WAITER Your drinks, gentlemen: one mineral water (not fizzy), one small espresso, one whipped chocolate milk (*with* extra chocolate chips). [*Deposits bill and turns to go, but hesitates.*] Excuse me, but I couldn't help overhearing your conversation just now, and, well...I know a bit about programming languages myself, and I couldn't help thinking that you're all wrong. Or all right, if you see what I mean.

HARRY No, I don't.

ED Not at all.

BERNIE Not even a bit.

WAITER You were talking about Perl. And, with respect, you all seemed to be getting rather worked up. I'm not sure why it is, but programmers *do* seem to get worked up about programming languages, and that tends to make them adopt extreme positions—the mathematicians get, if you don't mind my saying so, arrogant and unrealistic, the software engineers get dogmatic about telling other people how to write their programs, and the Perl fans seem to think the whole world is against them. You can see it happening all over the Internet. But it doesn't have to be like that, does it? People are different. The same person is different at different times. So it's good that programming languages are different. We should be able to move among languages and programming methods, and work with them all creatively...

ED As I was saying, I despair sometimes. Take this Java...

HARRY   Ah! Java—the Great Leap Backwards.

BERNIE   A complete travesty…

WAITER   …But I could be wrong. (*Mutters*) I'd rather take Blue Mountain any day.

Index

Entries consisting entirely of punctuation characters and mathematical symbols appear together before the alphabetical entries; they are arranged according to the following collation sequence:

! " # $ % & ' ( ) * + , - . / : ; < = > ? @ [\ ] ^ _ ` { | } ~

Entries consisting of an initial punctuation character or mathematical symbol followed by letters and numbers are arranged within the alphabetical entries, ignoring the initial character (e.g., $ARG appears as if it was ARG).